Other books
by Michael Baisden

Men Cry in the Dark

The Maintenance Man

God's Gift to Women

• • •

Love, Lust & Lies (DVD)

Do Women Know What They Want? (DVD)

MICHAEL BAISDEN

BESTSELLING AUTHOR OF *THE MAINTENANCE MAN*

NEVER SATISFIED
Do Men Know What They Want?

PUBLISHED BY BAISDEN PUBLISHING

LEARN MORE BY VISITING WWW.BAISDENLIVE.COM
Follow Michael on Facebook at BaisdenLive and on Twitter @BaisdenLive

CONTENTS

Do Men Know What They Want?

Food, Sex and Silence 5

R-E-S-P-E-C-T 7

A Woman Who Has His Back! 9

Let Freedom Ring! 11

Men 101 13

Smooth Operator

The Hunt 15

Call Me 25

The Escape 35

Night Court 57

A Man Is Gonna Be a Man . . . Really?

It Starts at Home 69

No More Mr. Nice Guy 87

Nothin' But the Dog in Me 117

Everything I Miss at Home 137

You, Me and She

Vamp, Tramp, Traitor 167

Wake Up! 191

Pay to Play 193

Starting Over! 245

Afterword 263

About Michael Baisden 267

DEDICATION

*To my daughter Michae', who was only three years old when
I self-published the first version of this book.*

*I'm proud of the beautiful and bright
young woman you've become.*

*I hope you were taking notes during our conversation about
relationships and men. Trust me, you're going to need it!*

I love you, Princess

Love, Dad

NEVER
SATISFIED
Do Men Know What They Want?

1

DO MEN KNOW
WHAT THEY WANT?

Do men know what they want? I'm not sure they do, but they definitely know what they don't want, drama! But are men responsible for creating conflict in their relationships because of their lack of honesty? On one hand they demand monogamy while at the same time exercising their options to see whomever they want. Most women believe that men are never satisfied, and they may be right! But the question is, are women willing to listen to what men say they want and accept it? Or will they try to change them?

Never Satisfied

It's hard to believe it's been almost seventeen years since I updated this book. It was my first, my baby; it was the book that started it all! I can remember traveling around the country with that raggedy old suitcase stuffed with books going from town to town raising hell on the local morning shows. That was before all the national syndication that I would unknowingly become a huge part of. Those were the days of the standing room only *Love,*

Lust, and Lies relationship seminars. It was just me, a hand-held microphone, and hundreds of fired-up women ready to kill me. I was so cocky back then. I thought I had all the answers. Life has taught me so much since then. The older you get, the more you realize how much you don't know.

I released the original version of *Never Satisfied* back in January of 1995; I was still driving trains for the Chicago Transit Authority waiting on a sign that it was time to take that leap of faith. And that day came soon after I published the book. It was a bitter cold day and I was working on the tracks with the rail workers. I boarded a train headed back to O'Hare airport and saw a family on their way out of town to someplace tropical. I remember how happy they were laughing and joking around with their straw hats on. At that moment I said to myself, why can't that be my family boarding a plane? I wanted a better life for myself and for my daughter Michae', who was three years old at the time. So, three months later I woke up, rolled out of bed onto my knees and prayed. I told God I was ready. I know my Christian fans are going to freak out when they hear that. But I did pray. And tears rolled down my face because I knew from that day my life would never be the same.

Since then I've hosted two television shows, *Talk or Walk*, and *Baisden After Dark*. I've had two of my novels adapted to stage plays, *Men Cry in the Dark* and *The Maintenance Man*, and produced two relationships films, *Love, Lust, and Lies*, and *Do Women Know What They Want?* Currently I host my own nationally syndicated radio show. But my proudest moment came in 2007 when I led the Jena 6 Civil Rights March. It was incredible to see thousands of people from all over the country of every age and race coming together to get justice for those six boys. I'll never forget that moment for as long as I live. Also, campaigning to elect the first black president was a huge landmark as well. It felt good to have his camp tell us how instrumental we were in getting him elected.

Yes, a lot has changed since then, I'm older and hopefully wiser. Which is why I felt compelled to update this book. I wanted to share what I have learned in the past seventeen years with my readers and my radio family. We've discussed so many topics over the years and I felt this was an opportunity to put my thoughts down for the next generation to read. When *Never Satisfied* was first released in 1995, it became one of the most successful self-help books on relationships written by an African American male. I knew it was going to shock some people and spark dialogue about everything from cheating men to the women who tolerate it.

And that's what my entire career has been all about, provoking conversation. Although it's been many years since I self-published the original, we are still hesitant to move the relationship model forward. Sometimes it's due to our religious beliefs, old fashioned thinking, and yes, the fear of change. I realize how difficult it can be to change the way you look at relationships but let's face it; relationships and the institution of marriage are in real trouble. If you were in school and you got a 50 on a test, that's not passing, that's flunking. And right now we're flunking out of relationships and marriage 101. When people hear terms such as open relationships, swinging, and polygamous, they freak out. But the reality is most people are in open relationships already. They either don't know it, or don't want to admit it. It's like they have a case of selective amnesia.

Well, this is your wake-up call. And just as I did back in 1995, I'm going to smack you in the mug with a hard dose of reality. Not according to me, but based on what everyday people have to say. I took the liberty of updating some of the stories based on some of the entertaining e-mails and calls I've received on my radio show over the years. I can promise you two things, you won't be able to put it down once you start reading, and you won't stop laughing. Sometimes when you see people so caught up in the game of cheating, you have to laugh to keep from crying.

So here it is, the new version of *Never Satisfied*. I kept all the good stuff from the original with a lot of new ideas and different perspectives.

Thanks again for all the years of laughs, great music, and the education. You guys have taught me more than I could have ever taught you. Enjoy!

FOOD, SEX AND SILENCE

Do men know what they want? According to comedian Chris Rock the answer is simple, "Food, Sex, and Silence!" His statement may have been meant as a joke but for a majority of men he was right on point. Let's face it! Men are simple when it comes to relationships. If our woman is not rationing sex, is cooking great meals, and is willing to give us our space, chances are we're happy, at least happy enough to stay in the relationship. However, if the wife or girlfriend is unable to consistently satisfy these needs, most men will likely use it as an excuse to seek satisfaction elsewhere. We are the consummate fair-weather lovers; at the first sign of sex rationing or being smothered we're out the door and into the bed of another woman. Of course, this does not apply to all men, but I think it's fair to say that the majority of men will not tolerate going without or being locked down, especially if we have options.

It's been said, "A man is only as faithful as his options." And generally speaking, it's true! It's easy for a man to boast about being faithful when nobody is interested in having sex with him in the first place. But for those men who are in demand, such as athletes, actors, and yes, radio personalities, the temptation can be overwhelming. It's easy to understand how pastors, politicians, and celebrities get caught up in sex scandals. There is so much pussy being thrown at them you wonder how any mortal man can resist. At some point, that moment of weakness creeps in and…bam! Next thing you know she's looking up and you're looking down. After it's over you lie there asking yourself, "How did this happen?" The answer to that question is simple, Ego! Most women know that the easiest way to get a man's attention is by stroking his ego, especially if the wife or girlfriend is not stroking it at home. Every man wants a woman who will tell him how brilliant he is and that he's the greatest lover she's ever had! Just as women have emotional needs, men have egotistical needs.

What Men Say They Want

When I asked men on my radio show what they wanted out of their relationships, the top three responses had nothing to do with food, sex, or even physical attraction. I'm sure that will come as a shock to most women who see all men as sexual predators with no conscience or emotions. But men fall in love, too, and many of us want to be in a monogamous relationship. Yes, ladies, some of us want families, someone to grow old with...all that other mushy stuff. All men are not dogs; some of us just need a little training. Women need a better understanding about what's really going on with us. Yes, we think about sex all the time, but it goes deeper than that! So get your pens and paper ready and write down what I'm about to share with you. The top three things men say they want is respect, support, and freedom. Let's examine respect first.

R-E-S-P-E-C-T

The Webster dictionary defines respect as: to take notice of; to regard with special attention; to regard as worthy of special consideration; hence, to care for; to heed; to consider worthy of esteem; to regard with honor.

It is clear that no man can be the king of his castle without respect. If his woman won't submit to his authority then how can he move the family forward as the leader? Now, keep in mind, I'm only referring to good men, not the cheaters, not the players, and not the irresponsible boys masquerading as men. With that being said, why are some women so adamantly against the word submission? It does not mean to abuse. It merely implies that a woman should yield to her man, to comply with the decision he has made. The responsibility of the woman is to choose a man whose decision-making she trusts in the first place, and to choose a man who is wise enough to consult her before making important decisions. But once her choice is made both people cannot have the last word. Both people cannot lead! Someone has to submit!

It's amazing to me that on one hand these same women who are dead set against submission have no problem submitting to the pastor at church or their bosses at work. They are careful to use a respectful tone and to comply with whatever direction they are given by these men; however, the man who has committed to them as a life partner often gets less respect than these men who have no stake whatsoever in her well-being. These are also the same women who are shocked when they discover their man is cheating with a less attractive and less educated woman. Well, guess what? She may not be beautiful or have a degree but she understood how to talk to him and how to treat him. Equality may sound idealistic but the reality is we all have a role to play; my advice for women is to find yours and stop picking and choosing when to play wife.

A WOMAN WHO HAS HIS BACK!

A ny man who is serious about pursuing his dream must make sacrifices and work long hours. If his woman is not his biggest cheerleader then what good is she? When times get tough, a man needs a woman in his corner who will put her arms around him and say, "Hang in their baby, you can do it!" Some women have supported their men financially, some have provided important contacts, and others have put in time to help build the business.

A woman from New York put it this way, "An ambitious man will never be happy unless he's pursuing something worthwhile, so why not support him and help make him successful, then you both win!" Unfortunately, some women are afraid to see their men succeed. They worry that as soon as he "Makes it" he will leave the marriage or relationship. My response to that is simple. Never help your man expecting something in return, that's not being genuine. If you truly love your man, you want to see him win regardless if you stay together or not. This is a classic case of women claiming to love their men unconditionally, while at the same time expecting a payoff for the time they put in. In many ways, women can be just as selfish as men. They just don't want to admit it.

LET FREEDOM RING!

During the taping of my relationship film, *Love, Lust, and Lies,* a woman from Atlanta was asked, what do you think men want? Her response was, "Men want their freedom!" The men who were on the set started to applaud and so did I. There is nothing more important for a grown man than to know his freedom has not been taken away simply because he says, "I do." When he promised to love, honor, and cherish, he meant it. But most men don't expect their lives to change just because they give you the label of wife or girlfriend, especially when it comes to hanging out with friends and having a curfew. A healthy relationship should expand your world, not reduce it!

Regardless if the man is being faithful or not, trying to control his comings and goings is a recipe for disaster! Men will tolerate nagging, excessive shoe shopping, even having their closets and bathrooms hijacked with feminine hygiene products, but no real man will accept that his relationship will forever restrict him from having a sense of freedom.

Notice I said a sense of freedom because as husbands and boyfriends we understand that we must be accountable to our partners, but there is a thin line between accountability and imprisonment! Come on, ladies, if we're going to keep it real, men are going to do what they want to do anyway. You're not going to make the situation any better by making his escape more difficult. It will only add stress to the relationship. In the end it all boils down to trusting your man to be responsible. Wasting your time trying to control where he is and whom he's with is just plain silly. Let it go, or let go of the relationship. It's that simple!

MEN 101

Ok, ladies, it's time to break out your note pads. Now that I've given you an overview of what men want, I want to prepare you for an even more interesting lesson on how men think. Initially, I was going to write an entirely new book on the topic of, "Do men know what they want?" But after filming my documentary, *"Do Women Know What They Want?"* I discovered that most of the issues that men have in their relationships were in the original version of *Never Satisfied: How and Why Men Cheat*. So, instead, I added new stories from the men and women I interviewed on the show over the years. I also changed the perspectives I wrote between the stories. I've learned a lot in the past sixteen years and I wanted to share that with my daughter and nieces as well as all of you and yours.

I realize that some people will always consider my views to be controversial and over the top. But the truth will always be controversial. But this book is not about my truth, these stories are your stories, from the CEOs to the stay-at-home moms. I promise that you'll be enlightened by the stories on all sides. The most important lesson I learned during this project was that men and women do want the same things, good sex, respect, honesty, security, but sometimes our insecurity, lack of self-esteem, and even our cultures get in the way of us having healthy relationships. Sometimes we need a new perspective to find a better way to reach our goals. And trust me, this will be different.

So, look at this book as edutainment: education and entertainment! I always found that combination to be the best way to hold an audience's attention. And what could be more engaging than a debate about what men and women want? My documentary film will address the issues of what women want, so now let's see if we can agree on what men want. And the best way to understand what men want is to understand what men think about everything from sex, relationships, and, of course, why they cheat. Let the games begin!

2
SMOOTH OPERATOR

What methods will a man utilize to conceal his affair? And how many lies will he tell to maintain these sordid relationships? These tricks, or games as women refer to them, have been the reasons behind many break-ups and divorces. It seems technology has made the game of cheating much simpler to play with the innovation of social networking sites such as Facebook and Twitter. But regardless of scientific advances one simple fact remains: a man must forever keep his lies straight because with one slip of the tongue his world could come tumbling down around him.

The Hunt

Any successful hunt must begin with the selection of the ideal location to find a particular animal. The cheating man understands this fact and has carefully considered where he will lay his insidious traps. The most commonly preferred places are the bars, nightclubs and lounges. These meat markets provide the perfect stalking grounds for any man with the desire to temporarily resign from his relationship. Nowhere else can such an alluring combination of women, alcohol, and immorality be found under one roof. And because so many women lack self-esteem and role models of how a man is supposed to treat a woman, men don't have to possess intelligent conversation or good manners. All he has to do is appear to have money and walk around with enough "Swagger" and the panties come flying off. Usually without last names being exchanged or the use of a condom!

Considering that those women who frequent these establishments are aware of the perpetrating and shallow nightlife, one might wonder, "Why do they continually go back for more?" Well, men have formulated their own ideas; they believe these women are desperately lonely, bored, or simply hard up. Are they right? Most women would probably say no, but actions speak louder than words. Every weekend they pile inside overcrowded clubs wearing tight skirts, heavy makeup, and their breasts pushed up to their chins. Their piercing stares and suggestive body language declares, "Tonight is the night." There is no doubt many of these women, while not openly admitting it, are romantically entertaining thoughts of finding that special man, *Mr. Right*. Unfortunately, this obscure fantasy plays right into the hands of the hunter who will most certainly use it as leverage to get what he really wants, uncommitted sex.

Some women do eventually wake up and realize the club is no place to meet a decent man. After years of putting up with the exhausting and childish games associated with nightlife, they grab their coats and purses vowing never to return. However, this rude awakening is of no concern to the hunter who is confident that next week will bring countless others to take their places. They will be lined up halfway around the block in the cold and rain, desperately waiting to get into the club, like lambs being led to slaughter. And it is from amongst these unsuspecting creatures that the next "other woman" will be chosen. The question is, who will it be, and why was she chosen?

Choosing the Other Woman

The attitude of many women is, "Men will lie down with anything with a heartbeat." That indictment may well be valid if the cheating man is only interested in a one-night stand. However, if he intends on maintaining an ongoing affair, specific requirements must be met, one of which is empathy. The other woman must be willing to accept his current relationship without "rocking the boat." Most cheating men, especially the married ones, will come right out and tell her the details of his situation. With such a large number of women to choose from, the odds are in his favor. Many women today are so desperate for a man they will accept that he's married, living with another woman, or has several other women. As one woman told me, "A piece of man is better than no man!"

Sexual inhibition is another requirement. John from Chicago stated, "If the other woman won't allow me to be sexually adventurous then what the hell do I need her for? I can be bored at home." His comment is typical of most married men who cheat. The other woman must be willing to do all those things they are afraid or unwilling to ask their wives or girlfriends to do. In the mind of the cheating man, the other woman isn't held to a high moral standard. The fact that she is settling for a man who is already taken is the perfect excuse to treat her like a whore, which in many cases is exactly what she is. Why should any man respect a woman who knowingly allows herself to be hidden from his wife and the rest of the world? If she wants to play this game then she must play by his rules, and believe it or not, some women play this role for years, giving up the best years of their lives to be put in the second, third, or even fourth position.

Loyalty is another important attribute for the other woman.

The cheating man, despite his own infidelity, needs a woman whom he can trust not to "Run The Streets." If he calls at midnight on a Saturday night, she had better pick up the phone. He doesn't want to hear any excuses about her being too busy hanging out with her girlfriends. In his mind, she is his personal sex slave who is at his beck and call 24-7. As the relationship develops, she is restricted from pursuing other intimate relationships and is expected to be completely loyal to him. Any breach of this unwritten contract will prompt him to terminate the affair and go hunting elsewhere. Women see this as hypocritical since he himself is cheating. But surprisingly many women tolerate this nonsense. In their minds his jealousy is evidence that he cares about her. When the only thing he really cares about is what he's getting out of the relationship. It's all about him!

Physical beauty would have to be the least most important attribute. Don't get me wrong; I'm not implying that men who cheat are only interested in ugly women. What I'm merely saying is, a woman who is exceptionally attractive and terrible in bed is not all that valuable an asset to the cheating man. He would prefer a woman of moderate looks who's great in bed, and who has her own place where he can go to creep. Oftentimes, the overly attractive woman is seen as a liability because she is more likely to make demands of his time and money. And since most cheating men are broke, the last thing they need is an additional expense. The philosophy is, "Keep it simple, keep it cheap, and keep it on the down low."

The process of choosing this qualified other woman from out of the crowd is a complex one. As you well know, the nightclub is a very dense place. Therefore, the hunter must keep his eyes sharp and position himself in the areas where his efforts can be maximized. Often you will notice him sitting at the bar, standing by the door, or looking down over the crowd from atop his perch. He wants to be the first to move in for the kill if a vulnerable woman should arrive, or should I say, a wounded animal? Once he spots his target, the chase is on. Armed with a fresh haircut, splash of cologne, and hopefully a breath mint, he sets out on his lustful safari.

Just as the animal hunter relies on guns, traps, and camouflage to capture his prey, the cheating man depends on smooth talk, good looks, and the low self-esteem of his victims to accomplish his goals. But determining whether a particular woman has the characteristics that will suit his purpose is not such an easy task in the nightclub environment. Loud music, incurable perpetrating, and the woman's blocking girlfriends make the process all the more difficult. This leaves him with little else to go on except a woman's attire. More precisely, what she's wearing and how she's wearing it. This is the first indication as to her level of availability, class, and morality. But due to the fact that short, tight outfits are commonplace wherever you go, the perception is that most of the women in the club are dizzy, promiscuous whores looking for action. Some men may perceive it as an invitation to touch, grasp and be disrespectful. There is no doubt many women expect these types of impulses since they go to such great lengths to expose so much of themselves. They are shamelessly sending a message regarding their availability, while adamantly demanding to be acknowledged. The hunter is merely reimbursing her for her troubles. And it doesn't help that women are on the dance floor bouncing and grinding to songs that refer to them as bitches and hos, while at the same time demanding to be respected. It's a complete contradiction!

On the other hand, the woman who elects to dress conservatively is viewed as more ethical and self-assured. The message she sends is, "I'm confident enough in what I am wearing to attract a man who respects me and is not out just looking for sex." Some men also perceive her as more intelligent and classy. Mature and self-confident women constantly complain about how difficult it is to compete for attention when the majority of women are willing to stroll around half-naked and throw themselves at men. And since the majority of men on the club scene are not interested in your IQ, advanced degrees, or the last great book you read, the more provocatively dressed woman wins nine times out of ten! After all, he's not looking for a lifelong wife to take home to mamma, only a part-time hoochie to take home to bed.

Clearly, the nightclub is nothing more than a weekly production specifically designed for play, profit, and perpetrating. The music is loud, the drinks are expensive, and everyone is dressed to impress. So what if many of the women don't have furniture in their apartment or even an apartment. And who cares if the guy has a 300 credit score or three baby mammas. On this pretentious stage nothing is what it appears to be. When the doors open, the curtain goes up and it's show time. Unemployed men suddenly become record producers and women on welfare masquerade as fashion models. With all the role-playing and B.S. going on it's no wonder women complain about not being able to find a good man at the club. Hell, even a so-called good man will step out to briefly forget just how good he is.

However, not all men seek their mistresses and lovers at these "night spots." Most prefer surroundings that are more comfortable and familiar, a place where they can mix business with pleasure.

Fooling Around on the J-O-B

While the nighttime may be the right time, the daytime has become prime time...for fooling around that is. The workplace has become the "hot spot" for infidelity. Every statistic shows that the J-O-B is the number one place where affairs begin, and although many companies have strict policies against fraternizing with co-workers, that hasn't stopped the avalanche of affairs and inappropriate flirting.

For the first time in American history, female workers represent nearly fifty percent of the work force, occupying every position from secretary to CEO. This reality puts men and women in direct contact with one another on a daily basis. In the morning they board crowded buses and trains together. And for eight long hours they work in cramped office spaces, brushing up against one another by accident and by choice. It was only a matter of time before the fireworks began. A cordial invitation to have a quick lunch passionately erupts into an indecent proposal to have a quickie for lunch. All the while, the cheater is getting paid.

There should be no mystery as to why extramarital affairs are flourishing in the workplace. It is the ideal place for the cheating man to meet a woman who is compatible, desirable, and accessible. Unlike the club scene, the workplace allows for a more gradual progression towards intimacy; there is no rush. In this environment the cheating man appears more like a scavenger, leisurely waiting for the slow death of an existing relationship so he can swoop down like a vulture and pick up the scraps of the emotionally torn victim. He is a great listener, too, especially if it's a negative story about the woman's husband or boyfriend. He appears to be a reliable shoulder to cry on; never realizing the support he really wants to give is in the form of his erect penis.

Workplace affairs are mutually pursued involvements where

both parties are generally up front about their marital status and living arrangements. The woman complains that her husband doesn't appreciate her, and the man swears his existing relationship is on the rocks. However, one or both of them is usually lying. Most cheaters know that honesty isn't always the best policy. The trick is to bend the truth a bit until the woman's heart is firmly secured in the trap. How many times have you heard the lie, "My woman doesn't understand me?" Or "My wife is married but I'm not." And if all-else fails, he'll give her his best line, "I'm just waiting for the kids to get older then I'm getting a divorce," when he knows damn well he's not going anywhere with three kids to support and a mortgage to pay.

The real question is, do women really fall for these tired lines? Or do they simply accept them in order to justify the relationship in their own minds? The cheating man doesn't care one way or the other. His only objective is to relax her defenses long enough to reel her in emotionally. Any lie will do.

Inconsistency

Men who elect to tell these lies about being miserable at home must continue to show signs of their unhappiness. Now the game becomes more complicated and the likelihood of getting caught increases. The wife or girlfriend begins to notice a sudden change in his attitude and his routine. First, he starts showing up late from work. "I had to work an extra shift, baby," he'll say. But his overtime is usually doing it doggy style at the motel with his mistress. Then he'll discourage her from visiting him on the job. No doubt to avoid running into his work *whore*. Finally, the most obvious signs of infidelity, working out more at the gym, buying new underwear, or his wedding ring abruptly disappears.

Of course, he'll try to use the lame excuse of, "I lost it." When that doesn't work, the next step is to merely find a reason to leave it at home altogether. Men are notorious for using their work as a reason for taking off their bands. "It's interfering with my ability to do my job," he says. Now, that excuse may not be much of a lie, since his new job is chasing pussy.

The dead giveaway that an affair is going on is simply this, inconsistency. Men are notorious for changing their habits. The once-a-week night out with the boys becomes two or three times a week. Sexually he does not perform the same, if at all. And there will certainly be a shift in his attitude. Men are so bad at cheating that they consciously and unconsciously begin to pick fights to justify their cheating. Recently I did a topic on my radio show during Sloppy Cheaters Monday. I asked women if there was such a thing as a respectful cheater? Mind you, I know that cheating is wrong and that men are already being disrespectful when they decide to cheat, but I wanted to make a point. Not surprisingly, most women agreed that there is a right way and a wrong way to creep. The expression that you often hear is, "Just don't bring it home!"

During the taping of my film, *Love, Lust, and Lies*, a woman from New York made it clear as to what that meant. "She better not call me, she better not know where I lay my head, and she damn sure better not be able to describe my house or what's inside my bedroom." Her point was simple; don't allow another woman to impact my day-to-day life. No diseases, no outside children, no significant monetary investment, and no drama! But because men allow their smaller head to do all the thinking, one or more of these situations usually become an issue. But even after being busted over and over again the hunt will continue. The next task is to find a way to communicate with his new lover without being detected. Now the real games begin.

CALL ME

" Communication is the key to any successful relation-ship." This is the claim of many therapists and marriage counselors. The cheating man absolutely agrees with this theory, particularly where communicating with the other woman is concerned. Some men have elevated this phase of cheating to an art form. While others are so stupid you suspect their wives and girlfriends are deaf, dumb, and blind. Regardless of what the man's level of sophistication is, the technology of today has made it simple to make a lust connection. One innovation that has revolutionized infidelity is texting. For the cheating man this was the best invention since the TV remote control. And you know how big a deal that was! Texting on your cell phone is one of the easiest ways to stay in touch with a mistress without having the phone ring, but it's also the most frequent way men get busted. If a woman suspects her man of cheating, the first thing she's going to do is check his cell phone. And if he suddenly puts a security lock on it, he's automatically guilty. Not just because he locked his phone, but also because he never locked his phone in the past!

Inconsistency in behavior is a dead giveaway that a man is stepping out. And most men, no matter how slick they think they are, will become inconsistent in one way or another, whether it's inconsistency with his time, sexually, or temperament. Cathy from New York said she knew when her husband was cheating because he would suddenly become argumentative. "The minute he started picking fights over little things like laundry and me not answering my phone at a certain time, I knew another women was in his life." In her case, her husband's temperament changed and he became inconsistent. There had to be a better way. Enter Facebook!

Currently, I have over 500,000 friends on Baisdenlive on Facebook, and 50,000 friends on Baisdenlive on Twitter, the vast majority of them are women. Now, given the fact that I use these social networks to promote the topics on my national radio show every day, it's obvious why I use it regularly. Not to mention, I'm a single heterosexual man who loves the contact with all my beautiful, intelligent, and single women, let's keep it real!

But why would a married man be on Facebook and Twitter beyond chatting with close friends and family? I've been told by many of my single female friends on Facebook that they get hit on by more married men than single men. The married guys also list their status as married, and they post pictures of themselves and their wives. Is that bold or what? This is another example of how out of control and disrespectful men have become towards their significant other. It's also a reflection of how desperate they perceive single women to be. Larry, who is a married 38-year-old teacher in New Jersey, made his point crystal clear. "Why should I hide the fact that I'm married? That's just one less lie to tell when we hook up. If she takes the bait with the understanding that I have a wife and kids, she's accepting that it's all about having sex, period!"

I recently did a show titled, "Does Facebook cause divorce?" It was based on a study done by the American Academy of Matrimonial Lawyers. In it, they stated that an overwhelming number of the nation's top divorce attorneys said that over the past five years they have seen an increase in the number of cases where cheating using social networks has been used as evidence.

Mark, who is 42 years old and lives in Ft. Lauderdale, FL, is one of those statistics. After six years of marriage, he was on his way to divorce court, all because of one click of a button on a social networking site. Casual chatting turned into flirtation, flirtation into texting, texting into phone calls, and phone calls into hooking up. Don't get me wrong; I'm not blaming Facebook, no more than I would blame my social networking site Minglecity.com. But sites like these do allow people to have access to millions of single, lonely, and sometimes desperate people, and it can all be done anonymously. And because the communication is lacking in most relationships, it's easy to understand how people can get lost in these fantasy relationships rather than deal with the reality of their own situation and try to work things out! Mark learned the consequences of flirting on line the hard way! I call this story "Poke me!"

Poke Me

I joined Facebook towards the end of the year; I remember because it was right before Thanksgiving Day. I loaded all my information and photos into my albums and send out a friend request to all my Frat brothers, close friends and family. The first time I had any contact from Kyla was on January second. My wife was visiting her family in Miami and I was home alone working on a graphic project on my computer. Right before I powered down I logged onto my Facebook account to see if I had any messages. That's when I noticed that Kyla had poked me. If you're not familiar with Facebook, poking is a feature that let's you know someone noticed you; it's like saying hello. Now, keep in mind, my relationship status on my profile read "Married to Kimberly" and there was a photo of my wife and me posted as my main picture. It was the one of us in Cancun; I had on my black swim trunks flexing my muscles and she had on a one-piece bathing suit. Ever since our son was born five years ago she was self-conscious about her stretch marks, not to mention, she never did lose the weight around her stomach.

Anyway, out of fun, I poked her back and send her a friend request. She accepted. Shortly after that, I sent her a short and cordial message.

"Thanks for accepting my friend request, have a happy new year!"

Mark

Then I turned my computer off. Early the next morning I started back to work and noticed there was a message from Kyla. It read:

Thanks for the Happy New Year shout out! I'm already headed to the gym while my lazy friends are still getting over their hangovers. Another year, another challenge!

Chat with you later.

Kyla

This time I went to her profile page. Her main photo was of a waterfall so I had no idea of what she looked like. When I clicked on her profile photos, my first reaction was, "Damn!" She was gorgeous!

She had short hair and cinnamon brown skin. It was obvious from her pictures that she was into fitness; she posted several photos of herself working out in the gym. Her abs and leg muscles were toned and her ass was round and tight. My dick instantly got hard.

At that point, I knew I was in trouble. I should have clicked the unfriend button and blocked her right then and there, but instead I decided to flirt. I tiptoed back into the bedroom to make sure my wife was still asleep. Once I was sure she was knocked out, I started typing.

Good morning sexy, thanks again for the poke and accepting my friend request. I wanted to tell you how impressed I am with your commitment to taking care of your body. I work out myself. Maybe we can exchange health tips from time to time.
Have a great day!
Mark

There was nothing innocent about my message, I was trying to be cordial hoping she would take the bait. Not that I was expecting to have sex with her, but I wanted to at least start a dialogue. Later that day after my wife and I came back from shopping, I rushed to put away the groceries so I could check to see if I had any messages from Kyla. My wife went straight to the bedroom and tuned into her reality TV show. She knew I hated those programs so she was accustomed to me going to my office and closing the door. "Perfect!" I was thinking.

Sure enough when I logged on to my Facebook account, Kyla had left another message.

Well, hello Mark, and thanks for the compliment. I work out 4 to 5 days a week at a gym on Alton Rd. in South Beach. You and your wife should come down and join me sometimes. I noticed you're in pretty good shape yourself. It's all about diet and discipline, right? Hope to hear from you soon!
Toodles!
Kyla

Why did she have to mention my wife, I thought to myself. But I looked past that and was glad she was leaving the lines of communication open. I thought about keeping it cordial, but I figured, what the hell, she knows I'm married, so why not go for it! All she could do was say no, and I would go back to living my life. I took a deep breath and started typing.

Just name the time and place, I'll be there! I work from home not too far from you in Coral Gables so my schedule is flexible. Not sure if my wife can make it, she's not really into working out. You know how some black women are about sweating their hair out! lol

   I'm looking forward to throwing some weights up with you soon! Have a great day!

Mark

In hindsight, that was the e-mail that stepped over the line. Not only had I indirectly made a date to meet this woman, I was dogging out my wife by saying she was lazy and out of shape. But like so many men, my little head was doing all the thinking so I pressed send. Kyla's response came within ten minutes.

Mark, are you being naughty? lol The invitation was for you and your wife. But I kinda figured she was not a regular in the gym when I saw your profile picture. You were buffed and she was clearly not in shape. I never understand why black women let themselves go once they get a man. Each time I go, the gym is full of White and Latino women working out to keep it tight. I guess some people just get comfortable, right?

   Let's meet up tomorrow morning around 10, the 9 to 5ers will be gone by then and we can have the gym to ourselves and really work up a sweat! (smile) Text me your cell number and I'll text you the directions. See you then Marky!

Kyla

These are the moments that every married man knows is the proverbial "crossing the line" moment. First of all she asked for my cell phone number. "Big mistake!" I was thinking. But I sent it anyway. Secondly, she added to my negative comments about my wife being out of shape. Another red flag, but I ignored it! And lastly, she clearly made a conscious effort to reach out to me based on my swim trunk photo showing off my biceps. Stalker tendency and home wrecker was written all over that one! But like so many other bored and horny married men, I took the bait. Of course, I justified it by saying to myself, "We're just going to work out." Yeah right! I was already fantasizing about fucking her against the Stairmaster.

Once my wife was off to work, I packed up my workout gear and dropped my son off at pre-school. In the six years of my marriage I had never cheated. As I merged onto I-95 North I was nervous and excited by what might happen. Let's face it; married life can be very mundane. Every day it's the same routine, breakfast, work, drop off kids, pick up kids, do homework or play time, eat dinner, watch Reality TV, no sex, and go to sleep. Kyla was right about my wife getting comfortable; there was no excuse for her still being out of shape five years after our son was born. The local gym was less than five blocks away. I offered to pay for her membership and a personal trainer but she always had an excuse. She was either tired, had dinner plans with her girlfriends, or she had just got her hair done. Kyla was right about that, too; too many women, especially black women, put their hair before their health. I still was in love with my wife but the handwriting was on the wall; she was never going to lift a dumbbell or go to a spin class. At least that's what I told myself as I pulled into the parking lot of the gym. I had to find some way to justify what I was doing.

The gym was practically empty when I walked in; there were

two muscle bound guys bench-pressing in the free weight area and a woman jogging on the treadmill. Suddenly, Kyla came rushing in the door behind me; sweat was dripping down her face and across her bare stomach. She had on a pair of running shorts and sports bra, which showed off her erect nipples.

"Hey Marky! You look exactly like your pictures," she pressed herself against me tightly and hugged me around the neck like we had known each other for years. "Come on in, make yourself at home. I'm going to grab a quick shower and I'll be right back."

I took off the shirt I had over my wife beater and began to stretch. The gym was laid out perfectly for real bodybuilders, nothing but free weights and cardio machines. I was on my second set on the bench press machine when Kyla came out of the locker room. She stood over me to spot me as I added more weights to the bar.

"Don't try to show off and hurt yourself!" she laughed.

"This is what I do everyday," I told her. "So, you can just stand back so you don't get hurt!"

"Hurt me, daddy!" she said while standing over me with her legs straddling my head. "I like it rough!"

I damned near dropped the bar on my chest looking up at the imprint of her pussy through her shorts. But I managed to get in the rest of my set. Once I got up from the bench, I noticed that the gym was completely empty.

"Where did everybody go?"

"Let's just say, I'm closed for lunch!"

"So, this is your place?"

"No, I just manage it for an old boyfriend of mine. But I set the hours and make the rules."

"I bet you do!" I laughed.

"What's that supposed to mean?"

"It means that it's obvious that you do what you want to do, and…!" I paused.

"And what?"

"And you get what you want!"

"Am I gonna get what I want today, Mark?" she said while sitting in front of me on the bench and putting her hands on my dick."

"And what's that?" I said playing dumb.

"Come on now, you didn't think I invited you down here just to pump iron did you?"

"Well, you did invite me and my wife."

"Chile please, I knew she wouldn't show, and if she did it wouldn't be long before she stopped coming! One look at her in that photo of you and her on Facebook and I knew she was retired."

"What do you mean, retired?"

"You know retired, as in done working, as in done competing, as in done fucking!"

I wanted to act offended that she tried to read my wife, our marriage, and me but she was right. My sex life was non-existent. And the energy she was giving me was so strong; there was no way I was leaving that gym without touching and tasting her. She was confident, beautiful, and sexually creative, everything my wife used to be. I felt like I owed it to myself to take what she was offering, if only for that one time. So, I did.

That affair went on for several months, but my affair with Kyla was not what broke my wife and me apart. Kyla was the first of three women I connected with that year on Facebook and other websites. She was just the woman who opened the door. By October of that year my wife had hacked into my e-mails and read every letter I ever sent out. She even saw all the provocative photos of the ladies I was sleeping with. Now my son is being raised in a single-parent household, and I'm paying alimony and child support all because I chose to avoid my problems instead of addressing them. So, married men beware, if your relationship is on the rocks, the Internet is the last place you want to be. Your whole life can be shattered with a single e-mail, just as mine was. It all started and ended with a poke!

Getting Busy

Keeping in touch with the other woman is no simple task. It is often a stressful process. With every new lover comes a renewed battle with the suspicious wife or girlfriend to see to it that his whorish plans are not interfered with. Facebook and Twitter apps loaded, cell phones turned off, undercover texting, and alibis set. Whew! It's enough to make your head spin. But that's just the tip of the iceberg. Once he's resolved his communication issues, the desperate and horny cheater must face yet another challenge, devising a plot to justify leaving out of the house long enough to "Get Busy." I call this process, *The Great Escape*.

THE ESCAPE

Many women may view "The Escape" as an overly exaggerated term to describe the man's desire to get away to see the other woman. But if you present this same expression to the man who cheats, he'll understand precisely why it fits perfectly. Past experiences have taught him that getting away to fool around is not so easy, especially if he's shacking or married. Some men spend hours, if not days, thinking up elaborate excuses to explain their temporary or overnight absences. They sometimes enlist the help of close friends and family members to pull off this charade. And that's the problem with lies, you always have to build on them and involve other people. At some point the lies don't add up, or you tell so many lies you start tripping over them.

The most interesting thing I discovered over the years of discussing infidelity and relationships in a series I call "Sloppy Cheaters" is that the same men who feel trapped were often the same ones who insisted on being in a committed relationship in the first place. Yes, men are usually the ones who suggest or pressure the woman into being a couple. That's right, I said it! Men are greedy but they're not stupid, at least not when it relates to recognizing a quality woman. The biggest dog in the world knows when he has a good thing and he'll try to hold on to it at all costs. So, we try to tie the woman down by selling her a fantasy, putting a ring on it, or whatever, and all the while we're out there poking every Mary, Jane, and Shaneequa.

Now, I realize how confusing this must be for most women. Many of them ask, "If men value their relationships so much why would they risk cheating in the first place?" Or they ask, "Why can't men just be upfront about wanting to see other women and spare all the time and energy it takes to creep?" First of all, no man cheats with the expectation of getting caught. For whatever reason, men think their game is so tight that they're going to get away with it. WRONG! Most men are very reckless when it comes to cheating. Ninety percent of the time our women know we're cheating; they either ignore the obvious signs, or accept it and keep their mouths shut. Hell, the wife or girlfriend might be cheating, too, as the expression goes, "What's good for the goose is good for the gander!" And to answer the question as to why men aren't honest and upfront about wanting to see other women? Simple; men don't want their woman to exercise the same option to see other men. Bottom line! So instead of being truthful and open, we have a nation of grown-ass men, some as old as 60, telling lies to get out of the house so they can go cheat. How pathetic!

As the night's secret rendezvous draws nearer, the walls seemingly begin to close in on the horny cheater. His comfortably furnished living room is subconsciously transformed into a cramped jail cell. "What in the world can I tell her to get out of here tonight?" he contemplates. As the clock ticks, the tension mounts. The man of the house now sees himself as the inmate of the house; likewise the innocent wife or girlfriend is also transformed. Where there once stood a docile woman in hair rollers now stands the fierce warden with the keys to his freedom. What drama! And to think, all of this hallucinating because we as men are not mature enough to be truthful in the beginning of the relationship. For the majority of us the truth is never an option. As far back as I can remember not one man in my life has ever told me, "Michael, always be honest with women." To the contrary, young men are encouraged to have sex with as many girls as they want, just don't get caught! Little do we know some women will accept the truth and continue to date us, and most importantly, there's never a loss of respect. It's unfortunate that men don't put a value on that. Nothing hurts a woman more than being disrespected and nothing is more unforgivable than being humiliated!

Since the warden, I mean, the wife or girlfriend won't issue a temporary pardon, the desperate cheating man must devise a plan of escape. Carl, who lives in Detroit and has been married for 8 years, admitted that he's mastered the art of escaping for most of his marriage. "When you meet someone new, the desire to be with them is so intense, you just want to be with them." he says, "And it's almost as if my wife can sense it and she comes up with last-minute plans to keep me busy. I look at the challenge of getting away to cheat like the movie, *The Shawshank Redemption*. You have to chisel your way out, one bar at a time!"

Playing Ball

Sporting events such as baseball, basketball, and football are the most common excuses men use to lie their way out of the house. Supposedly, they are either watching or playing. My guess would be playing. And since one or more of these sports are being played year round, it's become the perfect alibi for getting out day or night, summer or winter. I know men who play so much golf their wives don't expect to see them for hours at a time. Every Saturday morning they leave home hoping for "a hole in one," pun intended. When they return home exhausted from a long workout it's not from playing tennis or flag football.

This is another example of how the cheating man misman-ages his affairs. Instead of holding his ejaculation, he empties himself into the other woman, usually without a condom, and has to avoid intimacy with the wife/girlfriend because he can't perform. And since most women know their man is cheating, this becomes the proverbial slap in the face. Not only is she expected to tolerate his lying and cheating, but she has to do without sex because he is giving the other woman his energies, too. This is the straw that breaks it for many women who often declare, "Two can play that game!" We'll address that concept in a later chapter.

But let me get back to the horny cheater trying to escape. It's not just the lie about playing sports that helps men get out of the house, it's the lie about going to watch sports. It's the perfect excuse to get away with cheating because most women are programmed to unlock the cell and allow their men out on game nights. This custom has been passed down from generation to generation. Most women have experienced this with their fathers, uncles, and brothers, so it's usually no big deal. Even if the wife or girlfriend loves sports too, she understands that she is not invited unless the other guys invite their wives or girlfriends, which is almost never.

But even with the perfect alibi the cheating man always finds a way to mess up. Phil found that out when he tried to slip out of the house for a quickie. He has been with his wife Liz for 6 years, married 4, and the sports alibi was his patented move. It was working perfectly, until he did what most cheating men do over time, he got comfortable.

Phil's Story

When I want to use sports as an excuse to get out, I arrange to have one of my buddies call my house about an hour or two before game time. For example, if the game comes on at seven, the call comes in at around five thirty or six. The time factor is critical since receiving phone calls too early or too late would make leaving out of the house more awkward. You want to make it seem like it slipped your mind, "Oh, that's right, the game is on tonight! Baby, I've gotta go!" That way it seems more spontaneous! Get the point? Another important part of the set up is choosing the right caller. I prefer someone who my wife is familiar with, like a close friend or co-worker. Having a perfect stranger call is a definite no-no.

The last time I used this scheme was last season during the NBA playoffs. I planned a hot date with my lady friend Karen at 7:00 p.m. Friday. She was bragging all day about what she was going to do to me so you know I had to get away to shut her up. At 6:00 p.m., my best friend Brian called. I made sure my wife was in position to answer the phone. This way she could identify who it was. Right after they said their hellos, I went into my act.

"Brian, what's up? A basketball game you say? Who's playing? The Chicago Bulls and The Miami Heat huh, cool! The MVP Derrick Rose is gonna take LeBron and Wade to school tonight!"

I made sure to talk as loud as possible so that she would overhear our conversation. I didn't want her to get the impression it was my idea to go out. When she tried to walk out of the room, I followed her around the house with the phone. This performance was especially for her and she was gonna hear all of it whether she liked it or not.

"So, what time did you say the game starts, eight? Cool, I'll bring the chips and pretzels, and you pick up the beer. I should be there around 7:30 p.m., catch you later."

Talk about Academy Award for Best Actor. There I was running off at the mouth about our fake plans while my buddy Brian was laughing his ass off on the other end. When the presentation was complete, I casually began putting on my blue jeans and Bulls jersey; I wanted to look the part. Meanwhile, my wife was giving me one of those suspicious looks. But because I've done such a great job of acting, I fool myself into believing I was actually going to watch basketball. As I walked towards the door, I put on my Chicago Bulls cap to look authentic.

"See you later baby," I said. "Don't wait up!"

"Ok sweetheart," she said sarcastically, "have a nice time," she paused, "with the boys."

Now, what the hell did she mean by that remark? I thought as I shut the door behind me. At the time, I didn't care. I was a free man, and Karen was anxiously waiting at her place buck naked with a bottle of wine on ice. I got in my car, put in one of my old Isley Brothers CDs, and hit the road. At 8:00 p.m. I arrived at Karen's apartment. She answered the door wearing a sexy red bra and panty set. I wanted to commit a few flagrant fouls of my own, if you catch my drift. By 10:00 p.m., I had gone through two glasses of wine and three condoms. She was screaming so loud the neighbors must have thought someone was trying to kill her. Or maybe they figured she was an overzealous basketball fan. At 11:00 p.m. I washed up, put on my clothes and headed home. "What a game," I joked to myself. But on this night, my wife would take me into overtime.

When I walked in the door, she was still awake watching television. My first impulse was to run to the bathroom and check myself out, but I wanted to act normal. So I calmly hung my jacket in the closet and went over to give her a kiss. But before I could put my arms around her, she began questioning me about the outcome of the game.

"So, how was the game?" she asked.

"It was great! The Bulls looked pretty good tonight."

"Yeah, they did alright," she said. "But they need much better scoring off the bench."

"Since when did you start watching basketball?"

"I watch it all the time," she said sounding smart. "But I guess you wouldn't know that since you're gone every time there's a game on. By the way, did you see that vicious dunk by LeBron in the fourth quarter?

"Oh shit!" I thought to myself. I was so busy laying the pipe to Karen that I forgot to take in a few of the highlights of the game. She had me with my pants down, and I sensed that she knew it. But instead of accusing me of outright lying, she played it cool and allowed me to cut my own throat.

"No, I must have missed that when I made a run to the store for more beer."

"What about the clutch free throw Derrick Rose made right before halftime?" she asked. "I couldn't believe he missed it."

"I couldn't believe it either, baby. You would think a professional basketball player could at least make a lousy free throw, right?"

"Oh, and what about that hard foul Carlos Boozer gave Dwayne Wade at the end of the game?"

"Yeah, that was pretty bad. I love how the Bulls play physical. It's like watching football."

Why in the world did I say that? I fell right into her trap. She grabbed the remote and switched the television channel to Sports Center on ESPN. Right on cue, the basketball highlights came on. She gave me a nasty stare and excused herself to go to the bathroom. I stood there like a fool while the sports announcer commented on the Dallas Mavericks game. "What was the big deal?" you ask. Well, I told her I was watching the Bulls-Heat Game, but the game on that night was the Dallas Mavericks and The Oklahoma City Thunder. Needless to say, I flunked her unexpected pop quiz. That incident taught me one very valuable lesson. "Don't forget to watch a little ball while you're out "Playing Ball."

Escaping Labels

Are men really this sloppy and immature when it comes to cheating? Or are women so tolerant that men don't have to reform their cheating ways? I think it's a bit of both. The unfortunate part about Phil's story is that his wife didn't leave him or even threaten to leave. She did what most women do, fuss for a while and then go back to life as usual. Why are women so shocked that nothing ever changes, there are rarely any real consequences.

At times it can be frustrating for me as a forty-something year-old man to report these ridiculous stories about adults who jump through hoops to arrange sex with the other woman. However, when you consider the unrealistic expectations we put on our relationships, it should be no surprise that we end up in the same place over and over again.

The definition of insanity is to repeat the same act expecting a different result. Well, isn't that what we're doing in our relationships? We meet someone, have sex, fall in love or lust, and put a label on him or her. Then we expect them to act in accordance with that label.

But what does that label really mean? For example, if a man tells you he's married, should you assume he's monogamous? If a woman admits to having a boyfriend, should you assume that she is exclusive to him sexually or emotionally? My point is labels alone mean nothing without a verbal agreement! An understanding of precisely what the boundaries and rules are within that relationship.

The reason why we have so many men scheming on ways to get away to cheat is because the label of husband or boyfriend for that particular man did not mean he would stop having sex with other women. Maybe the label meant, "I want to raise a family with you." Or "You'll be the person I introduce to my family as my primary partner." Or it could mean, "I will only love you." But how will a woman ever know what that label means to that man if all she does is slap a label on him and say, now we're together! Without any real understanding of what that togetherness means to him. Monogamy and commitment are two separate issues for men. Don't ever forget it!

I'm not trying to minimize the responsibility of men to be honest but let's face it, women don't ask enough questions. In part because once they find "The One" they are hesitant to do or say anything that will scare that man away, especially after she's bragged about him to all her friends and family. Now, the pressure is on her to play the part.

To give you an example of how irresponsible and naïve women can be at times, I produced a documentary in 2011 titled, "Do Women Know What They Want?" The first question I asked a group of women was, "When you meet a single man, do you assume he's dating or having sex with other women?" Over half of the women said they assume he's celibate or not dating anyone else. That's right! In 2011 women of all ages and races, educated and blue collar, stated that they would believe that a single, heterosexual man is celibate or at least not dating! How is that ratio even possible considering women's attitude towards men in general?

On one hand women will profess, "A man is going to be a man!" Or, "A man will sleep with anything with a hole in it!" Or as a woman from Orlando said to me, "I teach my daughters not to pay attention to what a man says, but what he does!"

I actually agree with all three of those comments and so do many of you who are reading this book. But here's the twist, if the vast majority of women believe this is the nature of men, why in the world would they assume he's not having sex with another woman when they meet him? That's a classic case of living in denial. Even if a man tells you he's not having sex with anyone else, DON'T BELIEVE HIM!

The fact that over fifty percent of women admitted they would take a man's word for it, indicates to me that most women are so desperate, lonely, horny, or determined to find love, that they will allow themselves to believe anything to achieve their goal. Some women claim they are simply giving him the benefit of the doubt but if you really think about it from a psychological standpoint, what she's really doing is ignoring protocol in hopes that it will lead to something more. A lady friend of mine put it like this, "If the woman is attracted to that man, she's already past the introduction, has already started sizing him up for husband, boyfriend, sex partner, whatever. To accept the idea that he is already emotionally or sexually involved with someone else is a buzz kill!"

But here's my point, this man is a total stranger! You don't know him from a can of paint! How did he get elevated to potential husband, boyfriend, or whatever, without even so much as a credit check! Not to mention a Google search of potential criminal history! Funny how women would never advise their friends to be so trusting but when it comes to managing their own lives, it's often a train wreck!

The After-Work Getaway

So, what does this have to do with men escaping, you ask? Men creating lies to leave home to cheat begins with the lie that he wanted to be monogamous in the first place. That lie was created to make the woman happy and to secure her from being with other men. In the end, men get tired, bored, or scared and eventually cheat anyway, and the woman at some point shuts down, settles, or decides to cheats, too! A woman I interviewed for my documentary film, *Love, Lust, and Lies* called it revenge sex! So, the elaborate schemes to escape home to cheat continue oftentimes with disastrous results.

Earlier I mentioned the workplace is the most common place where men and women hook up for affairs. It makes sense then that the cheating man would use his job as an excuse to get away. The way it works is simple. He calls home to tell his usual lie about working overtime and then leaves directly from work to see the other woman. Sometimes he's actually having sex on the job with a co-worker. You'd be surprised by how many ass prints are on your boss's desk. Men are notorious for breaking the golden rule in business, "Never mix business with pleasure." Or more to the point "Don't shit where you eat!"

The reason why the cheating man prefers to cheat on the job, or after work, is because he can avoid explaining why he has to leave the house again. No man wants to be subjected to the guilt feelings of getting dressed to go out in the presence of his woman, especially since he's not taking her with him. The mere sight of him standing at the mirror, combing his hair, and splashing on his most expensive cologne will surely piss her off. Meanwhile, a subtle inspection is taking place to check that his attire is appropriate for hanging out with the boys, and not for picking up skeezers. She will definitely know something is up if he changes out of his stained boxer shorts into the silk bikini briefs he's been hiding in the bottom of his drawer. Of course, this entire situation can easily be avoided if the proper arrangements are made ahead of time.

One of the most ingenious methods men use to avoid going home to change is taking an extra set of clothes to work, better known as "The hide the clothes in the trunk trick." Better known as a Ho bag! There isn't a cheating man alive who hasn't tried this trick, at least once. The problem, however, is sneaking the clothes inside the car without getting busted. One man said he waits until his wife falls asleep. Another man was so desperate he folded his garment bag up and placed it inside the garbage. Now that's ridiculous! Most cheating men avoid all this drama by purchasing a complete wardrobe and leaving it at the other woman's house.

The single cheating man who lives alone is no less pathetic. He must also devise clever methods of escape to keep his playboy façade intact. Lawrence, who is 34 years old, is the perfect example. He began dating a beautiful young lady four months ago and promised not to have sex with anyone else. As a matter of fact, he also promised not to have other female guests over to his apartment. How stupid can you get? During the first two months of their relationship, he was loyal to his word. But after three months of this torturous treatment, Lawrence began to question his decision to be faithful. "I know a responsible man should stand by his word," he said, "but I was too greedy and too arrogant to do the right thing."

Could he continue to pull off this stunt without alerting his girlfriend to the fact that he is a no good, low down, dirty dog? Let's find out. The preferred method of cheating in this situation is a technique called "Nobody's Home."

Lawrence's Story

I thought that having my own place would allow for some sense of independence, but no. The second you lie down with a woman she starts trying to move in and stake a claim. I've been on my own since I was 21 and I'm not about to give up my freedom just because some woman believes her multiple orgasms grant her the mineral rights to my penis. I don't really like playing these games, but women don't give you any alternative. They come off as sweet and innocent, sex you to death, and then drop a bomb on you, "I want a commitment!"

That's what happened with Terry. We met about four months ago at a poetry reading. When the event was over, we exchanged numbers. We dated for a couple of months before she was comfortable enough to come by my place. We talked for a while and had a few drinks. It wasn't long before things got heated. I damn near ripped my clothes off before she could change her mind. I reached for the condom inside my nightstand drawer and rolled it on. That's when she grabbed my hand and said, "I can't have sex with you unless we have a commitment."

What in the hell did she expect me to say at this point? I mean, really, there I was lying in bed with a firm breast in one hand and a dick as hard as a Chinese calculus in the other. I was liable to say anything, which I did. I told her I would be monogamous. And up until three weeks ago, I kept that promise. But everything began to change as she became more insecure and possessive. She quickly developed the habit of trying to keep track of my whereabouts, or as my nephew would say, she was clocking me. I couldn't even take a piss without my cell phone going off. "Where have you been? Where are you going? What time will you be back?" Her insecurity was enough to drive a man to drinking, or as in my case, cheating.

As the weeks passed things only got worse. Terry began showing up at my job without calling, "I just wanted to surprise you and take you out to lunch," she said. Yeah right! Then there were the late night phone calls to make sure I was home alone. Finally, she made the ultimate mistake of coming by my place unannounced. At the time, I wasn't up to anything, but that was beside the point. She was out of line and had to be put in check.

"You must be out of your damned mind!" I told her. "I pay the bills here! The next time you pull this stunt, your ass is gone, do you understand?"

"Baby, I'm sorry, I was just in the neighborhood and thought I would surprise you."

"First of all, I don't like surprises. And secondly, you live on the other side of town. How in the hell did you just happen to be in the neighborhood?"

"Well, I was ah."

"Ah, ah, is right. Just don't do it again!"

That incident upset me, and it robbed me of the peace I had created in my little cave. There's nothing more valuable to a single man than knowing he controls his space. I should have dropped her ass right then and there but the pussy was too good. "Why is it that the craziest women always seem to have the best coochie?" I was thinking as she drove off. "Damn, damn, damn!"

Three months into the relationship Terry was still trippin', the late night calls slowed down but she was still doing drive-bys ever now and then. So, I developed a strategy to have my cake and eat it, too. One of my most effective moves was to volunteer for the rotating shift at work. This made it impossible for Terry to keep up with my hours and days off. When she called on Sunday afternoon, I told her I was on my way out the door. When she called on Saturday night at 11:30 p.m., I told her I was just getting in. After a couple of weeks of this alternating schedule, I felt comfortable enough to make a test run of the single life. My first date was with Linda. She was a fitness freak I met at the health club a few months back. We had been flirting for months and the time was finally right. I invited her over for dinner on a Saturday night to watch the movie, *Mahogany*, starring Diana Ross and Billie Dee Williams.

First, I set things up by telling Terry I had to work that

evening. Another precaution I took was to park my car three blocks away in another apartment complex. This may sound extreme, but Terry had a habit of circling my neighborhood like a vulture. The next order of business was to dim the lights and close the curtains. Even though I live on the 15th floor, I wasn't taking any chances. Terry was the type who would carry a pair of binoculars inside her glove compartment. I played it off by lighting candles so I appeared to be creating a romantic atmosphere.

At 8:00 p.m. sharp, just as I finished putting all my safeguards in place, the doorbell rang. I apprehensively walked to the door and looked out the peephole, it was Linda. "Whew!" I said under my breath. I invited her in, took her coat, and escorted her into the living room to have a seat. Her outfit was what I call sexy classy. She had on a long sheer dress, high heels, and nice accessories. I pay a lot of attention to details. After she was situated, I offered her a glass of wine. It was a relief to finally meet a woman from the gym who wasn't one of those health nuts afraid of having a cocktail every once and a while.

Not long after we finished our first drink we began to click. We both had a passion for classic rock, hard exercise, and wild sex. "What a coincidence," I laughed, "those are my favorite hobbies, too." I decided to impress her with my CD collection. I played some old songs by Sting, Journey, and the Wall album by Pink Floyd. While she got into the music, I refreshed our drinks and casually unbuttoned my shirt so she could get a good look at my chest.

By 10:00 p.m. we had finished eating and were relaxing on the living room floor. She asked for something to get comfortable in, so I gave her one of my T-shirts. You know I gave her the shortest one I could find, right? Up to that point, things were going smoothly with no interruption, until the phone rang. The answering machine picked up, but there was no message. I know having an answering machine is old school but it allows me to monitor who's calling my house.

I didn't think much of it, and went back to what I was doing. About thirty minutes later, while we were in the living room listening to The Dream album by Fleetwood Mac, there was a gentle knock at the door. "Oh shit," I thought. I was thankful that we were quietly talking with the stereo playing low. I excused myself and walked towards the front. When I got to the hallway, I quietly tiptoed up to the door and looked out the peephole. Can you believe I found Terry with her ear pressed up against the door? That blew my mind. She must have waited for someone to open the outer door, or either pushed a bunch of buttons until someone buzzed her in. You know how easy that is. Judging by the look on her face, she wasn't able to make out any sound, but she knocked again anyway. I took a deep breath and walked back into the living room trying not to look distressed.

"So who was at the door?" Linda asked.

"It's just one of my obnoxious neighbors," I lied. "He always drops by to borrow things and talk my ear off."

"How long is he going to keep knocking?"

"He'll get the message in a minute or two," I prayed.

"Don't mind him."

I guess she bought it, because she didn't ask any more questions. And besides, Terry quit knocking shortly thereafter. As the night went on, her clothes came off. I felt like a free man again, if only for one night. She turned out to be everything I expected, mentally and sexually. I was sure this wouldn't be the last time we saw one another. "All I have to do is keep the lies flowing smoothly," I kept thinking to myself. "And I can have it all." When the time came to say good night, I reluctantly walked her downstairs to the front entrance. I kept worrying that Terry was going to jump out from behind the bushes. After she made it safely to her car, I breathed a sigh of relief. "I made it through my first trial date without being busted," or so I thought.

The following morning was bright and sunny, perfect weather for car washing. When I walked outside, I was momentarily stunned because my Jeep wasn't out front where it is usually parked. Then I remembered that I had to hide it from Mrs. Ear to the Door. As I approached the far end of the lot, I could see it right where I left it, parked between the large dumpster and U-haul moving van. "I really tried to bury that rascal," I laughed to myself. Checking to make sure all the tires were still on, I got inside and started up the engine. That's when I noticed the note under the windshield wiper. It read as follows:

"You picked one hell of a place to park. Are you hiding from the Repo man or something? By the way, I came up to your job to surprise you with dinner, but I see you decided to *eat out* instead. I hope you can survive off hamburger from now on because as of today you're all out of Filet Mignon."

Needless to say, I was totally shocked. My first reaction was to jump out of the car and check for damage. I also looked under the hood for a bomb, just in case. After making sure everything was ok, I got back inside, shook my head and declared, "I'm getting too old for this shit!"

No Place Like Home

This life of the single cheating man is an intriguing one. He is a sexual predator who insists on entertaining at home where he can impress the women with his cheap art work and king size bed. His shelves are stocked with beer, wine, and other liquors to loosen up the sexual inhibitions of his victims. In fact, his little sex trap is so nice and comfortable, ladies don't seem to ever want to leave. But once playtime is over, he wants his space back. As soon as he climaxes, he begins plotting his strategy for her subtle evacuation. More to the point, he got what he wanted, now it's time for her to get out!

Darryl, a 31-year-old police officer, said he would have a fellow officer call and leave an official-sounding message concerning extra duty assignments. Then he plays it back with the speaker button on his cell phone so the women will hear it and get the idea to leave. On a few occasions he has gone so far as to put on his uniform and drive around the block until his guest was out of sight. I know you're saying to yourself "Is it really that serious?" Darryl says it most definitely is. In his words, "Women don't have the courtesy to leave when their welcome is worn out. Sometimes they need a little nudge."

Darryl's Story

Some men are too afraid to say what's really on their minds when it comes to escaping, but not me. After I have an orgasm and I can't or don't want to get it up again, I begin plotting a way to tactfully ask the woman to leave. This may sound cold but I don't care. It is the truth for most men, whether they want to admit it or not. When I meet a beautiful woman I see her as the most desirable creature on earth. But as soon as I get my orgasm, she is instantaneously transformed into an instant pain in the ass, always trying to cuddle and talk about her feeling. That's a major turn off for most men. I don't care how fine the woman is.

Last month, for example, I met this drop-dead gorgeous woman at the grocery store. Two weeks later we were in my bed sweating and going at it like wild animals. After the sex was over, she insisted on spooning me from behind and getting all mushy—I hate that. Men need some space after we cum, room to stretch out and breathe! Then she started going on about how special she thought I was, and how she was looking forward to seeing me again. Meanwhile, I'm thinking to myself, "I wish I could blink like Bewitched and make this woman disappear." I know this may sound cruel, but I'm keeping it real. I've dealt with so many average women in my life that I've developed an assembly line mentality. Basically, I just want to process her from the door to the bedroom. Everything in between her arrival and the time we have sex is simply a waste of time. It's the same old routine. First I welcome her in, offer something to drink or smoke, then we have sex. But after the thrill is gone, I want her gone! Believe me, there are a lot of women who feel the exact same way! They just don't want to admit it.

The worst part about this time-consuming process is that frequently I am totally disappointed with the end results. Here I am wasting my valuable time trying to maneuver the woman into bed, only to find out she was barely worth the trouble. It's just like Eddie Murphy said in his stand-up comedy "Raw." He did an excellent job of describing how women try to trap men by holding out on the sex. Over time, the man starts believing the woman's pussy is something special. "At first you think it's a Ritz," he joked. "But after you've eaten it for awhile, you find out that it's a plain old cracker." Once I find out that all I've got is a plain old cracker, my mind starts reeling with all kinds of schemes as to how I can get rid of her. Sometimes I'll yawn very noticeably to give her the hint. However, this doesn't usually work because most women see this as an invitation to offer to lie down with you. "Baby let's take a nap together." Inside my mind, there's a voice screaming, "I don't want a nap partner, dammit, that was your cue to leave!"

I've also tried acting busy around the house hoping she would get the hint. But no! What does the woman do but ask if she can help out. That really pisses me off. I end up trying to dust and vacuum around her while saying, "excuse me" every five seconds. And even if I do allow her to help, she doesn't know where anything belongs. She puts the forks where the spoons are supposed to be, and the Grits in the Oatmeal section. That just drives me all the more crazy. When all else fails, I resort to extreme tactics to escape this situation, I call it Mr. Freeze, when I turn off the heat and tell her my furnace is out.

She didn't last long with that thin sheet I gave her to keep warm. Within 20 minutes she was making excuses to leave herself. There was another time I had to practically starve the woman out of my house. The worst mistake I ever made was feeding her on the first date. Let this be a warning to men everywhere, don't ever let a woman find out you know how to cook. She'll be at your house so often you'll have to list her on your taxes as a dependent. And chances are she'll come over empty-handed and hungry each and every time.

Trying to understand the way I feel is pointless for any woman. Only another man who has been where I'm at can relate. They know as I do that it's not about being cold-hearted and insensitive. It's about having your space. Believe it or not I'd like to put aside these games long enough to really get to know someone, but women are very deceiving. For example, the woman I mentioned earlier was attractive, intelligent, and open minded. And to be honest with you, a damn good prospect for marriage. But two weeks into the relationship, I saw the signs of the real person. As Chris Rock said in his stand up, "You don't meet the person, you meet their representative." She stopped putting herself together before she came over to visit. Her energy was bad when she answered the phone. And her hygiene was not what you would expect of a classy woman. I'm not saying she was dirty, but a woman should never let a man know she took a dump in his bathroom; that's a complete turn off. I was like damn, did something crawl up in you and die.

Once I realize I'm dating "The Representative," intimate sex turns into target practice. After the sex is over I start wishing she would get the hell out of my bed so I could stretch out the way I really wanted to. All too often, the highlight of our date was hearing the door close behind her as she was leaving.

Honey, I'm Home!

The idea that men actually have these cynical feelings will surely cause many women to shake their heads in disgust and disbelief. At this very moment, you're probably asking, "Do men spend every waking moment plotting ways to fool around? Are men really this cold-hearted and calculating?" And more importantly, "Where do I fit into these schemes of Escaping?" Before you try answering these questions, there is one last trick of the trade. For his final feat, the cheating man of steel will leap over his wife or girlfriend in a single bound and stop a pair of speeding panties with his bare teeth. In other words, he'll try to sneak back into the house, take off his clothes, and slide quietly between the sheets without being detected. Sounds easy, right? I don't think so. It's not a simple matter of walking through the front door and announcing, "Honey, I'm home!"

NIGHT COURT

As the cheating man returns home from his night of mischief, he is consciously aware of the inevitable trial, which will ensue the moment he sets foot through the front door. The wife or girlfriend, who should be asleep, will be waiting with a gavel and magnifying glass in hand. His humble abode will be transformed into Perry Mason's courtroom, and the case of the cheating man will be in session. In this court of law, the defendant is guilty until proven innocent, and the prosecutor serves as both judge and jury. He's in a no-win situation!

The trial begins with a subtle inspection for any apparent physical evidence of his unfaithfulness, lipstick on the collar, the smell of a woman's perfume, and the dead giveaway guilt-ridden look on his face. If she is unable to prove that he has been up to no good based on these obvious signs, she will then build her case on circumstantial evidence. His coming late from work, hurrying to get to the bathroom, and most incriminating of them all, his inability to "get it up" in the bedroom. Cheating men often make the mistake of climaxing with the other woman and then coming home empty and expect the wife or girlfriend not to notice. Carol, who has been involved with two married men, confessed that it's no accident. "I make sure he cums before he leaves to go home. It's like a competition for his energy. I know that his wife will know he's been with me when he can't perform with her!"

Of course, the cheating man will come up with the excuse of being tired or start a fight to avoid having sex, at least until he re-charges his battery. In most cases however, the sex with the wife or girlfriend has already stopped, which only adds to the frustration and suspicion of his partner.

Here Comes the Judge!

How far will a man go to hide the physical evidence of his crime? And how far will the woman go to uncover the truth? Well, based on what I have witnessed, there is absolutely no extent to which these two parties will not go to accomplish their goals. The cheating man, while guilty as hell, will do his best to cover all tracks of his unfaithfulness. The suspicious wife or girlfriend, who is not as stupid as the cheating man thinks, will prepare a case that would rival even the best "L.A. Law" episode. Who will win? Or are there ever really any winners? I'll let you be the judge.

In the following case, Andre is the defendant. He is 29 years old and has been married for three years. His wife, who has suspected him of cheating for the last six months, is the prosecuting attorney. On this particular night he would find out that tricks are for kids. All rise, court is now in session!

Debra, The Innocent Housewife
Plaintiff
-Vs-
Andre, The Cheating Husband
Defendant

The Case of "The Truth Coming Out in the Wash"

There was one incident in particular when I felt that I truly did need a lawyer. It all began at 9:00 p.m. on a warm summer's night in August when I went over to my mistress Alise's apartment for our usual Friday night sex date. I know that doesn't sound very romantic, but it is what it is. As usual I fell asleep after going nonstop for almost two hours. When I woke up, it was two o'clock in the morning.

"Why didn't you wake me up?" I yelled at her.

"You were sleeping so good, I didn't want to bother you," she said, trying to sound convincing.

I quickly put on my clothes and shot out the door. She knew damn well I usually left no later than midnight. I drove home at one hundred miles an hour, all the while checking myself for signs of my night out. I tried to fix my wrinkled clothes and comb my hair but I still had that fresh fuck look.

By the time I made it home, it was 2:30 a.m. The smell of sex was all over me, and my hair was looking crazy. Right away, I knew what I had to do. The bathroom in the basement was my only chance of washing up without being busted. So, I walked around to the back door, and quietly slipped my key into the lock. As I pushed open the door, it began to squeak like hell. And the slower I tried to push it open, the louder it squeaked. Why is that?

Once I finally managed to make it downstairs, I quickly stuffed my clothes into the bottom of the hamper and jumped in the shower. For the next 20 minutes I thoroughly washed myself from head to toe. I had to make sure the sex smell was completely gone. It's amazing how women can detect the scent of another woman, not just the smell of her perfume, but also the aroma of her body juices on your penis. How do they do that? I damn near scrubbed the skin off my dick trying to wash Alise's scent off me.

After toweling off and finding a clean pair of underwear in the laundry room, I heard my wife, Debra, rattling pots and pans around in the kitchen. She was up for her late night inspection, but once again it was too late. All of the evidence had already been washed down the drain. I threw on my robe and confidently headed upstairs for a snack. When I got to the refrigerator, guess who was looking over my shoulder? No, not my wife, but Angela Lansbury of "Murder She Wrote."

"Where have you been all night?"

"I was out, what's with the interrogation?"

"You said you were going to be out with David, but he called here at 10:00 p.m. looking for you!"

"We did plan to get together, " I said confidently, "but I wasn't able to catch up with him."

"You two should do a better job of getting your lies straight."

At that moment, I couldn't have agreed with her more. I had told his dumb ass I had a date that night and needed him to cover for me. I had to come up with a diversion, and fast.

"Wait one damn minute!" I demanded. "What about this filthy kitchen?"

"What are you talking about?" she said with a stunned look on her face.

"It's your week to wipe down the counters and wax the floor. But judging by all the crumbs lying around here, I can see you haven't done shit all day."

"What in the hell does that have to do with you coming in late?"

To be perfectly honest with you I really didn't know. My intention was to divert the issue, I was reaching for whatever I could find. And believe it or not, it worked. Before you know it, we were arguing over who washed the dishes and who emptied the garbage last. By 3:30 a.m. I was exhausted. My head was spinning and my eyelids were getting heavy.

"This is pointless," I said while yawning. "You can stay up and argue by yourself. I'm going to bed."

She stayed downstairs pouting for another 30 minutes or

so, then came to bed. No doubt frustrated by the fact that she couldn't break me down.

When I woke up the next morning, she was already downstairs doing laundry. I decided to vacuum the living room carpet and clean the kitchen. Ordinarily this was a full-proof way of getting back on her good side, but not this time. As I began running the water for the dishes, I heard Debra shout from downstairs, "I'll be damned!" About ten minutes later, she called for me to come down. As I approached the basement stairs, it dawned on me that I had forgotten to take my clothes out of the bottom of the hamper. "Oh well, it's too late for that now." I said to myself. When I opened the door to the laundry room, she had all my clothes from the night before laid out neatly on the folding table.

First there was exhibit A, the lipstick stain on my collar. Exhibit B, the smell of woman's perfume all over my sweater. Now, I could have probably come up with a quick believable lie to explain those two items, but when she pointed out exhibits C, the condoms from out of my pants pocket, all I could do was throw myself on the mercy of the court. She was upset for weeks, but we managed to work things out. But why does it seem that no matter how hard you try to remember all of the tricks, something always seem to find a way to slip by? Oh well, I'll have to be much more careful, next time.

Second Chances

Yes, he did say, next time. The reality is that if a man cheats once, he will more than likely cheat again. Getting caught is merely a temporary setback and an opportunity to sharpen his skills. Let's not forget that the wives and girlfriends are tolerating this disrespectful behavior, in some cases for years. Even when she finds out that the cheating man has a baby outside the relationship or brings home an STD, the majority of women don't leave! They're either blinded by love and believe he will eventually settle down and change, or they're afraid to be alone. We'll address those issues in a later chapter. As for now, let the games continue.

More Games

Not every cheating man is fortunate enough to get away with sneaking in through back doors and jumping into basement showers. To the contrary, most men have to prepare themselves for an immediate inspection the second they hit the door. There is little or no time to suppress evidence. The wife or girlfriend, who is on constant alert, is waiting for the sound of his car to pull into the driveway to leap out of bed to deliver her opening statement. She has a bionic ear and can hear everything. A slow-turning key in the door lock may as well be a noisy police siren. Alex, who is 37 years old, understands exactly what I'm talking about. He has been shacking for the past two years, and his girlfriend, Sonya, is prepared for battle at all times. She is a hair roller-wearing super sleuth with a keen eye for lipstick and foreign hairs. And because she is so perceptive, he was forced to raise his game to another level. As he put it, "If you've got a woman at home like mine, you better have your shit together when you walk in the door." I wonder what he meant by that.

The Late Night Interrogation

Sonya, The Restless Girlfriend
Plaintiff
-Vs-
Alex, The Composed Boyfriend
Defendant

As I pulled into the driveway, I prayed Sonya would be asleep. But after taking a deep breath and slowly pushing open the door, I could see my prayer had gone unanswered. There she was at 1:00 a.m. with a pot of coffee brewing on the stove and an empty box of NoDoz on the counter. "Boy, I'm in for it tonight," I thought to myself. I played it cool and acted as if I had nothing to hide. Which of course, I did.

"Hi baby, what are you doing up so late?" I reluctantly asked.

"I heard a loud noise out back, and couldn't go back to sleep."

"Yeah, right," I said under my breath.

The only noise she heard was the sound of my car pulling into the driveway. I hung my jacket in the closet and headed for the stairs.

"Well, I'm going to take a shower and get ready for bed."

"Wait a second, sweetheart, I haven't seen you all day. Can I at least get a quick hug?"

I knew what she was up to. This was her sly way of getting a sniff of my clothes and a close look at my collar. But, of course, she was wasting her time. There was no evidence to be found.

When I made it into the bathroom, I turned on the shower and slowly began unbuttoning my shirt. And just as I was about to take off my pants, my wife abruptly walked in.

"Excuse me baby, I forgot to take my pill," she said while casually looking me over.

"Do what you have to do," I said trying not to laugh.

I knew she kept her birth control pills inside her purse. This was just another one of her surprise inspections to uncover evidence. Maybe she was looking for lipstick on my underwear, who knows. Whatever the reason was for her unlawful entry, she came up empty-handed once again. My body was odor free and my back was without scars. I make it clear to any woman I'm seeing that fingernails on the back and strong perfumes are prohibited. Sexy lingerie is fine, but if we're having sex they must shower first and don't put on any makeup or scents. That's just creating another opportunity to get busted.

After unnecessarily going through the medicine cabinet for five minutes, Sonya suddenly remembered that her birth control pills were in the bedroom. "No kidding," I thought. But instead of leaving the room to give me some privacy, she stood there in the doorway observing my every move. I looked straight into her eyes and busted out laughing.

"What are you giggling about?" she asked.

"Oh, nothing."

What I was laughing at was this detective role she was trying to play with me, and a bad one at that. I remember staring at her thinking to myself, "Ms. Sherlock Holmes really thinks she has her man tonight." But little did she know who she was dealing with.

You see, unlike most men, I don't worry about being inspected when I get home. I am extremely careful about concealing the evidence of my affairs. I was having sex with two other women at that time, one happened to be our babysitter and the other was a woman I work with; both ladies were married. That's rule number one in the cheating handbook: never cheat with someone who doesn't have just as much to lose as you do. And another mistake is ejaculating inside of the other woman. First of all, I'm not trying to contract a STD or have a baby. And second, having unprotected sex creates a chemical bond; I only want that kind of connection with my wife. My affairs are strictly for entertainment purposes. When men cross that line they are sending a mixed message and that's when all hell breaks loose.

Anyway, back to Ms. Columbo. When I went back downstairs to grab a snack, she began questioning me about where I had been all night. Of course I had an airtight alibi. But then she threw me a curve by bringing up events from months long past.

"Remember when you came home back in April and I found that woman's business card in your pocket with her personal cell number written on the back?" she asked. "And what about three months ago when you told me you were going out with Derrick and he called here looking for you that same night?"

I was stunned. My confident grin turned into a look of complete confusion. All of a sudden the kitchen counter she was sitting behind started to resemble a judge's bench. I had to retaliate.

"What in the hell are you talking about? I shouted.

"You know what I'm talking about! You and Derrick are always up to something. I just haven't caught you yet!"

"That is totally unfair, Sonya, and you know it!"

Of course, what I really wanted to say was, "I object!" But what was the point? She would overrule me anyway. I was clearly being railroaded with no jury of my peers to hear my case. The accusations and cross-examination continued.

"And what about the Saturday night back in June when you said you had to work? Not more than an hour after you left, your job called asking if you wanted to work overtime. Explain that one, Mr. Gigolo?"

Now I was really starting to get pissed. Not because of her aggressive questioning, but because I knew I had perfectly good lies to explain those charges...at the time. Isn't there some kind of statute of limitations? I was thinking. I fired back fiercely, determined to turn the case in my favor.

"Ok, wait one damn minute!" I insisted. "You can't pull up shit from a two years ago just because you suspect me of cheating. Either you have proof or you don't. Otherwise, get off my back!"

Women know damn well a man can't keep up with his lies if they're more than a week old. This was simply her way of getting back at me for not being able to come up with concrete evidence. I had a solid defense and she couldn't stand it.

After two hours of this nonstop Spanish Inquisition, she finally retired to her chambers. I mean the bedroom. When I woke up the next morning, the case had been dismissed. No doubt due to the lack of proof. She apologized for her paranoid behavior and we left it at that. Now, let this be a lesson to cheating men everywhere, Stand firm on your lies, and never, I repeat, never, confess to anything!

Do Women Really Want the Truth?

Do women want the truth? And if so, how much of the truth? Do they want details or just an overview? Do they want to know how long the affair has been going on, with whom, and how good the sex was? And do they want to know if you love the other woman more than her? I honestly believe that most women do want the truth, unless it's something they don't want to hear! Sometimes the truth can be overrated when it's being told to a woman who loves you and has invested in you. If she had made up her mind that she has found "The One!" the truth is often the last thing she wants to hear. Of course, there are exceptions.

If the man is marginal sexually, struggling financially, and lacks charisma and confidence, by all means she wants the truth.

She's probably looking for a reason to dump him anyway. But in the case where the woman is in love, financially secure, having great sex, or if kids are involved, why in the world would she allow something as painful as the truth get in the way of her fantasy life?

Ask any woman who has tried to alert her sister or girlfriend that her man was cheating and they will advise you to mind your own business! Most women have learned the hard way that the majority of women already know or suspect their men are cheating; confronting them with the evidence will only destroy the relationship between the two women because most often the man is not going anywhere. Not until she gets sick and tired of being sick and tired.

However, there are some women who do want the truth, not only about how men cheat but what motivates us as men to tell the lie about being monogamous in the first place. Remember, cheating is not defined as men who have multiple partners; it's telling the lie to be committed to just one woman that makes it cheating. So, why do men lie?

3

A MAN IS GONNA
BE A MAN . . . REALLY?

Like any other negative behavior, infidelity is learned from watching and imitating bad examples. Show me a cheating father and I can probably show you a cheating son. However, infidelity is not simply a reaction to negative influences; it is also a choice, a choice that has more to do with low morals than complex psychology. But regardless of what the reasons are for this deceitful conduct, one thing is absolutely certain: there is no such thing as a born cheater. The question then is, "How was he created?"

It Starts at Home

If women are serious about trying to understand why men cheat, they should begin by examining men's upbringing; it's possible he was raised by parents who have accidentally or purposely planted negative impressions in his mind concerning the way in which women are to be treated. And with the help of ignorant relatives and narrow-minded friends of the family, he could very well be ruined for life.

The mis-education of the young male usually begins with the so-called Men of the family. They are usually the first to offer their pessimistic views on today's woman. First there's good old Uncle Charlie, "All women are good for is cooking, cleaning and making babies. You can't trust them either. They're natural born liars, every one of them!" Then Cousin Jesse adds his two cents. "Women only want you for your money," he warns. "When it's gone, they're gone!" Of course, much of this worldly advice is based on nothing more than chauvinism and their own failed relationships. Nevertheless, they pump the impressionable young man full of this garbage and send him out into the world with a "Get them before they get you" mentality towards women. It doesn't help that the men he's taking advice from are listening to the same music and wearing the same clothes as he is. Our young men should see and hear distinct differences in the way adult men communicate and act. Unfortunately, we live in a country where forty-plus-year-old men walk, talk, dress, and behave no differently than a 19-year-old boy. Back in the day boys wanted to act and dress like our fathers and the older men in the neighborhood; now it seems that the older men are trying to act and dress like the teenagers. What's up with that?

And if that's not bad enough, the women of the family also add to this brainwashing. Aunt Betty, who always has her nose in other people's business, comments about the neighbors, "I can't believe the woman downstairs had another baby. I'll bet you a million dollars it's not her husband's." Cousin Barbara responds, "At least she's not screwing her boss trying to get a promotion like someone I know." Now, if this type of dialogue doesn't strengthen a young man's belief in the virtue of women, I don't know what will.

Don't mothers, aunts, and sisters realize the impact their conversation and conduct have on our young men? Every negative comment about other women and men is another brick piled on to a wall of ignorance that society perpetrates. Your sons are processing all those conversations you're having over the phone with your girlfriends about who's screwing who, how you can't stand another woman, and how man ain't shit! Well, guess what? You're raising the future husband of another woman. If he turns out not to be shit either, then maybe you raised shit!

It's hard to believe that not long ago the family home was the primary school of respect and good manners. Learning the proper way to talk to and date young ladies was a required course for graduation into manhood. But all that seems to have changed. Today's parents, much like our school systems, no longer appear interested in properly educating their young males. They set horrible examples and throw up their hands, surrendering them to the streets. As a result, boys are growing into men who are emotionally malnourished and morally bankrupt. How in the world can we expect these misguided souls to handle the day-to-day workings of an adult relationship? It's virtually impossible! The lazy and irresponsible parent then has the nerve to ask, "Where did I go wrong?" Well, as the saying goes, "The fruit doesn't fall far from the tree."

Who's to Blame?

Most men would prefer to leave their family history out of it when it comes to explaining why they cheat on women. No one wants to blame good old Mom and Dad for doing an ineffective job of raising the perfect gentleman. And besides, they know that using their upbringing as an excuse for infidelity will not wash well with today's woman. She is sick and tired of hearing these lame excuses about the lack of role models. Her attitude is,

"Damn, you're thirty five, when does maturity kick in?" There-fore, let me make it perfectly clear that none of the men whom I interviewed is expecting women to sympathize with their experi-ence. The whole idea is to establish a starting point from which to begin examining why men are so unfaithful. As Dorothy from *The Wizard of Oz* would say, "There's no place like home."

Raymond, who is 32 years old, comes from a long line of unfaithful men. His grandfather was a cheater, as were his father and uncles. And like so many other young men raised in this environment, he became a cheater, too. "After so many years watching the men in your family get away with it, you begin to see it as normal," he says, "and then you see the women in your family putting up with it. That just made it seem even more acceptable." Well, normal or not, he has successfully fulfilled the family legacy of infidelity. And with two sons of his own, it appears there will be heirs to the cheating throne. The question is, when will it ever end?

Raymond's Story

My father was a very intelligent and charismatic man who taught me everything I know about women, how to talk to them and, unintentionally, how to cheat on them. At the age of twelve, I began taking notes. First, there were the secret phone calls in the basement. My father always made sure he got as far away as possible from my mother's ultra-sensitive ears. The conversations were always brief and coded. He would say five or ten words and hang up. Within an hour after every call he was out the door. When my mother asked him where he was going, his excuse was always the same, "I'm going to play cards." To make his alibi appear more authentic, one of his brothers would call to confirm that he was playing poker or bid whist. But he became annoyed with being questioned every week, so he decided to sneak out the back door to avoid being interrogated. It was funny watching a grown man tiptoeing out the house like a kid who was on punishment. Everybody knew where he was going, but nothing was ever said.

As the years passed, my father's unfaithfulness became more apparent. I found all kinds of evidence such as condoms, secret telephone books, and pictures of him with other women hidden behind old albums and underneath the bar. Parents are so stupid. Don't they know you can't hide anything from a kid? But his most daring feat of all was seducing the next-door neighbor's wife. I believe it was the fall of ninety-one when Bridgette and Steve Jenkins moved in next door. They were a real odd couple. She was five foot nine, full figured, with dark brown hair that came down to the middle of her back. Whereas Steve was short, slightly overweight, and going bald. My father wasted no time in trying to cozy up to Steve. Twice a week they watched football and drank beers together. He even helped paint his living room. But all this buddy-buddy business was only a front. My father was using him to get next to Bridgette. I knew it was only a matter of time before he succeeded. And sure enough, his opportunity came when Steve went on graveyard shift midnight to 8:00 a.m. working bus supervisor at the Chicago Transit Authority.

Within a week of this new schedule my father had him timed perfectly. At 11:30 p.m. Steve walked out of the front door, and at 11:31 p.m. you know who came in through the back. From my bedroom window, which looked out into their backyard. I watched the whole thing like a bad reality show. He would creep out of the back door like a cat burglar, through the fence, and into the back door. One time he was so horny, he leaped over the fence instead of walking around to the gate. While all this excitement was going on, my mother never suspected a thing. If she did, she never showed any signs of it. She was accustomed to my father staying up late drinking beer and listening to music. And on the few occasions when she happened to wake up and catch him coming in, he would give her the old line about checking for prowlers. Of course, the only prowler who needed to be checked was him. This went on for six months before Steve became suspicious. And whom do you think he came to for advice? That's right, my dad. I could have died laughing as I listened in from the kitchen while they talked outside on the porch.

"Gary, I just don't know what to do," he said sounding depressed. "I know something is going on but I can't put my finger on it."

"Are you sure it's not just your imagination, Steve?"

"I'm not sure about anything these days. This midnight schedule has me walking around like a damned zombie!"

"If I were you, I'd stop worrying so much and try to get some rest. Bridgette loves you and would never do anything to jeopardize your marriage."

"I guess you're right."

"I know I'm right!" my father said convincingly. "You have got a good woman there, trust me."

"I'm glad we had a chance to talk, Gary. I was ready to pack up and take a job offer in Seattle."

"No, don't do that!" my father slipped. "I mean, why would you want to leave all your friends and family behind? This is your home."

What a masterful job he did of securing his next-door piece. Steve seemed completely fooled by his speech. Nevertheless, my father backed off for a few weeks, just in case. What a smart decision that turned out to be. I watched Steve drive off to work then double back several times trying to catch her in the act. But a few weeks later, when things cooled down, my father was leaping over the fence and into Bridgette's bed once again. This affair went on for two years until Steve decided to take the job in Seattle. On a cool autumn Saturday afternoon, he packed up his moving truck and drove off into the sunset with his furnishings and my father's mistress.

Those incidents all took place many years ago and today I have a family of my own. A beautiful wife and two handsome boys ages 6 and 4. When I decided to get married, I promised myself to be the perfect husband. No lies, no tricks, and no women on the side. However, old habits and family traditions die hard. Two years after saying "I do," I was out there doing the exact same things my father did to my mother. Whispering on the telephone, sneaking out of the house, and fooling around with married women. For years I didn't want to admit it, but I guess it's true. I'm a chip off the old block.

Father's Day Cards for Mothers, Just Stop It!

For an increasing number of young boys there are no positive male role models at home to imitate. As a result, women have been left to the difficult task of trying to mold their sons into respectable men with little or no help. And try they do, often times with great results, thank God. But no matter how hard women try to raise boys to men, they cannot be examples of men. Boys learn from observing. Ask any musician who has never taken a lesson and he will tell you, he learned from watching. The same principle applies to myself; I learned how to do radio,

TV, and writing books from mimicking others. I've never taken a class to do any of those things. Young boys need to see men to be men. Women cannot show men how to be men because they are not men, period! No more than a man can teach a girl how to be a woman or a mother; it's impossible! Yes, ladies, you can teach your son how to be a good person, have manners, and all the other important principles. But boys need to see good men in action so that they can emulate them.

Recently, I had a debate on my radio show about children giving their mothers Father's Day cards on Father's Day, and although I understand the message they were trying to send, it's this notion that women can play the role of a man that is adding to the problem. Women need to focus more on being a good example of what a woman's role and conduct should be. Too many women are getting caught in the middle and leaving our boys with an incomplete vision of what either sex's role is. Sometimes the best lesson a woman can give her son is how she allows other men to treat her. For starters, stop allowing your sons to see you date married men. Stop exposing your sons to men who don't care about you and don't have their best welfare at heart. And please stop introducing men whom you just met to your children. Having men bouncing in and out of your life sends the wrong message about the value of a woman. And lastly, stop accepting Father's Day cards on Father's Day and focus your energies on being the best role model of what a woman is. That's more valuable to our sons then bragging about how you are the mother and the father, because you're not, you're just a great mom!

Are Mothers Creating Cheaters?

Cedric, who is 29 years old, grew up in an environment where his mother was responsible for his negative attitude about women and relationships. Throughout his childhood he listened and watched as she used and abused men to get what she wanted. These bad examples contributed significantly to his cheating mentality. And like most men who've had bad memories of their mother's behavior, he remembers every detail like it was yesterday.

Cedric's Story

Watching my parents split as a 10-year-old was bad enough without the added burden of dealing with all the bitter feelings floating around. The divorce was supposedly mutually agreed upon, but you never would have known it by the way my mother verbally attacked my father. She talked to him on the phone like a dog, calling him all kinds of MF's and SOB's. I hated the way she treated him, and I told her so on numerous occasions. Shortly after the divorce was final, my mother's lifestyle began to change. She started smoking, drinking, and hanging out with a new set of friends. They were loud and obnoxious women who pried into our family business every chance they got. Her two nosiest girlfriends were Bertha and Agnes, names that fit them perfectly.

Bertha was 5'3" and weighed about two hundred pounds. She had a habit of taking off her shoes, exposing her crusty feet whenever she came to visit. And I'll never forget her bad breath; it smelled like a combination of spoiled cheese and hot garbage. Agnes was even worse. She had very bad skin and always smelled like cigarette smoke. When she tried to give me a kiss, I would run out the back door. But their appearance had nothing to do with why I despised them. It was their constant degrading of my father. Their conversations about him were mean and unjustified. The one I remember most took place a week after the divorce. Fatass Bertha instigated the whole thing.

"So, Valerie, how much alimony and child support did you get from that cheap bastard?"

"Not as much as I asked for," my mother responded.

"Just make sure you keep track of his raises, you can always take him back to court for an increase! When he gets paid, you get paid!" Then they gave one another a high five.

"Don't worry, he's not getting away with one thin dime if I can help it."

"What about visitation?" Agnes asked.

"Well, the judge said every other weekend, and two months during the summer. But I'll decide when and if he can see Cedric. I don't give a damn what the courts say!"

I like your attitude, girl," Bertha said. "He doesn't deserve to see his son after the way he treated you."

That statement upset me for two reasons. One, she didn't know my family well enough to make that judgment. And two, my father treated my mother like a queen. She was the one neglecting her responsibilities at home and running the streets. Besides, I was taught that family business should stay within the family. She was violating her own rules. But the really painful part was watching her torture my father over the years by cancelling visitation at the last minute, or not being home when he was supposed to pick me up. I could see the frustration in my dad's eyes while my mother cursed him nearly every time he picked me up. He never retaliated because he didn't want to risk not spending time with me. And that look in his eyes of being so powerless, that memory was burned into my mind forever. Women have no idea of the impact of talking negatively about the father of a child has on you at that age. It feels like you're being attacked right along with that man. My perception of women was never the same after that.

Two years and a thousand bitter conversations later, my mother finally met someone who could put up with her hostile attitude. I'll call him John. He was a nice man who was never too busy to talk or toss around a baseball. What I liked about him most was that he didn't try to take my father's place and he never once said anything negative about him. My mother acted completely different around him. Dressing up in sexy outfits, talking politely, and cooking meals like Betty Crocker. She never went through all of this trouble for my father, I thought. Maybe they would still be together. As long as she was happy, I was happy. And besides, with John in her life she was allowing me to spend more time with my father. It was the best time of my life; unfortunately, it turned out to be the calm before the storm.

About six months into my wonder years, my mother became pregnant. John wanted to get married, but my mother was dead set against it. The decision was made to keep the babies and address the issue of marriage at a later date. Oh yeah, I did say babies. My mother delivered twins, two girls. A year or so after the girls were born, my mother broke up with John. She said he was smothering her, but I knew this was only an excuse to get rid of him. Her mood turned gloomy, and her patience thinned. The whole situation exploded. My father was back in the doghouse and now John was right there with him. This was the point in my life where I specifically recall thinking of my mother as a bitch. Not in a disrespectful way, mind you, but she was giving these guys hell. And low and behold, guess who reappeared again, my mother's nosy instigating girlfriends. I guess it's true what they say, "Misery loves company."

By the time I turned sixteen, my mother had become a ruthless gold digger. She was determined to get what she wanted no matter how many men she had to go through. When the basement needed remodeling, she dated a carpenter. When her car broke down and needed major repairs, the carpenter was dumped for a mechanic. And when she wanted to spend the rent money to get her hair and nails done, she dated the landlord. Meanwhile, I'm sitting back watching and listening to everything, the lies over the phone, the late night booty calls, and the negative comments about John and my dad. She may not have been sexually involved with all of them, but she was definitely having sex if she had to get what she wanted. Witnessing all these lies and games caused me to lose what little respect I had for my mother. Deep down inside, I thought of her as an irresponsible parent and materialistic whore.

The day of my 18th birthday was the most dramatic of all the negative sights I had seen of my mother's loose behavior. I chose to spend the night at my father's house for the weekend to celebrate. We went bowling, to the movies and out to dinner. My mother wasn't expecting me back until Monday morning. But because of a power outage on Sunday night, our visit was cut short. I tried calling home to let my mother know I was on my way home, but there was no answer. When I arrived home at 7:30 p.m., I understood why no one could hear the phone ringing. There was a wild party going on. The music was loud and strange people were all over the house drinking and smoking marijuana. The only familiar face in the room was big Bertha. I tapped her on the shoulder to get her attention.

"What are you doing here!" she said with a shocked look on her face. "

What do you mean, what am I doing here? I live here. Where is my mother and where are the twins?"

"Your sisters are with the next door neighbor."

"And what about my mother?"

"I think she's upstairs, I'll go get her."

"I don't need you to play messenger," I said with an attitude. "This is my house."

"Wait Cedric, don't go up there."

When I made it to the top of the stairs, I could hear voices coming from my mother's bedroom. When I knocked on the door, a strange man's voice forcefully asked, "Who is it?" That's when I put my broad shoulder to the door and pushed it open. What I saw was disgraceful. There, lying on the bed buck-naked was my mother. She had a joint in one hand and the man's penis in the other. And no, this man was neither the carpenter, the plumber, nor the landlord. This was a guy I had never laid eyes on. My first reaction was to swing the door back shut. I just stood there in shock while my mother excused herself to put something on.

"I'll be right back," she told him.

"Who in the hell was that anyway?" he asked.

"My son."

"Your son! You didn't tell me you had a son."

"She's got two daughters, too!" I yelled from the hallway. "I guess she didn't tell you that either."

My mother came storming out of the bedroom and dragged me to my bedroom. But instead of explaining to me in a calm manner about what had just happened, she had the nerve to bawl me out as if I had done something wrong.

"Who do you think you are busting into my bedroom like some kind of mad man?"

"How was I supposed to know you would be in there fucking somebody?" I angrily replied.

Smack! She slapped me across the face and grabbed me by the shirt.

"I'm the adult in this damn house, you understand. I pay the rent, I buy the food, and I put the clothes on your back. So don't you get smart with me!"

I was so upset I couldn't even bring myself to cry. I wanted to pop her upside the head, but that was still mom. So, I got myself under control and calmly began packing up my belongings. Things were getting too deep for me around there, and it was time to leave. Meanwhile, my mother was standing with her hands on her hips, as if she thought I was bluffing. Within fifteen minutes I had stuffed as much as possible into my bags. I pulled the car keys out of my pocket and headed for the door. Everyone in the party stopped what they were doing to watch the show.

"Where in the hell do you think you're going?" my mother yelled as she followed me downstairs.

"To my father's house!" I shouted. "I'm 18 years old and I can live wherever I choose."

"You're not taking my car."

"Here," I said as I flung the keys violently in her direction. "I'll walk if I have to."

"Calm down, Cedric," Bertha said as she put her hand on my shoulder.

"Get your hands off me, you don't even know me."

I gave my mother a mean look, grabbed my bags, and walked out the door. When I made it to the corner, I called my father on my cell phone. He must have run every traffic light because he made a half-hour drive in less than twenty minutes. On the way back to his house, my mind flashed back to all the terrible things my mother had done throughout the years. First, I thought about how disrespectfully she treated my father. Then I remembered the cold-blooded way she dogged poor John. Finally, there were the disturbing memories of all the men she used and had been used by. I promised myself that day, never to allow a woman to get close enough to break my heart or take advantage of me the way she did so many men throughout her life. And to this day, I haven't. So, for all the women reading this story, ask yourself, are you creating your own problems by setting the wrong example as mothers. How many women would date the sons they are raising? Just saying.

The Hood

The negative influences of what goes on inside the family are often compounded by what goes on outside in the streets, or in The Hood. This is the space through which the gullible young boy must travel to get to and from school, the local store, and the concrete basketball courts. Here is where the hardcore lessons of life are administered, how to walk with an attitude, cock a baseball hat to the side, and how to perceive young girls as bitches and hos. These disrespectful classes are taught on the streets each and every day while the irresponsible adults are off somewhere drinking, partying, or screwing. The peer pressure in The Hood gradually becomes the most powerful force in molding the young man's mind. Many desperate parents have packed up and moved to the suburbs hoping to shield their sons from these negative influences but those efforts are often in vain because bad examples exist everywhere. The educated businessman with a revolving door of women can be just as negative a role model as the pimp on the street corner. All images are potentially dangerous if left unchecked.

The Idiot Box

Television, better known as the idiot box, is also a contributing factor in male infidelity. This electronic entertainer, educator, babysitter, and brainwasher has a great deal of influence over our everyday lives. It tells us what to buy, who's hot, and bombards us with images of the rich and famous. But it also alters behavior and distorts reality. Consider this, males between the ages of 13-18 watch an average of 36 hours of television a week. That's a little more than 5 hours per day. And what are they watching, "Family Guy," vampire sitcoms, and reality TV shows. And with the addition of cable, they have access to literally hundreds of degrading or dumbed-down programming twenty-four hours a day.

When I was a kid growing up in the '70s, we were lucky to get 7 channels. And that was only if you had a good VHF and UHF antenna. The examples of promiscuity were limited to the secret agents and street pimp characters. James Bond, *In Like Flint, The Mack,* and *Superfly* were among the most popular. But today, it is the Rap artist and reality TV stars that have been promoted to the status of role models. Young boys are drawn to these celebrities like hormonal magnets. With all of the butt slapping, titty grabbing, and dissing of women going on, who's surprised? Even many adult men are glued to the television like zombies. And while some critics may argue that art simply imitates life, I say it also has the ability to define it. Now I don't mean to sound like some old fart who opposes the freedom of Rap artists and reality TV show characters to express themselves, but let's get real. Some of that stuff is downright disgraceful and degrading, don't even try justifying it! The bottom line is, parents must stand up and take responsibility for properly raising their sons. Otherwise the television, and the streets, will do it for them.

It's a Family Affair

I would be remiss if I concluded this chapter without exposing the adult cheating man who also receives support from his family. Despite the fact that his relatives know full well that he's married or in a committed relationship, they provide the cheater with an alibi to get away from home. In some cases they actually allow him to invite his mistresses over to their homes to engage in sex. The men of the family, who are often cheaters themselves, sympathize with the horny relative and provide him with a warm bed and clean linen to do his dirty deed. As one 40-year-old uncle said, "We men must stick together in our time of need." I guess he was referring to sexual needs.

But what was most surprising was how often the women in the family were adding to this problem. As a matter of fact, more men admitted to having used their mother's, sister's, and aunt's home for sex than any other relatives. This is just another example of women working against one another. While wives and girlfriends all over the country are complaining about the no-good cheating man, these shameless female relatives are conspiring with their brothers, sons, and nephews to work out weekly sex schedules to carry out their affairs. Close your mouths; you know who you are. Some of you do it because you don't know how to tell him no. But often it's simply a case of, "Why not?" After all, you probably don't like his wife or girlfriend anyway. And who knows, he might even return the favor someday, right? This type of mentality plays right into the hands of the cheating man who needs all of the support he can get to remain irresponsible. With an unsuspecting woman at home and a loving relative to "Watch his back," he can go on like this forever. The surroundings are comfortable, familiar, and, most importantly, economical. One woman's reaction concerning this issue was understandably bitter, "If my brother wants to lie up all day screwing his whores, his cheap ass will have to pay for a motel room."

Unfortunately, there are far too may relatives who don't share her values. They will continue to allow the cheating man to use their residences as a whorehouse as often as he wants. What they fail to realize, however, is that by supporting his sex habit, they are preventing the over-grown little boy from developing into a halfway decent man.

NO MORE MR. NICE GUY

"Where are all of the good men?" women cry. The answer to that question is simple; you've probably already passed them by. And if you haven't, you probably will. According to the so-called "Nice Guys" whom I've interviewed, "A woman wouldn't know a good man if he bit her on the ass." Now, before you denounce this statement as just another angry reaction from a few frustrated unattractive losers, take your own survey. Ask your brothers, uncles, male co-workers and friends. See if they concur with this assessment of today's woman. Are you surprised that ninety percent of them agree? Well, you shouldn't be, and I'll tell you why. It is a commonly held belief amongst men that women are not looking for good men but instead are searching for unrealistic images. The ideal man must look a certain way, be a certain height, earn X amount of dollars, perform acrobatic feats in the bedroom, be God-fearing, have a good relationship with his mother, be active in the community, a good role model for kids, be sensitive, and do whatever it takes to make the woman happy. Oh, and one last thing, he must be all those men and still present a challenge because no woman wants a man whom she can boss around. Whew! It's enough to make your head spin!

During the taping of my film, *Do Women Know What They Want?,* I asked a woman if she was being unrealistic about expecting all these qualities in one man. Her response was, "If you think you're worth it, you can have it all." Really ladies? Is that all it takes is to believe you're worth it? What about the nice guys who believe they're worth it? Can they have it all, too, if they just believe? Or is it more a matter of adapting to the game? For those of you who are single, you know the dating game is ruthless and all about posturing and playing games. Even if a man approaches you respectfully like a gentleman, he still must possess charisma, confidence, good looks, and be dressed in the right gear! But guess what, the nice guy isn't always the smoothest one in the bunch. In fact, he's usually rather clumsy when he approaches you. It's not because he lacks confidence, it's just not that easy to approach women in public, especially if she's with a gang of women blocking his approach. It's like walking into a den of lionesses. Not only does he have to worry about being rejected by the woman he likes but all the other haters whom she is surrounded by. And don't let them be drunk and start clowning him: the walk back to his boys, who are always watching, could be the longest walk of his life.

You see, ladies, when you're the nice guy you're under the impression that all you need is a pleasant personality and respect-ful mannerism to attract a woman. Of course, this is his attitude before he gets dumped for the ump-teenth time, is stood up twice in one week, and witnesses the bad guys having all of the success. Suddenly, he starts to re-evaluate his position. Late at night while lying in bed alone yet again, the nice guy begins to analyze himself. "What am I doing wrong?" he contemplates. "Maybe it's time to stop playing the fool and learn how to play the game?"

Bad Boys Usually Get the Girl!

What experiences could cause a man to permanently or even temporarily vacate his position of nice guy? Often times it's just a matter of observation. The nice guys have examined the cheating man's rate of success. Likewise the cheating man has observed the nice guy's complete and total failure. Vincent, who is 26 years old, says, "Amen" to that. He is sick and tired of being dogged out by women who claim to want a good man. As he put it, "Women don't appreciate good men anymore. They lie to you and play games just to get into your pocket. Once the money is gone, they're gone!" This is the attitude he adopted six months ago while at the nightclub in Dallas. What began as an evening out with the fellahs turned into an education about women he would never forget.

Vince's Story

It was 10:00 p.m. when I arrived at the club. My feet were killing me from standing all day at work, so I was hoping to find a seat. Luckily, there were still three unoccupied tables in the back, directly across from the ladies room. I rested my jacket on the back of the chair, flagged down the nearest waitress, and ordered a pitcher of beer and Buffalo wings. But if I had known about the show that was going to take place later that night, I would have ordered a box of popcorn instead. At ten thirty my best friend Nate shows up, late as usual. I could tell by the look on his face that he was pumped and ready to party.

"What's up, Vince!" he shouted. "I hope you're ready to throw down tonight."

"Sit your wild ass down, Nate." I laughed. "Pour yourself a beer and chill out."

"Good idea partner," he said while lighting up a cigarette. "Let's work on getting a nice buzz until more victims arrive."

Nate was a real dog but he always had great success at pulling women. And he isn't exceptionally attractive either. As a matter of fact, I'm much better looking. He is 5'8", a little on the chubby side, and wears glasses. I'm 6'2", slim, with 20/20 vision. However, picking up women has little to do with looks and more to do with confidence. Nate demonstrated that to me on a number of occasions. I may have been handsome and a gentleman, but he had the most important characteristic of all, charisma.

By 11:30 p.m., the club had really started to jump. Nate and I, now full of Coronas and Tequila, grabbed the closest women we could find and shot out onto the dance floor. My sore feet had been magically healed with a shot of Patron. The DJ was really mixing it up with some R&B and house music. My dance partner was deep into the music. She took off her jacket and tried to show me up, but she didn't know who she was dealing with. Meanwhile, Nate and his partner were standing around like two geriatric patients, swinging their hands from side to side. I don't know what in the hell they were trying to do. It looked like a bad imitation of an old dance called the Spank. After forty-five minutes of bumping, jumping, and sweating, we took a break. I rushed to the men's room to freshen up and Nate went back to check on our table. The club had begun to fill up and no seat was safe from hostile takeover.

After wiping off my face and spraying on a fresh coat of cologne, I headed for the bar. The bartender was a tall, good-looking woman with full lips. When she asked me what I was having, I wanted to say, "How about those lips, *on the rocks.*" But instead, I ordered a screwdriver and kept from having my face slapped. While I sat there sipping on my drink, I glanced around the bar searching for good prospects. That's when Sharon caught my eye. She was sitting on the far end of the bar with two other women, both of whom were attractive. I must have stared at her for at least twenty minutes trying to work up the courage to introduce myself. Women have no idea how uncomfortable it is for a man to approach them, especially when they're in a group. It's not as easy as you think. After checking myself in the bar mirror, I took a deep breath and made my move.

"Hello, my name is Vince, would you like to dance?" Without saying a single word, she grabbed me by the hand and led me onto the floor.

"I guess that means yes," I said jokingly.

The dance floor was packed with people Stepping, some people call it hand dancing or bopping. We shoved our way through and joined in. It wasn't long before people were stepping on my sore feet and scuffing up my shoes. The only benefit was getting a full view of Sharon's anatomy as she turned and dipped. She was about five-seven, with beautiful brown eyes, and a body like a Kim Kardashian. And the outfit she had on was hot, a gold sequin mini-dress with matching pumps. What a sight! It took everything I had not to palm her ass while we were dancing.

Twenty minutes later the DJ slowed things down. I expected Sharon to rush off, but she surprised me by putting her arms around my waist and leaning against my chest. For the next two slow songs she whispered the lyrics in my ear and grinded the shit out of me. I tried to keep my dick from getting hard but it was a losing battle. Halfway through the first song I was as hard as petrified wood. When the dance was over, I quickly shoved my hand inside my pocket and escorted her off the dance floor.

"Thank you for the dance," I said trying not to look too embarrassed.

"The pleasure was all mine, "she said with a seductive smile.

"If you have a minute, I'd like to sit down and get better acquainted."

"Sure, but let me go finish my drink and talk with my girl-friends for a second. Where are you sitting?"

"Directly across from the ladies room," I said while pointing.

"Ok, I'll meet you over there in a little while."

"Wait a minute!" I said. "I didn't get your name."

"My name is Sharon, what's yours?"

"Vincent."

"Ok, Vincent, I'll see you later."

As she turned to walk away, I took another look at her body in that tight dress. Boy was she filling it out. Her ass was so round you could have sat a drink on it and maybe even an ashtray. I jacked up my slacks and walked towards my table feeling like I had hit the jackpot!

Getting back to my seat was no easy task. Women were all over the place trying to get in and out of the restroom. Meanwhile, the men were standing around with empty glasses in their hands blocking the aisles. They were too cheap to get a refill and too chicken to talk to the women who were walking right past them. After excusing myself a thousand times, I finally made it through. Not surprisingly, Nate was sitting right smack in the middle of two tables full of women. He looked like a kid in a candy store.

"Man, do you see all of these women," he whispered. "I've already got three phone numbers and the night is still young."

"Congratulations, Playboy," I said trying to keep my voice down. "Now, if you don't mind I'm going to need your seat for a minute."

"So, you pulled one huh Vince? I knew it wouldn't be long before I rubbed off on ya."

"Just take your no dancing ass out there on the floor and try not to make a fool of yourself"

"Happy hunting, partner."

He took one last sip of his drink, and made his way through the thick crowd. Now I was left alone with a group of loud and flashy women on both sides of my table. Wouldn't you know that out of all the appealing females in the club, I ended up sitting next to the most obnoxious? Sure, a couple of them were attractive, but as it turned out, not very classy. Little did I know the broadway musical "Women from Hell" was about to begin and I was going to be in the starring role.

For the next 30 minutes I looked down at my watch a hundred times wondering what happened to Sharon. I didn't want to believe she faked me out, but my faith was weakening with the passing of every minute. After waiting restlessly for another 15 minutes, I resigned myself to the fact that she wasn't coming. My mood changed from exhilaration to aggravation. How could she play me like this? I thought to myself. "If she wasn't interested she should've just said so." Nate always told me never to get my hopes up too high when dealing with women. "They'll burn you every time," he would say. As I sat there with my feelings hurt, I decided to do what most men do, get drunk. All I wanted was a stiff drink and to be left alone. But the women sitting next to me had other plans.

"So, are you waiting for your wife?" one woman inquired.

"No, I'm not married."

"You must be waiting on your girlfriend, then."

"Well, I'm not exactly dating anyone seriously right now."

Why in the world did I have to go and say that? They were all over me like white on rice after that comment.

"Hey girls, he's single!" she shouted to her mob.

"Well, are you available or what?" another woman asked.

"Yes and no," I replied.

"Which one is it sweetheart?"

"What I want to know is do he have a job?" her illiterate girlfriend interrupted.

This interrogation was getting to be a pain in the ass. Some men may find all this attention to be flattering, but not me. I'm not attracted to overly aggressive women, especially not ignorant ones. I politely told them I was expecting a friend, hoping it would quiet them down. And for a while, it did. But this was the calm before the storm.

The women who were piling in and out of the ladies room only added to my frustration. They were talking loudly and using harsh language. As I listened in on their conversation, my young mind was disturbed and enlightened. And because they had such big mouths, it was easy to overhear every word.

"Did you see that cheap ass dress that bitch was wearing?" said one woman whom you never would have expected to speak in that way.

"Yeah girl, and she still had the price tag on it," her girlfriend laughed. "She'll be taking that bad boy back for a refund tomorrow."

Then I overheard another woman schooling her girlfriend on how to take advantage of men.

"Girl, you should have left your wallet in the car."

"And how was I supposed to pay for my drinks without any money?" the girlfriend asked.

"Simple, do what I do. Find a man with some money, show him a little cleavage, stroke his ego, and grind against him on the dance floor. He'll be buying you drinks all night long."

"Hmm," I thought. "So that's the game, huh?" I put that one in my mental Rolodex. Finally, there was a group of intoxicated black and Hispanic women coming out of the ladies room screaming.

"Where are all the real men?"

"Yeah, where are all the real men?" the women at the table next to me joined in.

At first, I bit my tongue hoping the men standing nearby would put them in check, but they were a bunch of wimps. So being frustrated, angry, and the drunk son of a bitch I was at the time, I took it upon myself to single-handedly defend the male race.

"Where in the hell are the real women?" I shouted back.

"The real women are right here," said a black woman wearing

a large nose earring who was to be the biggest instigator.

"Real women my ass! One of your girlfriends is rocking a cheap weave, the other one has on fake nails, and your nappy-headed butt is wearing blue contact lenses and big ass bone in your nose. So don't come up in here yelling about needing a real man. You've got to be real to see real."

The area exploded with laughter. The men were giving high fives and co-signing. Even some of the women applauded me for telling it like it is. As for the rowdy bunch that started the whole mess, well they somehow managed to slither their way to the opposite side of the club. I guess I must have hit a nerve.

Feeling somewhat redeemed, I polished off my drink and grabbed my jacket ready to call it a night. And just as I was about to go after Nate, guess who I see making her way over to my table? That's right, Sharon. After getting past all the big behinds and jealous looks, she sat her glass on the table and began explaining why she hadn't come over sooner.

"I wanted to come over earlier, but it was so congested over here I didn't think there would be any place to sit."

In my mind, that was bullshit. I should have cursed her out right then and there, but I didn't. Believe it or not, I was still happy to see her.

"Well, now that you're finally here," I said, "let me get right down to the point. Do you have a man?"

"Slow down, can a lady get a drink first?" she began fanning herself. "It's hot as heck in here and I'm thirsty as hell."

Although I thought her drink request was a little inappropriate, I signaled to the waiter to come over.

"What can I get for you?" she asked me.

"I'll have a crown and cranberry, and the lady is having..."

"Make mine a double shot of Patron Gold," Sharon blurted.

In my mind I was thinking, Damn! A double! But I played it

cool. Besides, she was rocking the hell outta that dress.

"That'll be twenty-eight dollars," the waitress said while reaching her hand out for my money.

I gave her thirty-five and told her to keep the tip.

"So, where were we?"

"You asked me if I was dating anyone seriously, my answer is, no, not at the moment."

"You've got to be kidding me. A beautiful woman like yourself without a man."

"It's true. All the men I meet are either married, shacking, or dealing with too many women. I don't have time for that." She paused. "But what about you, Vinny?"

"It's Vince."

"I'm sorry, I meant Vince," she said while touching me on the arm. "I know the ladies must be knocking down your door."

"My situation is the same as yours. I keep running into women who are into playing games. They claim to want a good man but they aren't bringing anything to the table except drama and expectations. So, lately I've just been concentrating on my job and taking care of my daughter. By the way, do you have any children?"

"Ah," she hesitated. "I don't like getting into my personal life until I get to know someone better."

"I thought that's what we were trying to do."

I thought her answer was rather vague, but at the time I was more interested in those seven digits than her resumé.

"Can you excuse me for a minute, Lance? "she said while popping up from her seat headed for the restroom.

"My name is Vince," I shouted at her.

I could understand why she had to go so badly, her breath smelled like a brewery.

While I waited for her to return, I searched for a pen and

piece of paper to write my phone number on. That's when I looked up and saw Nate making his way back over to the table. He was sarcastically applauding and sporting this silly grin on his face. "Now what?" I said to myself.

"Congratulations, Vince, I see you managed to get with the biggest skeezer in the club."

"Who are you talking about?"

"That slut Tina I saw you over here talking to."

"You must be mistaken, her name is Sharon."

"Is that what that trick told you? Her name is Tina. And she's been passed around more than a bottle of barbecue sauce at a picnic."

"Tina!"

"Yes, Tina, and I'll bet she ordered the most expensive drink on the menu."

"How did you know?" I asked curiously.

"That's her M.O. bro. That's her way of sizing up a dude's bank account. That nice suit you're wearing must have set off her radar."

"What about kids? She avoided that question."

"No kidding!" he laughed. "That chick has three little heathens all by different daddies."

"You're kidding me, right?"

"I'm telling you the truth, Vince. I met her about three months ago at a club in Plano. She was bragging to a lady friend of mine about how easy it was to get men to buy her drinks. I guess she chose you tonight."

"But wait a minute. If she wanted to take advantage of me, why didn't she come over with me after we danced?"

"Because another sucker was already buying her drinks. As a matter of fact, he was buying drinks for her girlfriends, too. I guess his money must've run out."

"I'll be damned, no wonder she smells like a tavern."

"Where is she now?" he asked.

"In the ladies room."

"Ok, this is what I want to do. Wait until she comes back and see if she asks you to buy her girlfriends a drink. If I'm right, she'll ask for something expensive. I'll be standing over on the stairs where I can see you."

"By the way, what did she order from the bar?"

"A double shot of Patron Gold," I replied looking like a sucker.

"Ca Ching!" Nate said while trying not to laugh. "Don't take it too hard bro, everybody plays the fool, sometimes."

At first, I didn't want to go along with this game. But the more I thought about all the lies she told, the more appealing it became. So, I settled down and tried my best to look and act normal. Nate didn't help matters much when he suddenly turned as he was headed for the stairs and asked, "By the way, what was she drinking when she came over?"

I picked up the glass she came over with and examined it.

"It's water."

He turned and continued on his way to the stairs barely able to keep from pissing on himself from laughter. All I could do was sit there like a idiot and think about how polite I had been to her, only to find out that I was being set up for drinks and God knows what else.

When Sharon, I mean Tina, returned from the bathroom she was refreshed and, wouldn't you know it, thirsty.

"I'm back," she announced. "Did the waitress make it back with our drinks?"

I got a drink for you alright, I thought to myself. Little did she know I was onto her game. I wanted to blow up, but instead I played along with her masquerade to see how far she would go.

When I spotted the waitress coming our way, I paused to see if she would order something else.

Once the drinks were set down, she immediately excused herself saying she had something to give to her girlfriend and that she would be right back. Nate and I watched her make her way through the crowd and over to her friends. Sure enough she sat the drink down on the bar, slapped them five, and headed back my way. The minute she sat down, she went into her act.

"Goddamit, I can't believe that fool knocked the drink out of my hand," she said while rubbing her hand on my leg. "I'm sorry, baby, can you get me another one, please!"

I guess she didn't want to take a chance on mispronouncing my name again, so she decided to call me baby! I was prepared to go along with a little game. I flagged down the waitress again and waited for Tina to order.

"May I take your order?" she politely asked.

"Yes," Tina replied. "I would like a Mojito and a shot of Grand Marnier."

"And what about you ,sir?"

"Actually, I'm good. I didn't spill my drink," I said sarcastically. "And you can cancel that first order. Give the lady here another of what she's already having. By the way, *Tina*, that is water, isn't it?"

The poised look on her face quickly changed.

"What did you call me?"

"Tina," I replied, "Isn't that your real name, you trifling heifer?"

Nate must have read my lips because when I looked over towards the stairs he was laughing so hard he damn near fell over the railing. Even the waitress was cracking up. Tina jumped out of her seat, gave me a sly grin, and took off without saying a word. But what was there to say? She was busted. After that altercation, I grabbed my jacket, shook hands with Nate, and went home. What a night?

The lessons from that night will stay with me forever. I learned that not only do nice guys finish last, but they also spend more money. I also discovered that women are great impostors. They dress themselves up to look like queens but in reality they're nothing more than well-dressed pickpockets. And while I realize that not all women are as conniving and ignorant as those women I encountered at the club that night, I am wise enough to know that many of them do exist, too many. Now I can set aside this nonsense about treating them all like queens. That's such a bullshit term. What woman do you know who actually treats herself with respect but then they have the audacity to demand it from you? From now on my motto is, "Burn them before they burn you." This may sound cold but I didn't create this world we live in, I'm only trying to survive in it.

Nice Guys and Churchwomen

Many men can relate to the humiliating experiences associated with dating and the club scene. It is an environment where perpetrating and game playing is the norm. The nice guy is out of place in this setting where perpetrators rule. He would be better off pursuing a meaningful relationship elsewhere. "But where is elsewhere?" The nice guys tell me they get burned no matter where they look. Some say the best place to meet a good woman is in church. But often times women in church are no different from women out of church, if not worse. Not only do you have to deal with the same level of materialism and promiscuity, but you have to tolerate the hypocrisy, too. Besides, I haven't seen a shred of research that proves to me that women in church are classier, more responsible, or more appreciative of a good man. Many of them raise hell all week at the club, drinking, smoking weed, gossiping, and yes, having premarital sex, then go to church speaking in tongues while giving the preacher ten percent of their salaries. Is it all in the name of God, or do they pray and pay to cover up their guilt? The nice guy doesn't care one way or the other, he simply wants a woman he can share his life with and treat like a lady. But where is she? And how many times does he have to get burned before he decides it's time to change his game if he wants to stop getting burned. The Bible speaks a lot about heaven and hell. But if you're a decent man looking for a quality woman in American today, you're already living in hell!

Material Girls

For too many nice guys, it's the same process over and over again. You meet a woman you're interested in. She insists on going out on several dates to get better acquainted, at his expense of course. And for the next two months he takes her out to dinner, buys her clothes, pays to get her hair and nails done, and helps her move five rooms of heavy furniture across town. And what does he get for his trouble? A well-fed, well-dressed, unappreciative woman living in a well-furnished new apartment. When he suggests getting intimate, she drops the bomb on him, "I just want to be friends."

After so many of these emasculating experiences, the nice guy begins to see the light. Although he has been raised in a home where women were put on a pedestal, he becomes fed up with these continuous assaults on his manhood and his wallet. At last, his innocent eyes have been opened to the cold world of the material girl. Now he must take a stand and look out for his own interests. Jason can relate to the negative feelings men can develop towards women as a result of their game playing. At 31 years old he's been trying to keep a positive attitude towards women and relationships. But after so many bad dates and expensive lessons, he says the nice guy role is getting old. After years of being used and dogged out, he proclaims, "Nice guys finish last! It's time for the players to play!" Was he looking for an excuse to play the field, or was he driven to it? I'll let you be the judge.

Jason's Story

Throughout my life, I have dealt with many scandalous women. Some of them were terrible liars, others who just couldn't keep their legs closed. And although I take full responsibility for my choices, at some point you feel that there are no good choices to make. Women say this all the time about men but they don't understand that men go through the same thing. At least the decent men do. We get cheated on, our wives and girlfriends get pregnant by other men, and we get sold the fantasy of marriage and kids, the whole nice package. When the reality sets in, you realize it's just about what they can get from you, and once they get it, they move on. Yes, it happens to men, too. We just don't like to talk about it because it destroys our egos to admit we've been hurt. Which is why I had to use an anonymous name for this story, because I'm not different. Men can't handle being hurt, so we hide it and carry that baggage on to the next woman. Sometimes that one painful experience can stay with us for the rest of our lives.

The baggage I'm carrying came from a woman I met two years ago; I'll call her Jennifer. We met at a card party my friend Stan was throwing at his place. He was forever trying to play matchmaker. He went out of his way to introduce us. He said we had a lot in common. And as it turned out, we did. We both loved working out, watching basketball, and playing cards. But what made us most compatible was that neither of us had children. I wasn't interested in a ready-made family, and she didn't want to play the stepmother role. "If I'm going to have a house full of kids spending my money and driving me crazy, you better believe they're going to be mine," she said. I couldn't have agreed with her more. I had no desire to deal with baby daddy issues. Anyway, after discussing everything from hobbies to politics, the topics became more personal.

"So Jason, are you seeing anyone special?" she asked.

"To be honest with you, I have friends, but nobody that I'm seeing on a regular basis."

"I appreciate your honesty. Most men would lie about not seeing anybody."

"I always say, relationships end the way they begin, so I like to begin mine with honesty."

"So, explain to me how someone as handsome and honest as yourself managed to stay single?"

"Well, at the risk of sounding conceited, I haven't met a woman who meets my standards."

"And what might those requirements be?" she asked while smiling flirtatiously.

"She must be attractive, not have any kids, have a sense of humor, and be physically fit. But most importantly, she must love sports." I laughed.

"Boy, what a coincidence! That woman sounds exactly like me. But hold on just a minute, Stan told me you only date older women. I'm only twenty-seven.

"Hey, there's an exception to every rule."

Jennifer was a gorgeous woman with a wonderful sense of

humor. Any man would have changed his criteria to get with her. She had beautiful dark brown skin, long jet-black hair, and a body that was right out of a fitness magazine. Even the loose-fitting jeans she had on couldn't disguise her small waist and big thighs. She was everything a man could ever ask for in a woman, and then some. As the conversation continued, I set aside physical attraction and concentrated on her personality and family values. I knew we had only just met, but dating is a process of elimination and I wanted to make sure we were on the same page. I mean, why waste your time getting a phone number and wasting valuable time if you don't want the same things, right? My facial expression became more serious and so did the subject matter.

"Look, Jennifer, before we go on joking around with one another, I'd like to tell you how I feel about relationships."

"Fire away."

"First of all, I'm a very busy man with a lot of responsibilities. I don't have the time or patience for game playing. I need a woman who is interested in building something."

"Well, I'm ready for a one-on-one relationship myself," she replied. "But I'm having the same problem you are, finding someone who meets my requirements."

"Ok, I'll take the bait, what are your requirements?"

"I want a man who knows where he's going in life, keeps himself well-groomed, and can hold on to a job for more than six months."

Although her remark was very funny, I understood exactly where she was coming from. We decided to put our conversation on hold for the time being and enjoy the rest of the evening playing cards and crackin' jokes. She treated me like I was her man by fixing my plate and feeding me at the table. I felt as if we had known each other for years. Sometimes you meet someone you click with that makes you feel that way.

When the party was over. I gave her a hug, a kiss on the cheek, and we exchanged phone numbers. She promised to call within a couple of days to arrange a date. While driving home, I thought about how nice it was to meet her. I was also wishing we would have the same chemistry the next time we got together. No, I wasn't being pessimistic. But those second encounters can get tricky. I call it "Second Date Syndrome." That's when you notice all the defects, which were either hidden or overlooked the first time. Some of these defects include the woman's butt appearing flatter or her breasts seeming smaller than you remember. Then there are the facial flaws, or the "Ugly Face," as I call it. This is when the nighttime beauty queen turns into a daytime tire biter. It's truly amazing how much women can cover up with makeup and a good weave. When the sunlight hits them it's like a scene out of *Dracula*. Lastly, you have the most unfortunate change of them all, the personality switch. There is nothing more disappointing than discovering that the woman you felt so cool being around has suddenly lost her pleasant personality. I was hoping this wouldn't be the case with Jennifer. Well, a man can dream, can't he?

It was late Sunday night and I hadn't heard from Jennifer. I figured two days was long enough to wait before calling someone, but she obviously felt differently. By the end of the week I began making excuses for her. "Maybe she lost the number," I thought. Or "Maybe she was in a car accident." After ten days of waiting, my compassion turned to aggravation. I began to think she had lied to me about not having a boyfriend, but Stan assured me she was single. That being the case, there was only one other possible explanation; she was playing the old "Telephone Hesitation Game." This is how it works. The woman either requests or accepts a man's phone number with the promise of calling soon to arrange a date. She then *intentionally* waits days, if not weeks, to use it. During this time, the number is taken through a process more complex than the U.S. mail.

It is sorted out along with all the other numbers she has collected over the weekend and put in a category. Usually this is done in the presence of her nosy girlfriends to add a little fun to the procedure. One by one each man is judged based on physical attractiveness, personality traits, estimated income, and penis size. After careful deliberation, a verdict is reached. If a man is labeled as too ugly, too boring, too cheap, or too light in the pants his number is thrown into the trash. Most women participate in this practice to one degree or another. And Jennifer was proving to be a part of this infamous sorority. "But why me?" I wondered. "What could I have done to deserve elimination?" At that point, it didn't really matter. All I wanted was the courtesy of a phone call. Just one lousy call, that's all!

After twelve days of subjecting myself to this mental cruelty, I copped an attitude. "To hell with her," I declared. "It's her loss." I sat around that entire afternoon and convinced myself it was over. And just when my mind was finally made up, guess who decides to call? That's right, Ms. Telephone Delay herself. I was hoping she was calling from either a hospital emergency room or a remote village in Africa. No other excuse would be acceptable.

"Hi, Jason, this is Jennifer, how are you doing?"

"Fine, how about yourself?"

"I'm doing great! Sorry I didn't get an opportunity to get back to you sooner, I've been kinda busy."

"Well, I understand how it is. Everybody has their priorities," I said sarcastically.

While she went on about how busy her schedule was, I was thinking about how she was all over me at the party like a cheap suit, and now she was talking as if everything was cool. I wanted to curse her out and hang up the phone, but I was too curious about what else she had to say.

"So, are we still going to get together to go out?" she asked.

"What did you have in mind?"

I could hear her take a deep breath before responding.

"Well, how about taking me out for drinks at Houston's and then to dinner at Ruth Chris Steak House."

I almost hit the ceiling. Not only did this woman ask me to take her out for drinks, but she had the audacity to request dinner, too. All this after she waited damn near two weeks to call me. This woman must be crazy, I said to myself. I had other plans for her. After debating the point back and forth about a half hour, I convinced her to come by for fried catfish and a bottle of white wine. At least that's what I told her.

When she arrived at 8:30 p.m., I had everything ready, a plate of hamburgers, a bowl of potato chips, and a cheap bottle of wine. She complained at first, but she was too hungry to turn down even that modest meal. Within fifteen minutes, her plate was clean and her glass was empty. I had never seen a woman eat like that before. You would've thought it was the last meal on earth. As the alcohol started to take effect, I decided to break out the hard stuff. I had a pitcher of jungle juice left over from a bachelor party earlier that week. For those of you who have never heard of jungle juice, it is a mixture of fruit juices, clear liquors, and grain alcohol. When blended properly, it tastes like fruit punch or Kool-Aid. But don't let the sweet taste fool you; it will get you seriously fucked up.

I pulled out the tallest glass I could find and filled it to the brim. Without even asking what it was, she drank every drop of it. And the more she drank, the more the real Jennifer came out. Her proper speech became increasing ghetto. Not because of the alcohol either; It was clearly a result of her inability to maintain her front.

"Jason, I cain't believe you didn't take me out to dunner," she slurred. "Nobody turns me down, not with this body."

By 10:30 p.m., I had lost what little respect I had for her. She was drinking like a fish and stumbling over my furniture. And to add insult to injury, she began taking inventory of my apartment.

"You have a nice place here," she said while inspecting my original artwork. "I bet you don't have any problems balancing your checkbook."

These remarks only added to my hostility since she still hadn't made any attempt to get to know me personally. That's right, men have feelings, too. And we want to be appreciated for our hard work, not just our hard dicks. As the night went on, I began to feel more like an animal on a hunt than a man on a date. I was waiting for a moment of weakness to move in for the kill. "One wrong move." I thought, "and your ass is mine." But believe it or not, I backed off. My mother did not raise her son to take advantage of women. Besides, who wants to have sex with an alcoholic? Not me! I may have been a little upset, but I'm no sex maniac.

I stopped serving her drinks, and put on a pot of coffee. There was no way in the world she was driving home in her condition. I had to sober her up. While the coffee was brewing, I started clearing away the dishes and wiping off the table. She moved out of my way and into the living room. I put on my favorite jazz playlist on my iPod and opened the patio window to allow the cool breeze to flow through the apartment. For the next twenty minutes, she lay quietly on the sofa listening to the music. I couldn't believe she kept her mouth shut for that long. When the coffee was ready, I poured a cup and joined her on the sofa.

"Here, drink this," I said while handing her the hot cup.

"Thank you, Jason, you are so sweet."

"You're welcome."

"I'm so embarrassed by the way I acted. Can you ever forgive me?"

"We'll see, just finish drinking your coffee so you can drive home."

The fresh air and the caffeine were definitely doing her some good. She sat up straight and began to speak more clearly. I decided to salvage what was left of this disastrous evening by showing her my vacation pictures and telling a few jokes. She listened attentively, and occasionally smiled to acknowledge my bad humor. And for a brief moment she reminded me of the classy woman I met at the card party. A very brief moment! Shortly after midnight, I began straightening up around the apartment and washing the dinnerware; it was time to say good night. That's when she made the terrible mistake of sizing me up for "Sugar Daddy Duty." As I put away the dishes, she came into the kitchen to check my qualifications.

"By the way, Jason, how is your credit?"

"Excuse me!"

She walked up behind me, pressed her breasts against my back, and went on.

"I was just curious because I'm trying to buy this new car and I need a co-signer."

My immediate reaction was to slap myself on the forehead with my soapy hand. I couldn't believe she had the nerve to form her mouth to say those words. She was clearly out of her damned mind, I was thinking. She had to go.

"Jennifer, do me a favor and go get your coat," I said. "It's time for you to leave."

"Why are men so tight?" she said while sliding her hand down between the sink and my crotch. "If I was your woman and needed help, wouldn't you be there for me? I mean, what if I was short on my rent or something?"

And that was the last straw. I wiped the suds off my hands, rushed to the closet, and pulled out her jacket.

"Let's go, Jennifer," I said while showing her the door. "The bank is closed."

"Come on, Jason," she whined. "I'll be a good girl. Just let me stay with you tonight. I'm not ready to go home."

"You don't have to go home, but you've got to get the hell out of here!"

With that I slammed the door in her face, turned out the lights, and went to bed.

Of course, this wasn't the last dream date that turned into a nightmare. As recently as last month, I experienced another doozy. A woman whom I met at a networking party called to invite me out to dinner. Remember, I did say she invited me out. Since she took the initiative to arrange the date, I volunteered to drive. I picked her up at eight, and we were on our way. When we arrived at the restaurant, our table was waiting. To make a long story short, the food was great and the conversation was even better. After finishing our meal and having a glass of wine, she was ready to go. I left a generous tip on the table and we walked towards the register. As we approached the lobby area, I stopped to help her on with her coat, and then I excused myself to go to the bathroom. When I came out, she was standing at the register still holding the bill in her hand.

"Do you need help with change?" I asked.

"No, I'm waiting for you to pay for dinner."

"Here we go again," I angrily thought. "Different woman, same old game." I was so enraged that I stormed out of the restaurant, got in my car, and left her butt stranded. I couldn't believe she expected me to pay. Not half the bill, mind you, but the entire balance. Like I said, women are all the same. They're only interested in what a man can do for them. Well, two can play at that game.

Heartbreak Hotel

The life of a nice guy is a difficult one. He lives in a world filled with women who don't appreciate his generosity or sensitivity. If he buys gifts and loans money he is viewed as gullible. And if he says, "I love you," and cries on his woman's shoulder then he's a punk. If he initiates the conversation about getting married he's too clingy. After years of being misunderstood and kicked to the curb he begins to feel the pressure to measure up to the macho, cold-hearted, playboy image. And with the help of an unfaithful wife or girlfriend, he is often pushed over the edge. Keith, who is a 21-year-old college student, recently caught his girlfriend involved in extracurricular activity. Since then his attitude towards women has become cold and bitter, especially toward his girlfriend. "This drama was totally unnecessary" he said. "If she wanted to fuck other guys, all she had to do was end the relationship!" At a young age he is learning what so many other men have as they mature, "Everything that glitters isn't gold."

Keith's Story

My mother always taught me to treat women with respect. She also taught me that if a man were honest with his woman, he would receive the same in return. But my mother never met anyone like Cynthia. She turned out to be a real heartbreaker. We met at City College two years ago. The moment I laid eyes on her in the cafeteria, I knew she was the one for me. She had hazel eyes, a beautiful smile, and she was a nerd like me. And because she ran track, her body was in great shape. What a package! But the problem with this perfect package was how appealing it was to the other guys on campus. They wanted to unwrap it as much as I did. As it turned out, she had been unwrapped and test driven several times before and during our relationship.

For the first twelve months we were together, life was great. Cynthia and I went to concerts, plays, and amusement parks together. You name it, we did it. However, the following year things began to get a little shaky. I was accepted at a university in Atlanta, and she was staying here in Chicago. I thought the distance might cause a problem between us, so I sat down with her and discussed having an open relationship.

"Look, Cynthia, I'm going to be away for three and four months at a time. I'll understand it if you want to see other guys while I'm gone."

"Is that really what you want, Keith?" she said sounding upset.

"Not really, but you are an attractive young woman and I know these guys are going to be sweating you left and right."

"Why don't you let me worry about that? I'm a big girl, and I can handle myself. But are you sure this idea of breaking up isn't for your benefit?"

"You know better than that, baby. I only wanted to give you an opportunity to call it quits without any guilty feelings."

"Well, don't do me any favors," she said as her eyes began to swell up with tears. "I know what I want, and it's you."

Needless to say, this was good news for me because I loved this woman and wanted desperately to be her first love. I had been waiting patiently for two years and I wanted to be rewarded.

During the first three months of school, Cynthia and I talked every day on the phone. But after only three months, once a day turned into once every other day, then once every three days. I didn't think much about it because mid-term exams were kicking my ass. And besides, Christmas break was coming up and we knew we would be getting together. The day of my last test, I called Cynthia and told her when to expect me home. I couldn't afford airfare so I decided to ride up with some friends who lived in Chicago. They were going to drop me off on Christmas Eve and pick me up the day after New Year's. Everything was set until the guy whose car I was supposed to ride in had an accident the day we were going to leave. How bad can your luck get? I asked myself. Of course, I had to call Cynthia with the bad news. She seemed very upset and disappointed that I couldn't make it. The emphasis is on the word *seemed*. As I sat in my dormitory room disappointed and horny as hell, good old Dad came through with airfare. I decided not to call Cynthia and surprise her for Christmas! And as it turned out, I was the one who got the surprise.

Once my plane landed, I thought about catching a taxi. But one look at the heavy traffic on the Kennedy Expressway and I was easily persuaded to take the train. I followed the signs to the CTA train station under the airport and hopped aboard the crowded cars. The ride to 95th street took about an hour, so I killed time by daydreaming about Cynthia. Man, it's going to feel good to hold her again, I was thinking. And who knows, maybe she'll even give me some pussy for Christmas.

Once I snapped out of my horny fantasy, I became more concerned about how lonely she must have been without me. Her mother was out of town on business and her best friend was spending the day with her boyfriend's family. I knew she would be home alone with no one to keep her company. I was anxious to come to her rescue.

When the train reached my stop, I battled my way through the heavy crowd and headed straight for the florist. By the time I got there all of the red roses had been sold out, so I bought a long stem yellow rose and a beautiful card instead. After all, it's the thought that counts. When I arrived at her place, I peeked into the living room window hoping to startle her. But all I saw was a bottle of beer on the table and a nightgown hanging over the chair. Although Cynthia hated alcohol, I didn't think much of it. I decided to go around back to knock on her bedroom window. She's really going to be shocked, I thought. But what happened next shocked only me.

As I tiptoed around to the rear, I began to hear faint sounds of a thumping and squeaking. The closer I got, the louder it became. "Squeak, thump, squeak, thump!" Somebody was getting busy, and I mean real busy. Once I made it around to her window, it was clear where those sounds were coming from.

"Whose is it, whose is it?" a man's voice asked forcefully.

"It's yours baby, it's yours," Cynthia's exhausted voice submitted.

"Is it good baby, is it good?"

"Yes, baby it's good. Don't stop, please don't stop."

My heart dropped to the ground. And yes, I cried. Here I was playing the perfect gentleman, waiting patiently for her to be ready. Come to find out she was ready all along. I was willing to let her pursue other relationships. But no! She elected to hold out on me, while sleeping with everybody else on the side. I stood for a moment leaning against the wall in total shock, listening to my girlfriend getting banged by some dude. Then I pulled out my pen and wrote her a message on the card I bought.

Dear Cynthia,

Today you broke my heart. I came home to surprise you, but it was me who got the surprise. For years I was fooled into believing your body was priceless. I waited on you to be ready so we could share something special. But as I have finally found out, you're worthless, nothing more than flea market trash.

But I want to say, Thank you. Thank you for screwing me as well as the man you were with today, although I'm sure he enjoyed it more than I did. But most importantly, thank you for a special kind of education about trusting women. It is one that I will carry with me for the rest of my life.

Signed,
No More Mr. Nice Guy

P.S. Let this flower be a reminder of how sweet and caring a man I used to be.

Vicious Cycle

Many women will argue that men being hurt in relationships has nothing to do with why they cheat. But it is clear to me from listening to a number of these stories, that the effects can be devastating. Any relationship that has a chance at longevity must be built on trust. And if that trust is damaged, whether it happens today or ten years ago, the man will be hesitant to trust or love again. Some people may call it putting up a wall, immaturity, or even insecurity. The point is a man will do whatever it takes to keep from being hurt again. And while he's about the business of blocking his feelings, getting even, or whatever you want to call it, guess who's getting hurt? That's right, the innocent woman who had absolutely nothing to do with his bad experiences. Of course, the vengeful man is unwilling to stop long enough to take this into account. In his mind, everyone must pay, the women who have injured him in the past and those who might play games in the future. Unfortunately, this type of mentality is destructive and creates a vicious cycle of manipulation. The hurt man makes the next woman in his life pay for something she didn't do; she in turn gets even with the next man she dates. This melodrama plays out over and over again from generation through generation. When will it ever end?

NOTHIN' BUT THE DOG IN ME

What examination of the cheating man would be complete without a long hard look at the infamous D-O-G? As one woman so eloquently put it, "Any man who cheats is a dog, Atomic Dog, Under Dog, Mighty Dog, and last but not least, Deputy Dog." Now, after you have collected yourselves off the floor from laughter, we can look deeper into the mind of this pathological sex addict and player. To begin with, he has a chauvinistic attitude towards women. In his mind, women are sexual objects put on this earth for the sole purpose of satisfying his needs. Forget about qualities like personality, education, and sense of humor. Those traits are unnecessary for the duties he needs performed. As one man boldly stated, "A woman's reading skills and Ph.D. won't be of much use when she's lying on her back."

The dog cheating man is a habitual liar who has mastered the art of insensitivity. While looking his wife or girlfriend squarely in the eyes, he can say, "I love you," and then sleep with her best friend without an ounce of guilt. To put it frankly, he can marry you on Sunday and screw the bridesmaids on Monday. And what does the dog have to say in his defense? Not a damned thing! He is a cold-hearted, selfish-minded, menace to female society who makes no apologies for his conduct. As a matter of fact, he actually believes he's doing women a favor by spreading himself around. Matt rationalized his behavior this way, "Let's be honest, there aren't enough good men to go around. If every man chose to be monogamous, who would all these single women have sex with?"

This arrogant remark is just one example of how crude the Dog can be. He has an ego the size of the Grand Canyon and a little black book that resembles the Yellow Pages. Women are merely numbers with notches next to their names to indicate their level of sexual performance, orally and otherwise. The act of sex has no emotional significance; he has mastered the art of emotional detachment. Sex is nothing more than a sport to measure against previous conquests or simply to pass the time away. The Dog cheater is the star of every reality series and the subject of most Rap songs. The titles may vary but the message is all the same, hit it, split it, punch it, and drop it. Meanwhile, the dance floor is packing with dizzy women pumping their hands in the air singing along to these disrespectful lyrics. The dog is watching from the bar with a drink in his hand, thinking, "That's right, keep on singing, because I'll be punching one of you tonight when the party is over!"

Thirty-seven-year-old Ron is one of those scheming men watching from the sidelines. He has been divorced for three years and says that his desire to be with other women is too overwhelming to control. In his own words, "Men are warriors who must venture out and conquer. It's not that we're not satisfied at home, every now and then we need new pussy, it's that simple." Well, it's quite obvious this guy won't receive any awards for deep intellectual thought. However, you must admit his statement is typical of how most men think. They see themselves as animals trying to be spiritual, when in fact they are spiritual beings fighting against their animalistic selves, or flesh. This is the distinct characteristic of the Dog. He is a self-proclaimed beast who is unwilling to elevate himself above primitive behavior. For the purpose of this chapter, so be it!

The Dog Pound

Understanding the Dog is as simple as 1-2-3. One, he has no regard for the feelings of anyone except his own. Two, he will do whatever it takes to get women into bed. And three the Dog proceeds with his sexual assault on women simply because he loves the game. And I mean LOVES! How does the Parliament song go?

"Why must I feel like that?
Why must I chase the cat?
Nothing but the dog in me!"

This is his anthem, his motto, and his mentality. Forget about negative role models. This guy has made a conscious choice to have as many women as humanly possibly. Of course, I'm still referring to 37-year-old Ron. He is the epitome of the cheating Dog. As far back as he can remember, he hasn't been able to keep his hands off of the girls. While the other little boys were out playing baseball and basketball, he was organizing a game of Spin the Bottle and Catch a Girl Kiss a Girl.

As an adult, he has never managed to remain monogamous for more than two months at a time. Which obviously explains why he's divorced. The controversy surrounding Ron had nothing to do with his lack of sexual control but his unwillingness to accept 100% of the responsibility for his behavior. He actually had the audacity to blame women for at least half of his dogish deeds. What does he mean by that, you ask? Don't ask me. Let's get it straight from the horse's mouth or should I say, "Straight from the pound?"

Ron's Story

First of all, I resent the term "Dog" to describe what is simply a lifestyle choice. I choose to have several women; it's that simple. In my opinion this is the only sane way to carry on with relationships. No commitment, no worries, and no headaches. I can come and go as I please, no questions asked. Sure, I may have to lie every now and then to keep the peace, but women expect that anyway. I just keep my business under cover so nobody gets hurt. Now before you get the idea I'm being cold-blooded about this whole monogamy thing, let me explain something to you. I've tried to be faithful on a number of occasions, but I just can't do it. No matter how attractive and sexually satisfying the woman is, sooner or later I get bored.

Like most men, I need a little variety to keep things spicy. And having sex with different women provides me with that. I try to explain to women that there's nothing they can do to stop a man from creeping. I don't care if they do a striptease and pole dance for their man every night; at some point it's going to get old. It's not about another woman's sex being better, it's just different. There's no feeling in the world that can compare to meeting someone new and taking them to bed. You get a rush as she unsnaps her bra and pulls off her pants for the first time. It's kind of like Christmas and New Year's rolled up into one night. First you unwrap the gift, then you celebrate until the break of dawn. I know this may sound raunchy, but it's real. I love the idea of lying in bed with a tender young thang on Friday and waking up next to an experienced vet on Saturday. After all, a man needs more than one pair of shoes to wear, right? You need a pair for jogging, a pair for work, and a dress pair. Women are no different. You've got to be able to mix it up a bit.

The most upsetting thing about being a so-called Dog is

listening to other men beg and kiss women's asses just to get into their pants. They use stupid lines such as, "Sex isn't everything you know." Or, "I prefer a woman who has something to offer intellectually." Fuck that! I'll take a great blowjob over a spelling bee any day. The only academic requirements I insist on are basic reading and writing skills. If she can scribble her phone number on a napkin, and decipher the street address to my apartment, she's a rocket scientist as far as I'm concerned.

Then you have these hypocritical married men who stand on their soapboxes preaching monogamy. They brag about how wonderful married life is and try to convince you to settle down. But those are usually the same horny bastards who end up on the ten o'clock news getting busted at The Starlight Motel with some hooker named Trixie. The truth of the matter is all men have a little dog in them. If they had the opportunity to lie down with a sexy woman without being found out, most of them would do it without a second thought. I don't know of any man in his right mind who fantasizes about having sex with only one woman for the rest of his life. If he tells you he does, he's either lying, gay, or impotent.

Now let me explain what I meant by women being responsible in part for my behavior. To begin with, I think they should take a long hard look at just how provocatively they dress when leaving the house. Today's fashions can make even the most innocent choirgirl look like a whore. Women have begun to dress in ways that puts more emphasis on what they have to offer downstairs as opposed to upstairs. I can go anywhere downtown, during business hours mind you, and see women walking around with half of their behind showing and their nipples sticking through their blouses. And these same women will have the nerve to ask, "What are you looking at?" And "Why are men so doggish?" Give me a break! Women know men are only human. If they truly wanted us to stop acting like dogs, they would make more of an effort to cover up those delicious looking bones.

Women also have the nerve to expect men to be 100% honest about their marital status. But again, their attire makes it virtually impossible. How can any mortal man resist telling a lie when he's confronted by a woman wearing a short skirt, a fresh paint job, and a push up bra with her breast on the verge of popping out? Then they have the nerve to ask, "Do you have a girlfriend?" or "Are you married?" One look at her small waist, thick thighs, and those 36 double Ds and he's going to instantly become the most eligible bachelor in America. Even the most loyal of men have been known to crack under the pressure of a beautiful face and a pair of large breasts. The fact that he has a wife, two children, and a dog at home doesn't even cross his mind until after he has sex with her. "Selective Amnesia," I call it.

Revealing clothing isn't the only reason why I feel women contribute to infidelity. The Dogs like my friends and I are bombarded daily with examples of how lonely and desperate women are. So desperate in fact, that I recently saw a program where a woman was getting married to herself. Now, tell me there isn't a need for the dog to pitch in. Women have bought completely into the "Male Shortage Theory," which is perfectly fine with us. I love to watch reality shows where women make fools out of themselves fighting over half a man. Every week there's a new show on TV, shows like "The Bachelor," where overly anxious women literally fight over rich men hoping to get married. And what type of message do you think this sends to the so-called Dogs of the world? I'll tell you what the message is, "Sex them all and take no prisoners!"

Dogs also don't discriminate. We're not looking for this idealistic woman to marry and have our kids; our only requirement is that she be sexy and sensual. Full-figured, short, tall, we love them all. One buddy of mine, for example, will date a short, slim woman on Friday, and turn right back around and tackle a 6-foot 250-pounder on Saturday. As he put it, "I don't mind a lightweight every now and then, but I prefer a winter woman with a little meat on her bones." Then you have the overachieving corporate types who love to be dominated. At work they make multi-million-dollar decisions, call all the shots, but in the bedroom they want to be slapped, choked, and have the roots pulled out of their hair. The nice guys may give her the romance but I give them the orgasm and flashbacks. When a woman has an aftershock in the middle of the day, it's not a romantic thought that triggers it, it's usually because a guy like me has fucked her so good that her walls are still swollen and pulsating. Nice guys not only finish last, they usually cum too quick.

And to all of you married and involved women out there, you need to get off your hypocritical high horse! You know how valuable a service we have rendered to your group. Over fifty percent of women have cheated on their partner at least once. How many of you reading this have stepped out or know someone who has stepped out on their partner because she wasn't getting enough attention or affection? The number of women going without sex in this country is epidemic! Answer these questions honestly. When your husbands have come up a little short, who is it that saves the day with a few more inches? The Dog! When you get tired of having his fat stomach crushing your pelvis, who is it that provides you with a nice firm body to jump up and down on, all night long? The Dog! And finally, when your man refuses to take a dive between your thighs, who is it that goes down below where he won't go? The Dog! With that in mind, the only question I have left is, "Have you hugged your Dog today?"

Stroking His Ego

While most men are unquestionably motivated by the sexual pleasures of cheating there is another factor which seems to be just as significant. That is the pure emotional and psychological rush men get from having sex with different women. I label this type of Dog as the Egomaniac. This scoundrel is often more concerned with being admired than getting laid. He is an arrogant, self-absorbed, wannabe playboy who must be constantly reminded of how great he is. Paul, who is 45 years old and has been married for fifteen years, fits this description perfectly. He admits that his affairs with younger women play an important part in how he sees himself. In his words, "Being able to attract beautiful young women makes me feel good about myself. Having sex with them makes me feel energetic and it motivates me to stay in shape." Many older men who date young women share the same story. The idea of being with a woman half their age can be an incredible boost to the male ego, just as cougars have started dating younger men to keep up with them sexually and to add a spark to their lives. But this is not just about feeding egos. Remember, we're talking about a man who has been married for fifteen years with a grandchild. It's no big deal if he wants to date younger women, but at 45 years old, he's still lying about it. I hope the young woman he's dating is worth it.

Paul's Story

Let me say this before we get started. I've been married for over 15 years, and there is no way I would have been able to tolerate a traditional marriage without having affairs. And most of my friends who have been married for ten plus years, feel the same way. And since there was no way I could introduce a different lifestyle to my wife, the only alternative is to step out every now and then. I love my wife, and I enjoy the life and security we've built together, but I'm still a man and I have needs that my wife is not comfortable with fulfilling. So what am I supposed to do, divorce my best friend because I want to have something new every now and then? That's just ridiculous! Hell, if she were getting some on the side, I would understand. What woman wants the same old dick for 15 plus years, right?

Since I travel often in my business, meeting new women and keeping it away from home comes easy. My last affair was with a flight attendant I met on my way to New York for a sales conference. While she was serving peanuts and coffee, I was serving up the old charm. By the time we landed at JFK, she was hooked. She wrote down her cell number and email address. When I called her the next evening to invite her over for drinks, she didn't waste any time getting straight to the point. "I'm attracted to older men," she admitted. "I know you're married, but I would like to get to know you better."

Needless to say, she got to know me very well. Since she had four other flight attendants sharing her apartment, we reserved a room at a motel outside of the city. The moment we walked through the door, she reached inside her small suitcase for something comfortable to slip into. I caught a quick peek at what looked like a tiny bra held together with dental floss.

"Oh my God," I said. "Are you going put that skimpy thing on?"

"Stop looking," she said while shielding it from my view. You're going to spoil the surprise."

"Baby, I don't think anything could spoil that surprise, especially with a body like yours."

She blushed and headed for the bathroom with her bag of goodies.

"I'll be back," she said seductively.

Once she closed the door, I went into action. First I took my clothes off and folded them neatly on the chair. Then I used the sink outside of the bathroom to touch myself up a bit. Just in case you ladies didn't know it, men are notorious for washing their dicks in the sink. Finally, I got down on the floor and did 50 push-ups. I wanted to be buffed for my new lover. The second the shower shut off, I leaped onto the bed and did my best to look athletic.

"Are you ready, baby?" she said as the bathroom door swung open.

"Ready like Freddy," I laughed.

When she walked out into the open, all the blood rushed out of one head and into the other. She had on a crotchless black lace teddy, with garter straps, and high heel pumps. I was in heaven. For the next two hours we did it in every position humanly possible, on top of the sink, in the shower, and against the wall. When it was all over, she collapsed on top of my chest and fell asleep. I just lay there staring at her thinking to myself, "Another first round knockout. I've still got it!"

At 45 years of age, not many women will criticize me for not conducting myself more responsibly, especially since I'm well-educated with a professional job. However, being a Dog has nothing to do with economics or intellect. Don't fool yourselves for a moment into believing this is some sort of low-income or low-education thing. It's simply a man thing. I hear men talking about their sordid affairs and kinky sex on the sixteenth hole of exclusive golf courses, at political fundraisers, even after church on Sunday. That's right, the Dogs are everywhere. Cheating is a universal game played by men from every social, economic, and cultural background. As a matter of fact, the wealthier they are, the more resources they have to play. The vice-president in charge of marketing is my favorite to watch. He is 54 years old and has been married for over twenty-five years. Nevertheless, he loves to show off his prize catch, just like a cocky high school kid. Without an ounce of shame, he allows his mistress to come upstairs to the office to pick him up for lunch. And she always has on a sexy outfit. I'm thoroughly convinced he insists she wear something provocative to shock the rest of the staff. When they first began dating three months ago, she was dressed conservatively. Now she appears to have raided Cher's wardrobe. Last week she stepped off the elevator wearing a suede mini-skirt, see-through blouse, and four-inch Stilettos. I had to roll my tongue back into my head. And you should see him when he returns from their lunch dates. He struts around with his chest all poked out like a peacock. This may all seem very juvenile from a woman's perspective but some men need to use attractive women to feel good about themselves, including me. I guess the old saying is true, you can't teach an old dog new tricks.

Insecurity

The cheating man's sexual and egotistical need for having sex with multiple women is often nothing more than a clever camouflage of the larger problem of insecurity. The problem, however, was finding a man willing to discuss this topic from that perspective. It's not easy to walk up to a grown man and say,

"Excuse me, Sir, I'm writing a book about infidelity and I'd like to interview men who cheat because they are insecure." I don't think so! Men will never admit to insecurity being a factor any more than they will admit to having a small penis or being horrible in bed. Our egos just won't allow it! Why, because insecurity is synonymous with weakness. And I don't need to tell you how offensive that word can be to a real man. The trick now was to come up with a word, or term, which would address the issue of insecurity, without calling it insecurity. I thought about it for a moment, then it came to me, "I'll call it 'Back Up,' and just as I expected, they took to this term like fish to water."

The cheating man's need for "Back Up," is based primarily on control. But it also has a lot to do with fear. First let's examine the control motive. Most men, regardless if they are cheating or not, have an innate and socialized need to be in control. Of course, this is not a problem if he simply wants to open a tight jar or drive around the block lost for an hour. However, when matters of the heart are at issue, the idea of control cannot be dealt with by using a socket wrench or a road map. This is a major concern for the alpha male who has been accustomed to having a solution to every physical problem. The key word of course is physical, not emotional. Sure, he's willing to submit to the mechanical expertise of a repair man if he can't start his car, or ask the gas station attendant for directions when he is lost. But whom does he call when his relationship isn't working and he feels lost in it? His buddies? His mama? A therapist, perhaps? Are you crazy! No man with an ounce of pride is going to surrender himself to the embarrassment of his friends, the scrutiny of his mother, or the nosiness of some pencil-pushing therapist. In his mind, there's only one way to maintain control over his relationship and that is simply not to get too emotionally involved in it. As one gentleman candidly put it, "The one who is least in love usually controls the relationship."

It is because of this type of mentality that more and more men are subscribing to the player's doctrine that states: "Never love a woman more than you love yourself." Sounds harmless, right? Wrong! For the defensive and emotionally apprehensive man, this philosophy translates to, "I will not allow myself to get so intimately involved that I might lose control over my relationship." Does this sound familiar? Sure it does. The cheating man's interpretation is skewed only because he is constantly looking for a reason not to love anyway. Now, let's flip the script and present this same slogan to a woman: "Never love a man more than you love yourself." She would likely comprehend this to mean, "I will love and care for my man, but I will take time out for myself, too." This is a classic example of just how differently men and women think. The woman is always prepared to love again, no matter how many times her battle-ridden heart has been broken. Whereas the man treats love like a Jehovah's Witness knocking at the door, hoping it will go away if he draws the curtains to his heart and keeps quiet.

The issue of fear is another dominant factor as to why men feel the need for "Back Up." Fear of what, you ask? The fear of falling in love and being hurt. Most men will strongly disagree with this remark simply because they have no idea what it's like to be close enough to a woman to give a damn. They passionately deny any woman could ever hurt them while at the same time they are too afraid to get close enough to give it a try. What are we afraid of, you ask? The unknown. The cheating man has a warped and over-exaggerated idea of what love is all about. Subconsciously he is afraid that once he falls in love, he will be instantly transformed into a mindless, spineless, pussy-whipped robot that will lose complete control over his life. Therefore, he remains in his comfort zone where the emotional territory is familiar and controllable. Men know that having sex and sharing themselves emotionally with several women creates emotional distance, which in turn allows them more control. So when the time comes to end the relationship, he is already invested in another woman. The ties can be cut without the pain of rejection or heartache.

As for the cheating man who has tried love before, he is too chicken-hearted and paranoid to go down that dark road. All alpha males are secretly guarding against having their emotions at the center of their relationships. This is why many of us steer clear of any woman who represents true affection and strong commitment. It's kind of painfully funny when you think about it. With all of our bulging muscles and bold talk we cannot handle emotional injury half as well as women can. Some say it's because women have had much more painful practice, while others contend it's nothing more than social conditioning. Well, I have my own theory, "Men are simply more sensitive than women are to begin with." That's right, I said it. I know all hell is going to break loose when my male peers get a load of that statement. No matter, I'm going to stick by my guns on this one.

Before we allow sleeping Dogs to lie, there is one last story I want to share with you. It is an interesting look at how one man covered up his insecurities, and/or fears, by keeping as many women as possible on hand. His name is Maurice. He is single, conceited, and has 29 years of experience to certify his Dog license. What I found most interesting about him was the way he viewed his relationships with women. He expressed his attitude about cheating with a very colorful basketball metaphor. I know the women are going to scream foul on this one.

Maurice's Story

I look at my relationships with women like a game of basketball. I'm the coach and they are the players. The first order of business for the coach is to find a star player, a woman to build the team around. She will be expected to come through under pressure, night in and night out. Her responsibilities will include coming to all practice sessions and scoring on a consistent basis. If she performs up to standards, her contract will be extended and she'll get all the perks that go along with it, dinners, meet the family, be introduced to close friends, etc.... Then you have your two backup players. They are an integral part of the team because they provide you with leverage to renegotiate with your star player. If expectations start to get too high, you move one of them into the starting rotation and start recruiting again. Finally, you have your benchwarmers. Although they don't get much starting time, don't sell them short. In a pressure situation they will give you everything they've got. Many times they play the hardest because their goal is to get more playing time.

All jokes aside, I feel it's necessary to keep as many women on stand-by as possible. This is the only way I can put up with all the games women play. What do I mean by that? Let's start with the average date from the man's perspective. You call up a woman to arrange a date, drive twenty miles across town to pick her up, spend your hard-earned money on expensive dinners and movies, then drive her back home. If you're lucky, you'll get sex. And nine times out of ten the sex isn't that good. I don't play that. My attitude is this; if we're not having sex you can stay at home. Why should men have to pay to get to know you, waste weeks if not months dating you, and hope that he will eventually have sex with you without a guarantee that the sex will be any good. That's insane! My attitude is, let's get the sex out the way so we can get to know each other. The reality is, you don't really meet the real man until he's getting sex on a regular basis. Until then, it's all posturing on both sides.

Another reason why I need to have more than one woman is because women can sense when a man is hard up, like a lioness smelling fear in a wounded animal. Those chicks at the club are the worst. They sit back with their noses all turned up acting as if Denzel Washington is waiting at home naked in bed with champagne on ice and a dozen roses. When they know damn well the only welcome home they get is from Morris the cat or Fi Fi the poodle. Nevertheless, these lonely heifers play you like they have good men knocking down their door. And without any consideration for how much you can afford to spend, they start making demands on your wallet, buy me a drink, take me out to breakfast, let's go shopping! You're sitting there thinking, "Damn, what am I getting out of this again?"

But the ultimate insult is when a woman expects you to help her out with her rent. As Michael Baisden would say, "Now, that's some fragernackle bull!" And believe it or not, some men fall for it. The reason why is simple: he's whipped. Or he's giving up all of his other options and she is the only woman he is having sex with. That will never happen to me. I make sure to keep at least two women on stand-by, so when women start talking crazy about getting their hair done and paying rent, I can tell them to go to hell!

But dating multiple women is not always about the sex. As a matter of fact I spend most of my time alone. I work ten hours a day, play basketball three times a week, and I have my daughter every other weekend. With such a busy schedule I don't want the obligation and expectation of a full-time relationship. And I don't have the time, energy, or finances to wine and dine women. When a woman I'm seeing comes over to my place, it's all about the business. How was your day, what's going on in your life, do you want something to drink? Then it's time to handle the business. I mean, what it all boils down to in the end is sex. Good sex that is! Because if the sex is horrible, neither of you will be around long. The best way to keep life simple is to date women who want what you want. That means I stay clear of the wanna-be married types, the baby-making monsters, and the where-is-this-relationship-going drama queens. It's best to date women who've already been married, already have kids, are financially secure, and preferably over 35. From my experience younger women bring nothing but drama!

A young lady I recently met at a concert is the perfect example of why I need backup. Her name was Valerie. She was 30 years old with no kids. That was mistake number one and two. For two weeks she called me on the phone boasting about how she was going to turn me out and make my nose curl, blah, blah, blah. But on the night we finally got together, she was whistling a different tune.

She arrived at my place at 11:00 p.m. wearing a pair of cut-off shorts and a tank top. I escorted her straight to the bedroom and threw my tongue down her throat. Within seconds we were rolling on the bed feeling all over each other. When things really started to heat up, I made my move by unsnapping her shorts. Now, guess what her reaction was after talking all that shit on the phone. She grabbed my hand, pushed me away and said. "I need more time to get to know you better before we have sex." I wanted to curse her dick-teasing ass out. But instead, I kept my cool and took the opportunity to give her an education about men.

"Look, Valerie, I'm sexually attracted to you and you're obviously sexually attracted to me, so what's with all the games?"

"I just want to get more comfortable with you, that's all,"

she whined. "I only met you two weeks ago and I hardly know anything about you. We haven't really talked about a relationship or even gone out anywhere together."

"Let me tell you something, baby, I don't have the time or financial resources to see you every week or take you out a hundred times before becoming intimate. And besides, this idea you women have of getting to know a man better is the most ridiculous thing I've ever heard."

"Why do you say that?"

"Because a man will never show you his true self until after he's had sex with you, determined that it's good, and gets it consistently. And then he still may never reveal himself completely."

"So, what! I'm just supposed to give a man my precious temple without even knowing who he is? That's crazy!"

"No, what's crazy is that for the past week you've been having phone sex with me, then you show up with your ass and titties sticking out, and now you want to get to know me, woman please!"

After I delivered my speech, I politely walked her to the door and kicked her frigid butt out. My best friend Randy told me I was in the wrong and should've been more patient. However, he was more sympathetic two nights later when the same thing happened to him. A woman he met at a film festival came over to his hotel room at 1:00 a.m. dressed in a pair of shorts and a bikini top. She kissed him, grind him, and let him suck her. But when he tried to reach for a condom she pretended to be upset and threatened to leave. And since Randy is one of those nice guys who doesn't believe in having backup, he put up with her teasing all night. To top it off, she had the audacity to demand breakfast the next morning. And this fool paid for it!

Again, I don't have that problem. If a woman can't play by my rules, I'll put her on waivers just like the NBA. There are too many free agents out there who are more than willing to fill her slot. An unrestricted free agent, if you will. This process is known as Drafting. And if you live in a city like Miami, there are plenty of good recruits out there, too. Just go down to South Beach and watch the parade of fine women of every race, shape, size, and color. The grocery stores, for example, are great places to scout good rebounders. The laundromats, on the other hand, are prime locations to find that agile woman who can put it in the basket. Even church can be a great place to recruit if you're looking for an unselfish player who will pass the ball. The bottom line is this; I need a solid team to keep my life simple. You can call it immaturity, insecurity, or whatever. But I'm not going to be like these other suckers out there wasting my valuable time and money trying to find Mrs. Right, when all I'm looking for is Mrs. Right Now!

Do Good Men Cheat?

Now that playtime is over, let us turn our attention to the more serious examination of why a so-called decent man would stray away from home. Revered as the most honest, trustworthy, and family-oriented of them all, he, too, has needs. Needs which aren't being met at home, for whatever reasons. But unlike the D-O-G, he is not deliberately seeking out women for sexual conquests. In his case, sex with the other woman is driven by what he's not getting at home. Many times the idea to have an affair never entered his mind, but over time due to the close proximity to women in the work place, common interests and an appreciation for their professional talents brings them together. In other words, sex is often the unexpected result, not the motivating factor. Now before you men start beating your chests and slapping five over that assessment, consider this. Although these explanations for cheating are much less premeditated, they are just as painful for the wife or girlfriend who eventually finds out.

EVERYTHING I MISS AT HOME

Home Sweet Home. Home is where the heart is. And last but not least, A man's home is his castle. These are touching phrases used to express the attitude of the man who is looking forward to coming home to his woman. He may not necessarily live in a mansion or have a perfect life, but he has a roof over his head and his needs are being met. But what about the man whose needs aren't being met? What does he have to look forward to? Those catchy phrases mean nothing to him since he is often neglected, disrespected and misunderstood when he steps foot in the door. From his point of view, home is not sweet, but sour. And as for his castle, it may just as well be a ragged Hobo's shack because unless the queen is performing her duties, the King will be unhappy and unfulfilled. What are these so-called duties, you ask?

Well, at the risk of being labeled a male chauvinist, I would have to say there are basically three. One of which is satisfying the man's egotistical needs. Men are over-grown babies who must have their egos stroked constantly. We need to be told how wonderful we are, how smart we are, and how much you admire how we are handling our business. In other words, we need cheerleaders! Another responsibility of the wife or girlfriend is to see to the supportive needs of her man. If a man makes a conscious effort to educate himself or get ahead in life, he deserves a pat on the back. And he wants to know that she is behind him one hundred percent. One who is totally committed to standing by his side through thick and thin. Many men see the so-called independent women of today as having no staying power. At the first sign of trouble, she's packed and ready to move on. Over the years of hosting my radio show, men complained about the lack of support more than any other issue in their relationships. On one hand, you have women complaining that men aren't stepping up, on the other you have the men who are making an effort who are not being supported. Which one is it?

Finally, there is the issue of the man's sexual needs. Aside from long tiresome workdays, menstrual cramps, and other feminine problems, the man expects his woman to be sexually available to him 24/7. The last thing he needs is a mate who is never ready, and is rationing out sex as if the supply was limited. This is an area where most men are unwilling to compromise and must have absolute compliance, or else! "Or else what?" you ask. Or else he may decide to seek the affection of another woman who is willing to give him what he wants, when he wants it. No man wants to be put on a sex schedule. It takes all the spontaneity and fun out of sex. And once sex becomes a chore to a man, it's over!

If a woman neglects or refuses to provide her man with these so-called basic needs, is he then justified in pursuing outside relationships? Most women would say, "Hell No!" They believe men who feel dissatisfied at home should either talk it out, seek counseling, or leave the relationship altogether. However, men know their choices aren't always so cut and dry. Other factors must be taken into consideration, ones that are emotionally draining and economically costly. A gentleman from Los Angeles typified my point. "I've been with my wife for twelve years, married for ten." He says. "I can't just pack my suitcase, gas up the old Lexus, and drive off into the sunset. I have a mortgage to pay and two beautiful children who depend on me. Not only that, but my wife would take me to the cleaners in the California divorce courts." After making a thorough evaluation of his financial situation, he determined that a move would be impractical. For the moment, he is trapped. He sincerely wants to leave, but can't. So now what? The cheating man must make a decision. To leave or not to leave? Or rather, to cheat or not to cheat? That is the question.

Patrick faced this same dilemma in his marriage a year ago. He became fed up with his wife's constant nagging and attempts at trying to change him. Like so many marriages, things became routine and boring. "While we were dating she was a free spirit and seemed to accept me for who I was," he says. "But after we got married and started to make good money, she became snobbish and expected me to act differently." However, Patrick was not that kind of man. He was raised in Detroit by a hardworking, blue-collar, father who taught him to judge people by their human wealth not their net worth. His idea of a good time was watching basketball and drinking beer with his buddies. His wife, Nicole, in contrast, was from a well-to-do family in New Orleans. She was basically a spoiled brat who fit in very well with the uppity crowd. Watching basketball and sipping on beer was definitely not her cup of tea. A year after graduation, they both landed great jobs in Chicago. After four years of climbing the corporate ladder they decided to get married. But after only one year of what seemed to be the perfect relationship, he found himself becoming deeply involved with another woman. Inquiring minds want to know…what happened?

Patrick's Story

O ur marriage started out like a fairy tale. We were both college graduates and very much in demand in our respective fields. And with combined salaries of over $100,000, we were well on our way to living the American Dream. As it turned out, all that money could not buy a dime's worth of understanding and consideration. After getting settled in our new home in Schaumburg, IL we began aggressively pursuing our careers.

During those first twelve months, things were very hectic. Nicole was working sixty hours a week handling contracts and other paperwork for a government agency. Meanwhile, I was putting in long hours and routinely flying out of town on business. It got to the point where we hardly ever slept in the same bed together. How does the expression go? "Two ships passing in the night," that was definitely us. We accepted this chaotic lifestyle as the price of success. We knew it wouldn't go on forever.

Over the next year our workloads gradually began to lighten up, we spent more time together becoming better acquainted as husband and wife, and as human beings. But what I soon discovered was we weren't exactly on the same page, or even the same planet when it came to our social status and attitudes about the black community.

As the months rolled by, it was obvious Nicole had bought completely into the yuppie, corporate mentality. First she insisted on updating our wardrobes. "Something more sophisticated," she would say.

When I confronted her about spending too much money, she jokingly replied, "Sweetheart, I'm not trying to keep up with the Joneses, we are the Joneses!" Ha, ha, Hell! I was thinking to myself. That was the first sign that she was drinking the yuppy Kool-Aid. But I went along with it for a while to make her happy.

Then she wanted an expensive painting for the living room. I went along with that, too. Finally, she decided we simply had to have a new car. Something that would be, in her words, "more reflective of our status." She managed to drag me down to the Mercedes dealership to purchase a brand new 2012 SLS AMG. Now, keep in mind we still had to make our $2,000 a month mortgage payments, and repay my student loan. I know $100,000 sounds like a lot of money, but it doesn't mean you're rich. Besides, I was perfectly content with my faded blue jeans, dogs playing poker poster, and my Toyota Camry. Who is she trying to impress anyway? I wondered. But, since we didn't have any children or massive credit card bills, I didn't complain. What the hell, I told myself, we deserve to enjoy the fruits of our labor. It never dawned on me, however, that the atmosphere and identity she was trying so hard to create was for her comfort and my exclusion. Sure, I was intelligent, handsome, and ambitious, but I just didn't have the attitude which says, "I'm better than you."

Our differences were becoming more apparent with the passing of each day, especially with regards to our choices of friends. Most of my associates were postmen, bus drivers, and guys who hung out at the gym. Nicole's friends, on the other hand, were real Divas. Her friend Tiffany was the biggest bitch of them all. She drove a BMW and always had her nose turned up. The difference in our social lives became even more evident when she refused to allow her friends to mix with mine. She never once invited them over to the house, at least not while I was around. But to be honest with you, I really didn't give a damn. My friends and I were having a ball, and the presence of her stuck-up girlfriends would have only spoiled the mood. What did bother me was the disrespectful way she would greet my company at the door. Without even so much as a hello, she would turn her back and walk away after letting them in.

"He's downstairs," she would rudely say. "And don't forget to wipe your feet."

And then there were the sarcastic remarks about their economic status. My best friend, who just happened to be a plumber, was her favorite target.

"So, is Mr. Handy Man coming over tonight?" she wisely remarked.

"Yes he is. Why do you ask?"

"Could you ask him not to park his raggedy maintenance truck in front of the house? It brings down our property value."

This was her smart-ass way of attacking his blue-collar profession. I guess she figured he wasn't intellectual enough for her taste. What's so ridiculously funny about her whole attitude is he damn near makes more money than both of us put together. But it wasn't just about money with her; it was about status.

Because I loved my wife and wanted to keep our marriage from drifting apart, I sat down with her and openly discussed my concerns. I left work early, bought her favorite bottle of wine, and rushed home to cook. I wanted the mood to be just right. When she made it home at 5:30 p.m., a candlelight dinner was laid out on the dining room table. The wine was chilling and the curtains were drawn. She was clearly moved. I waited until after we were finished eating to tell her how I felt.

"Nicole, I don't like where our relationship is headed. We need to do something about spending more time together, more quality time. You are my wife and I love you; all I need is for you to meet me half way. How about it?"

As she listened to my words, tears began to fall from her eyes. "I feel the same way, too, sweetheart. Things are getting a little out of hand. Just tell me what you need me to do."

After talking it over for a couple of hours, we decided on two things. One, to take a vacation together in the fall. Either a trip to Hawaii or a seven-night cruise. Secondly, to throw a get-acquainted party for all our friends. We figured this would be a great way to spend more social time together. All of this took place on a Friday evening in July. But it wasn't until late Sunday that we began making specific plans for the party. I remember that discussion vividly because it was a very hot and humid night. And I'm not just talking about the temperature either. Her idea was to arrange a dinner party on a Friday night. Of course, I preferred something less formal, like having a barbecue on a Saturday afternoon. What began as a civil discussion turned into a revealing argument.

"Look, baby," I said. "This formal setting sounds very nice, but people don't want to be all cramped up when they're trying to get to know each another. After all, this is supposed to be pleasure, not business."

That's when she slammed her pen down on the table and gave me a look, which I had never seen before.

"I wish I had never agreed to go along with this stupid idea in the first place!" she shouted. "I knew you weren't going to approve of anything that would make your simple-minded friends uncomfortable. Let's just forget the whole thing altogether."

"Damn! Where did that come from?"

"I'm sorry honey," she apologized. "It's hot and I'm tired, let's just go to bed."

She gave me a dispassionate hug, walked upstairs and got in the shower. As I began to turn off the lights, I stopped to sit down on the sofa to fully absorb all that was said.

I realized then that her attack was as much directed at me as to my so-called "simple-minded" friends. Despite my good looks, education, and respectable position, my image was not polished enough to show off to her bourgeois friends.

I had a strange feeling from that day on things would never be quite the same between us. Unfortunately, I was right.

The weeks following that incident were filled with sly comments about my attire around the house and how I spent my free time. One day she went too far. I was sitting on the living room sofa, minding my own business, watching a basketball game when she walked in with an attitude.

"Why don't you put on that nice sports shirt and slacks I bought you? Don't you get tired of wearing gym shoes and jogging pants all the time?"

"Now she wants to play fashion consultant," I said under my breath.

I ignored her remarks and went back to watching my game. I guess she got the message because she stormed out of the room with a frustrated look on her face. But she wasn't through yet. One hour later, she was back to pick up right where she left off.

"Why do you have to go play basketball with those same guys every weekend?" she said rudely. "Why don't you try something new like tennis or golf?"

That was about all I could take from her. Trying to change my character and choose my friends was her worst mistake ever. I made one last effort to control my temper, but it was in vain. I sprang up from the sofa and got in her face.

"Let's get something straight!" I said while pointing my finger at her. "I work hard every day. And if I choose to sit around this house all day buck naked, with a beer in my hand, that's my business. And furthermore, I don't want to hear any more of your rich girl shit about who my friends are and stupid golf. Now leave me the hell alone and go play with your fake housewives of Chicago girlfriends!"

She grabbed her purse off the counter, gave me a mean look and slammed the door shut. I was upset, too, so I snatched my gym bag off the patio and jogged the half-mile to the health club.

I needed something to relax me, and the gym was always the perfect medicine. On that particular day, it was exactly what the doctor ordered.

By the time I finished my routine and changed into my swim trunks, it was about 9:30 p.m. The club was going to be closing in a half hour. So, I dashed out of the shower and headed for the pool. I was determined to get in a few laps before leaving. After splashing around like a mad man for about twenty minutes, I took a rest on the edge of the pool. That's when I looked up and noticed the aerobic class letting out. Jessica, who was one of the instructors, acknowledged me with a wave and began making her way down. What I liked about her was how polite and cheerful she always seemed to be. And she spoke in a soft sweet tone. No matter how down I was, she always lifted my spirits with her bright personality. As she approached me from behind, I was hoping her charm would work its magic again, especially with the way I was feeling.

"Hello, Patrick," she said with her usual smile. "I can see you're having one of those exceptionally funky days, aren't you?"

"You better believe it. How do you always manage to pick up on that?"

"First of all, the way you tossed those weights around today was a pretty good indication," she laughed. "Not to mention the fact that you are splashing half the water out of the pool like a big kid."

"You know, Jessica. I'm not one to discuss my personal problems, but answer me this. Why are women so fickle?"

She put her hands on her chin as if to seriously contemplate my question, and then responded.

"Probably for the same reason men are so horny, it's only natural."

I burst out laughing at that one. She had a wonderful sense of humor.

"Well, Jessica, thanks to you, I won't have to go to jail for killing my wife tonight," I said sarcastically. "That woman is about to drive me crazy."

"In that case," she said with her hand out, "I'll take my fifty bucks for psycho-therapy right now."

Now that was funny. She really made me feel much better, and boy did I need it. As the announcement came over the PA that the club was about to close, she threw me a towel and asked me to meet her at the front door.

"I have something I want to give you," she said. Without a single dirty thought in my mind, I showered, put on my clothes and headed for the exit. When I got there, she was talking with another female trainer.

"Here, Patrick," she said while handing me an invitation. "I'm having a Bulls Basketball Party at my place next weekend. Why don't you and your wife come by and join us? There's going to be plenty of food, and lots and lots of beer!" she laughed.

"Ok," I said, "I'll see what I can do."

After we exchanged casual hugs, I put the invitation in my gym bag and walked out the door. As the door swung shut behind me, I could hear the other instructor yelling out. "And don't forget to bring one of your handsome, single friends with you!" Leaving the club, I felt great. My muscles were tight and my frustration gone, thanks to Jessica. Although she wasn't the most beautiful girl in the world, she definitely had a way of making a man feel like a million dollars. When I returned home, I could see the Mercedes parked in the driveway. That kind of brought me down a bit because I really wasn't in the mood for another argument. "She's probably waiting at the door with a skillet," I joked to myself. But instead of being greeted by an angry woman I was overwhelmed by the aroma of food. Nicole was cooking some of her famous Cajun gumbo, and it smelled good, too. If this was her subtle way of saying "I'm sorry," I thought, apology accepted.

As I walked towards the kitchen, I noticed that the table was set with candles and a bottle of wine. She must really be sorry, I thought. The real shocker was what I saw standing at the stove. Nicole was cooking in a teddy. The one I bought her for our honeymoon. I wanted to jump her bones right then and there, but I waited until after we had dinner. She had gone through a lot of trouble, the least I could do was to enjoy it all. Besides, the food was looking almost as good as she was, and I was starved. After eating half the pot and drinking all of the wine, I carried her upstairs, Don Juan style. I made hot passionate love to my wife all night long. She didn't even complain about her hair getting messed up. And you know how black women are about you touching their hair during sex. It's like trying to hold a newborn baby and wrestle at the same time.

The next morning we both called in sick. This was the perfect opportunity to turn things around in our relationship. Who cares about paperwork backing up? I thought. After making love for the second time that morning, we decided to get dressed and go to the movies. While I ran her bath water, she went downstairs to start breakfast. At that point the day was going perfectly, until the phone rang.

Wait a minute, I thought. I know for sure that the ringer and answering machine were turned off.

Nicole had obviously switched it back on. I gave her the benefit of the doubt assuming it was either an urgent business matter, or a very brief conversation. What happened next completely and permanently diminished our relationship. She came rushing upstairs as if there was a fire.

"Honey, I'll be right back. Tiffany just had a fight with her boyfriend and she needs someone to talk to."

"You're kidding me, right? What about our day together?"

"This won't take long. I'll be back by the time you finish breakfast."

Within fifteen minutes she was made up, slipped into an outfit, and was out the door. I couldn't believe it. Instead of concerning herself with her own relationship, she chose to run to the rescue of her girlfriend. This time the gym wasn't going to be enough. Instead, I calmly went downstairs, picked up the spatula and finished breakfast. Afterwards, I called into work and told them I would be coming in that afternoon.

What's the point of sitting around the house alone? I figured. I may as well get some work done.

Before leaving out the door, I remembered to grab my gym bag. I usually went to the health club directly from work. As I cleaned it out, putting in fresh socks and towels, I came across the invitation to Jessica's party. "Boy, I could use some of her good spirits right about now," I said to myself. For the remainder of the day, I found myself anxiously looking forward to seeing her. I really needed someone to talk to.

At 5:00 p.m. sharp, I was out the door and on my way to the gym. This time the pool was my last priority. As I drove into the parking lot, I was hoping to see Jessica's Honda Civic parked out front. And sure enough, there it was. I can't remember the last time the sight of an automobile made me feel so elated. I was hoping to catch her at the door to say hello, but she wasn't there. That's when I remembered she was the instructor for the 5:30 p.m. high-impact aerobic class. So, I decided to change into my sweats and join in. She was surprised to see me because I usually stayed in the weight room or the pool. As far as I was concerned, aerobics was for sissies and fat people. Boy, was I ever wrong. Ten minutes into the session I was ready to pass out.

She took us through a workout more strenuous than Marine boot camp. It was clear to everyone in the class she was trying to kill me. Besides looking in my direction every five seconds, she made sarcastic remarks about my manhood.

"Well girls, do you think these macho men appreciate how hard we work to get into those tight mini-skirts?"

"Hell no!" they all yelled at once.

Of course, I was the only man in the class at the time. What a coincidence. After the class ended, she sympathetically came over with a towel and a container of water. In a friendly way, I wanted to choke her to death.

"How could you do that to me?" I asked with my hand on my chest.

"I was just trying to make sure all of your frustration was gone from last night," she laughed.

"You did one hell of a job, let me tell you."

"Here, you big baby. Sit back and let me help you relax."

She walked around to my backside and began massaging my neck, and it felt good.

"Why don't you take your shower and meet me downstairs?" she said.

"Good idea. I think your workout will last me until next week."

After freshening up and putting on my clothes, I walked towards the front door to meet her. When I got there, she was surrounded by a group of men hounding her for her number. As I said, she wasn't a raving beauty, but she had lots of appeal. When she saw me coming, she politely told them she had business to attend to. I could see they were pissed off and jealous. But hey, that was their problem. She pulled me into her office and partially closed the door.

"I know this may sound rather forward," she admitted. "But

how would you like to join me for a snack and cocktail at my place."

"Well, I think ..."

"Wait, before you answer" she interrupted. "I want you to know that I understand that you're a married man, and I would never..."

"Hold on for a second, Jessica..." I interrupted her.

"No, you hold on, please allow me to finish," she said as she cut in. "It's just that, I never get a chance to talk with you one on one, and I think we could be good friends. No expectation, no demands, just friends. Ok, now I'm done."

"Are you sure?" I asked.

"Absolutely!"

"In that case, let's go."

"Are you for real?" she said looking stunned.

"Look," I said. "I'm hungry and I'm thirsty. If your refrigerator is full and you don't have children from hell, I'm all in!"

"Cool, let me lock up and I'll meet you in the parking lot!"

We exited the club as discreetly as possible. People are forever in your business, you know?

I followed her for about twenty minutes to her place. When we got there she broke out a bowl of spaghetti and garlic bread. We spent the next couple of hours on opposite ends of the couch talking about sports and our personal lives. It wasn't long before she got around to asking me about my wife.

"So why doesn't your wife ever join you at the club?"

"She's too busy shopping and getting her nails done."

"Have you ever fooled around on her?"

"Well, aren't we getting personal?"

"I'm sorry," she apologized. "I guess that was going a little too far."

"No, I don't mind, I have nothing to hide. No, I haven't even thought about it. Now, let's talk about you. Where is that special man in your life?"

"Nobody wants me," she said as she walked to the kitchen to refresh her drink.

I believe women only say this because it puts the man in a position where he has to tell her how wrong she is. Of course, I took the bait.

"Jessica, you are one of the most desirable women I know."

"You really think so, Patrick?"

"Sure I do. Any man would be lucky to have you as his woman."

Although she set me up for that response, it was the absolute truth. Physically, she was in outstanding shape. No doubt due to the daily workout like the one she put me through. And as for her appearance, she was a little above average. She wore her hair in the old school Toni Braxton style, and she had thick lips like Sade. But most impressively, she was a basketball fanatic. What more could a man ask for? As I said, she had appeal.

That night was the beginning of a wonderful friendship. The following weekend I went to her Bull's Basketball Party, and had a great time. Needless to say, my wife did not attend. Instead my best friend, the plumber, came along. The day after meeting Jessica, he made a very interesting observation. In his exact words, "Man, that woman treats you better than your own wife." And then he said, "You two have a lot in common." That was not the last time someone made this same comment. But Jessica and I are only friends. And no! We haven't slept together, yet. Although I must confess, our relationship feels very much like an affair. Is that possible? I say this because she is the first one I call with good news, bad news, and when I need understanding. However, Jessica is not the woman I promised to be faithful to. And until that changes, I'm only going to call my wife when I desire sex.

But you must admit, it's a damn shame when another woman has to fill the empty void left by my marriage. Eventually, I will have to make a decision about whether Jessica and I can remain just friends. There is no way in the world I can guarantee my feelings won't grow stronger being this close to a woman who treats me so good. And the tone that she uses when she speaks brings out the masculine caretaker in me. I can't emphasize enough how much that impacts a man. I hope my story causes women everywhere to ask themselves two questions, do I speak to my man in a way that makes him feel like "The Man," and, most importantly, "am I my man's best friend?"

Unrealistic Expectations

One of the most significant reasons why both men and women find themselves in such disappointing relationships is because of the superficial standards they use in determining who will make a good partner. The man, who has watched too many Rap videos, is looking for a woman with the perfect magazine face and video vixen body. While the woman, who has seen too many reality TV shows, is searching for a man who is six-five, with a large bank account, and a nine-inch penis. Not once during courtship does anyone ask, "How do you feel about buying as opposed to renting?" Or, "What percentage of your income do you believe in saving and investing?" And equally as important, "Would you be willing to support me if I wanted to start my own business in the future?"

These are questions that should be addressed before getting married and most definitely before having children. A gentleman named Michael I interviewed from St. Louis thought he had made the right choice for a mate. That was until he told her about his idea to quit his job and start his own business. Her reaction was not what he expected. She did not kiss him and say, "Oh honey, that's a great idea, you can do it!" Instead, she put her hands on her hips and declared, "Not with my money you won't." All of a sudden her great cooking and physical beauty were irrelevant. She was instantly transferred into a selfish dream thief!

She failed to realize that her man was not necessarily seeking her financial support. However, he was hoping she would be there to rub his sore back and say, "Hang in there, baby, you can make it happen." Or at the very least, offer to lend a hand in her spare time. Obviously, that was asking too much. She turned her back on his dreams, and left him no other choice but to seek support elsewhere. That's right, another woman. She loaned him money, prepared late night meals while he worked, and provided much-needed encouragement when no one else believed in him. And today, thanks in large part to her efforts, his business is off the ground and prospering. "So, why doesn't he just leave his wife altogether?" you ask.

Again you are looking at this situation from the female perspective. As I stated earlier, other factors must be taken into consideration, the most important being his children. He realized a divorce from his wife would result in separation from his two kids and that was unacceptable. Not to mention the financial cost. Child support, alimony, and lawyer fees can be pretty expensive. It didn't take him long to do the math and decide the price of leaving was too high. With the business finally making money, and his girlfriend fully accepting his situation, he discovered what so many other wealthy and not so wealthy men have, "It's cheaper to keep her."

Give It to Me Right!

The reason why many so-called decent men cheat on their mates often has nothing to do with support or understanding. You know as well as I do that the number one reason why most men are dissatisfied at home is because of sex. Either they are complaining about the quality they're receiving or the quantity they're being denied. First things first, let's start with the quality issue. No man wants to come home to a woman whom he has to coach into good sex every night. Week after week, year after year, he patiently waits for his wife or girlfriend to elevate her sexual aggressiveness, physical endurance, and fundamental skills. "Ok honey, lift your leg a little higher," he directs. "Don't stop now, baby, don't stop." "Ouch, not that way sweetheart, I can feel your teeth!" he shouts.

These frustrating situations take all of the fun and excitement out of sex. And sometimes the level of satisfaction never increases, no matter how hard he tries. As one man put it, "I could tape a cheat sheet on my chest, and my wife would still find a way to mess up." Again, the man has to ask himself that all-important question, "Now what will I do?" For the conniving D-O-G the answer would be quite simple, "Get a replacement." For the so-called decent man, this decision takes a lot more studying. After all, he had every intention of living up to his commitment to be monogamous. When he pledged, "To forsake all others," he meant it. However, that was before he discovered her inadequacies in the bedroom. Now all contracts promises and bets are off, at least where sexual obligation is concerned. Aside from inexperience and clumsiness, the quality of sex can be affected by the woman's weight, or should I say, excess weight? Joe from Charlotte put it more colorfully; "It's bad enough when you have to play traffic cop in bed, but a crane operator, too. Now, that's just not fair."

Some men, however, prefer a full-figured woman. And to them I say, "More power to you," literally. You're going to need it. But I think it's safe to say that the majority of men would prefer a woman who was a bit easier to sweep off her feet. Of course, weight is only an issue if someone in the relationship makes it an issue. Nine times out of ten that someone just happens to be the man. Despite the fact he hasn't seen his toes in years, he wants the woman with the perfect body, or near perfect. And God help her if he's seriously into exercising. She'll never hear the end of it. "You need to work on those calves," he'll say. "One hundred more sit-ups a night should flatten out that stomach." This is very helpful advice coming from someone who can eat like a pig and never gain a pound. And, by the way, when was the last time he gave birth? Men have no idea how difficult it is to lose those unwanted pounds after a pregnancy. Nevertheless, we demand absolute flawlessness. And if they can't get it at home, they'll simply have to order out.

Tony, who is a 41-year-old electrician, is one of those men who demand perfection in and out of the bedroom. After being involved in a monogamous relationship for two years, he began seeing another woman to satisfy his sexual needs. When I asked him why he decided to do this, his answer was very direct and to the point, "I'm not satisfied with my girlfriend's performance in bed. The oral sex is terrible, and she's gaining entirely too much weight." The question many women will surely ask is, "How can he sleep with another woman and still claim to be in love with his girlfriend?" Come on, ladies, don't be so naïve. Love has nothing to do with it. Like most men, he does not equate love with sex. The other woman is nothing more that a temporary sexual bandage to cover the neglectful scars left by his girlfriend. Let's face it, when it comes to sex, women need a reason, while men only need a place. Women should stop torturing themselves trying to understand how men separate love from sex; it's just the way we're made up, just accept it! It's obvious that men like Tony have. In his mind there is no conflict. Love is forever, while sex is strictly for play.

Tony's Story

Iknow people will label me as insensitive for what I'm about to say, but somebody has to tell it like it is. When I met Tracie, she was 5'3", and weighed 127 pounds. Well, her height obviously hasn't changed, but her weight sure has. As of today she's tipping the scale at a whopping 150 pounds. In my opinion, that's entirely too heavy. And what's so funny is that I met her at a health club. She used to work out almost every day. Starting with the stair machine for warm up, then 30 minutes on the treadmill. Sometimes she would come into the weight room to pump a little iron. You name it, she did it. But that was then. Now all she does is sit in front of the television, eat Doritos, and watch recorded episodes of reality shows all day. It's like one day she woke up and said to herself, "Now that I've got a man, I can just let myself go." That's unfair, and selfish. Maybe couples should sign a contract that requires them to stay within ten pounds of their date weight. If either person violates this agreement, the other party has the option of sexual substitution. Doesn't that sound like a great idea? Most women would probably say no. But I bet the men are thinking, "Sounds like a plan to me!"

The only reason I even bother to bring it up is because I love Tracie and I want to marry her. But she is only 35 years old and I don't want to marry a woman with a weight problem. It's not just about what I want, even she knows that her weight is getting out of control. Just last month she was talking to me about what areas she needed to work on. "If I could lose about fifteen pounds I would feel better about myself," she said. "I've got to lose a few inches from my waist and thighs." I couldn't have agreed with her more. But my question is, when is all of this weight reduction and muscle toning going to begin, 2020? I miss the good old days when she was so confident about her figure she would walk around my apartment naked all day. Now she rushes to turn off the lights, covers up with towels, and dives under the sheets to avoid exposing herself. All that does is draw more attention to her problem areas. Don't women realize that?

The mental stress of dealing with the weight issue was compounded by Tracie's sexual inexperience. The first few times we had sex were disastrous. She was pulling while I was pushing. When I tried to put her on top, she just sat there as if the bed was going to do all the work. And as for oral sex, forget it! That was a journey into the unknown for her. She was reluctant to go down on me. I actually had to ease her head down with my hand while she was kissing me on the chest.

The more pressure I applied, the more comical her expression became. She would look up at me as if to say, "What in the hell do you think you're doing." I played it off by throwing my head back and moaning, "Awe, that's good baby, right there." Then I put the move on her by angling my body so my penis was right in her face. After I finally managed to get her down there, she spent the next fifteen minutes kissing around it, under it, and on top of it. She did everything except put it in her mouth. I'm lying there with a rock-hard dick thinking to myself, "Just suck it goddamit!" That was one of the most frustrating evenings of my life.

Two days after that dreadful experience, we sat down and talked about how we could improve our sex life. I promised to be more patient, and she guaranteed me the next time would be better.

Well, one year and two hundred next times later and the sex still sucks. Or as the Rolling Stones song goes, "I can't get no satisfaction!" True enough, she has come a long way in the rhythm department, but she still can't give good head. Her biggest problem is trying not to scrape my penis with her teeth. There is no way for a man to enjoy sex when his dick feels like it's going through a shredder. Ouch! Just thinking about it makes me cringe. And on those rare occasions when she does manage to do it right, she stops just as it starts to feel good. I hate when she does that. Ladies, when a man says, "Right There!" that means don't move! Not, stop and take a break.

I'm at the point now where I prefer not to have it done at all. Even a hand job every now and then is out of the question with her. She can't even perform that simple task without damaging the equipment. She grips it too tight and bends it from side to side like a damn Slinky. After so much frustration, I ask you, "What's a man to do?" Tracie has everything a man could ask for in terms of personality, natural beauty, and loyalty. There's no way in the world I'm going to let another man have her. No way! I will just have to keep working with her to better our sex life. But until then I'll be calling the other woman at 1-900-Do-Me-Right.

Conditional Love

Most women would probably agree that any man who cheats on his woman just because she puts on a few extra pounds, never truly loved her in the first place. However, men do not love as unconditionally as women do. We are visual creatures who are stimulated by what we see physically. In our minds, we expect the woman we love to remain beautiful, and thin, forever. The reality of weight gain is something many of us are unwilling to accept, especially in a new relationship. Can a brotha at least get the first five to ten years to admire our woman's figure before she blows up? Is that asking too much?

And if that means Jenny Craig and a membership at Bally's Health Club, so be it. I'll personally foot the bill. But I must say this in the woman's defense; most of this criticism about physical fitness often comes from men who are fat as hell. They have the nerve to demand perfection while their potbellies are bulging out of their belts. One man referred to his forty-two inch waistline as love handles. The reaction of a woman standing nearby set him straight. "Love handles my ass," she said. "You need to stop drinking all those damned beers and get some exercise yourself."

What's Too Freaky?

Most men, including myself, expect women to have it all! Nice figure, pretty face, wonderful sense of humor, well-paying job, good parenting skills, master chef, and sex guru. And if that's not enough, we want the perfect blend of all these qualities, a woman who can win the Ms. Congeniality award by day, and the slut of the year trophy by night. To put it frankly, we want Halle Berry the Super Mom, and a maid who's a Super Freak! But wait, it gets even more ridiculous! She must then be careful not to be too whorish; otherwise, the husband or boyfriend will suspect her of foul play. "Who did you learn that from?" he'll ask. She's in a no-win situation. Either she's too passive or too aggressive. What's a woman to do? My attitude is, stop being so insecure and just enjoy it! There's nothing worse than a sexually confident woman having to hold back on exploring sexually because the man is trippin'!

As for the issue of oral sex, let me offer this comment. I haven't met a woman yet who wasn't prepared to go all out to please the man she loved. The question is, will he return the favor? Men have a tendency of lying back like porno stars while the woman knocks herself out trying to satisfy him. But immediately after she's done, he's ready to saddle up and start riding. The thought in his mind is, "To hell with you, it's Hammer Time!" This selfish attitude is exactly why so many men have been cut off and left hanging. As one woman remarked, "If I can take the beef, he can go fish." Men who are successful at getting the most out of their sexual relationships have one thing in common, they ask questions. Instead of complaining and cheating after the fact, they communicate their needs prior to getting deeply involved. Questions regarding acrobatic positions and exotic appetites are not put off until it's time to get into bed, because by then it's too late.

While men have every right to ask for what they want, the woman needs to know in advance what those desires and expectations are. As one young lady remarked, "My boyfriend should have told me ahead of time he was into all that freaky stuff. Oral sex is one thing, but anal sex is for prison inmates, not lovers." Another woman was more comical about her experience, "My fiancé tried to pull a Star Trek on me. He tried to boldly go where no man had gone before. So, I sent him where plenty of men had gone before, right out the front door." It is clear these women refuse to submit themselves to the exotic sexual appetites of their lovers. And why should they? Not every sex act is natural or necessary to achieve total satisfaction.

One man who has no complaints about the quality of sex in his bedroom is 37-year-old Charles. After five years of marriage, he and his wife still engage in dirty talk, try new positions, and break out the sex toys every now and then. This kind of openness helped him resist the temptation to fool around with another woman. In his words, "My wife, Lisa, is everything I could ask for in a sex partner. She is aggressive, creative and vocal. There's nothing more erotic then sex noise. The more she moans the more I know I'm hitting the right spots! It's like having a sexual road map. All you have to do is follow directions.

But that was his attitude before his son was born last year. His wife's tune instantly changed from, *The freaks come out at night* to *Yearnin' for your love.* After spending years working towards the perfect sexual relationship, he now has to contend with his wife's habit of rationing sex. Even the most decent man can only endure this kind of torturous treatment before his hormones get the best of them. Charles was no different, he felt perfectly justified in stepping outside of his marriage to seek temporary relief from this frustrating situation. And you know, men spell relief S E X.

Charles' Story

Does anyone have any idea what it feels like to live in a candy store and not be allowed to taste the sweets? Well, that's my life. Since my son was born a year ago, my sex life has gone down the drain. Instead of doing it five times a week, I'm lucky if I can get some five times a month. At first I thought the problem was physiological, so I didn't press the issue until I thought she was fully recovered from giving birth. But after three months I was ready to explode.

"What's the problem, baby?" I asked her. "Is there something wrong that you're not telling me about?"

"I'm just not in the mood," she replied. "Maybe later."

What the hell does, "Not in the mood" mean? I asked myself. She may as well have said, "I just don't want to do it with you," because that's how I felt. As much as I love my wife, I couldn't take much more of her tired excuses. My patience was running thin and my morals were weakening. To make matters worse, she was breast-feeding right in front of me every morning. I thought I was going to go crazy. For three months I watched her feed my son thinking to myself, can I have some, too, please?

About five months into the miserable situation, I found myself doing things that were totally out of character. Like staying out late, flirting with strange women, and drinking way too much. My bowling buddies noticed the change immediately because I was no longer rushing home after the game. Of course, they started in on me about my change of lifestyle. And it didn't help one bit that my bowling nickname was Able. You know, like able to come through at crunch time. Well, as you can imagine, they really had fun with that one.

"Isn't it past your bedtime, Able?" my teammate Jerry laughed.

"Yeah, Able, we know you like to eat while it's hot" Roland added.

"Very funny, fellas, "I said trying not to sound too pathetic. "Can't we just have a drink without all the wife jokes?"

"What fun would that be?" my friend Jerry added. "Besides, we didn't give you the nickname Able for nothing. Now we might have to take it back since you're not able to get any pussy at home."

They all cracked up at that joke. And to tell you the truth, I wanted to laugh, too, to keep from crying. What I needed was something to keep my mind off of sex. So, before I left the bowling alley that evening, I pulled Roland aside.

"Remember last month when you asked me if I had some spare time to give you a hand down at the cable company?" I asked.

"Yeah, I remember. You turned me down cold. And you know

I could use your expertise."

"Well, I'm ready to take you up on your offer."

"Are you serious, Able?"

"Yes, I'm serious, but only under two conditions."

"Ok, let's hear it."

"One, I only work weekends."

"And two?"

"Two, I want a patch on my uniform top that says Able."

We laughed and shook hands.

"It's a deal. When can you start?"

"This weekend, I don't have a damn else to do!" I said. "I'm tired of jacking off!"

"I'll see you Saturday morning at 10:00 a.m."

"You better make it 11:00 a.m., I might get lucky Friday night."

"Like I said," Roland replied. "I'll see you at 10:00 a.m."

When I got home that evening, I told Lisa about the side job. She thought it was a great idea and seemed relieved. Not only was I making a few extra dollars but she also knew this would keep me from hounding her for sex over the weekends.

"I think working with Roland is a good idea sweetheart," she said. "At least you'll get an opportunity to utilize some of your electronic skills."

"Yeah, right," I thought. She just didn't want me utilizing any of my physical skills around the house, if you know what I mean.

As expected, the job started out pretty boring. During the first two weeks I didn't do anything except watch the other technicians. On-the-job training, they called it. I didn't care as long as I was getting paid. Things finally began to pick up after a few weeks. By then I was working on my own. I was assigned to do the troubleshooting on a new line that was being put into a high-end condo development. When that job was complete,

I volunteered to do some of the installations inside the units. That's when the old devil started working on me. Some of the female customers were beginning to ask for me by name when they had a technical problem. Of course, most of their problems were sexual. This went on for six months before I finally got myself in too deep.

It was 4:45 p.m. on a Saturday afternoon and I was getting ready to go home when the call came in from a customer in unit 2001. It was the penthouse suite. I had installed service there two weeks ago, but the housekeeper was complaining about a bad connection. So, I packed my supplies and headed over on my way home. When I arrived at 5:15 p.m., the door was open and the unit seemed empty. I shouted to see if anyone was there.

"Cable man! Is anybody home?"

"Come on in," a woman's voice yelled. "The problem seems to be back here."

When I opened the door to the cafeteria, I understood exactly what she meant by that remark. Regina, who was the owner, was bent over the television wearing short tight gym shorts and a white bikini top. I could see the nipples on her breast protruding through the material. My mouth was open, but I couldn't speak. I finally managed to gain my composure.

"So what seems to be the pr-problem?" I stuttered.

"Well, Mr. Cable Man," she said very seductively. "I'm having a problem with my reception."

"Let me have a look at it."

As I walked over to the television, I could see that the cable wire had been disconnected in the back. Now I was starting to really get the picture. This was a setup.

"Do you see the problem?" she asked.

"Yeah, I think I have it fixed." I picked up the remote and set to the guide channel. "Is there anything else you need looked at?"

Why in the world did I have to say it like that? She took advantage of my sarcastic remark.

"As a matter of fact, there's something else I need fixed. Did you bring all of your tools?"

"Excuse me!"

"Don't tell me you don't know what I'm talking about, Able."

"How did you know my name?"

With a seductive look on her face, she walked over to me and pointed at my nametag. We were so close, our lips nearly touched.

"You are Able with the cable, aren't you?" she said while licking her thick lips.

When she said that, I could feel the bulge in my pants growing. Too little sex and too much blood flowing from my brain caused me to hallucinate. Instantly, I had become a single, horny, and eligible bachelor. No wife, no kids, no guilt.

"Miss, I feel it's only fair to warn you," I said while she unsnapped my tool belt. "I've been sexually deprived for the last few months, and I'm liable to hurt somebody."

That's when she walked over to her purse and pulled out a pack of condoms.

"Is that a threat or a promise?"

Everything after that was a blur. For the next hour I corrected all of her reception problems, adjusted her satellite dish, and made sure her box was properly plugged in, if you know what I mean. By the time I finished, she had received basic and all of the super stations, all at no additional charge, of course.

Since that day, my marriage has been going much smoother. My wife doesn't feel pressured into having sex, and I don't feel frustrated being turned down. I simply put on my uniform, grab my toolbox, and head out for another love connection. And I don't mean for the company either. I'm going to quit that job in a couple of weeks. After all, the whole purpose was to find something to do with my spare time, which I managed to do. Now I install a different kind of cable, the kind that doesn't require wires or a remote. As a matter of fact, Regina was so impressed with my work, she turned me on to some of the other single female residence. If my wife is still rationing sex by the time she calls me back, I'll be ready, willing and Able to do the job again.

Sex As a Weapon

Are there any women out there who can sympathize with this unfortunate man? Remember I said sympathize, not agree. Surely there are plenty of men who will not only sympathize with him but also applaud his decision. They know, as I do, that some women ration out sex for the sole purpose of control. It is no secret that women have used sex, or the lack of, to manipulate men into getting what they want. It is nature's erotic tool to hammer out deals and adjust the situation to suit her needs. Likewise, it can be used as a primitive weapon to shoot down a man's ego and kill his masculinity. There is no excuse for playing games with a man's sexuality. Sex is for pleasure and propagation, not for payoff and punishment. For the women out there who have a legitimate physiological or psychological excuse for holding out, my advice to you is, "Seek professional help. Right away!" And to those of you who choose to continue using sex as a means to exploit, I say, "What goes around comes around."

4

YOU, ME AND SHE

In the game of infidelity, there are no innocent players. The other woman is a careless co-conspirator. The wife or girlfriend is a silent witness to the crime. And the cheating man is guilty as charged. In the end they will all pay for their part in this lust triangle, emotionally, financially, or with the loss of dignity. Play at your own risk!

Vamp, Tramp, Traitor

If it is true that men who cheat are dogs, then the other woman must be the dogcatcher. Because without her full and unconditional cooperation, the husbands and boyfriends of the world would have only one place to go, home. Single-handedly, she can turn a happy home into a house of horror. With little or no shame she will aggressively pursue, wrongfully date, and shamelessly screw any man who tickles her fancy. And she doesn't give a damn if he just happens to be married, engaged, shacking, or seriously involved. As far as she is concerned, the wife or girlfriend is his responsibility, not hers. This type of woman is cold-hearted and careless. She is out for herself and pledges allegiance to no one. Not to her co-workers, not to her best friend, and not even to her own blood. Any man who crosses her path is fair game, no exceptions. As one woman stated, "Women get along just fine at passion parties, business functions, and baby showers, but let an attractive man come into the picture and it's every woman for herself."

It is important to keep in mind that when I talk about the other woman, I'm referring only to those women who are consciously aware of the cheating man's other relationships. The innocent and unsuspecting other woman who has been lied to is not to blame, unless she continues to carry on the affair even after she discovers the reality of his situation. Then she too becomes an accessory to the crime. There is no legitimate excuse for any woman to stay with a man once the truth is out. Nevertheless, you and I both know they will still try to justify their dirty deed, either by declaring temporary insanity or blaming the man. For example, one woman said, "By the time I realized he was married, I was already in love with him." Please, give me a break! Women are fully aware when they are dealing with a man who has more than one oar in the water. They simply ignore the obvious signs to temporarily or permanently postpone confrontation. What she should have said was, "By the time I admitted to myself that I was playing the fool, I was already dick whipped." This confession would have been more accurate and honest. Then there is the ever-popular excuse of, "All of the nice men I meet are either shacking or married." That may well be true, but that doesn't give you the right to have sex with them, now does it?

For an increasing number of women, the concept of "Man

Sharing" is not only tolerable but preferred, or so they say. These are the women I label as "Vamps." They intentionally seek out men who are already involved in other relationships, preferably marriages. And their mentality is shrewd and to the point. One woman's statement expressed my point. "When I'm ready to have sex, I just pick up the phone and call my fuck buddy," she said. "But after the sex is over, I want him gone. If he's married, I know he has to go home to his wife." Women who fall into this category have accepted sex as nothing more than a physiological need. No commitment, no emotional attachments, no expectations.

The professional woman is a perfect example. She is too busy with high-powered meetings and quarterly reports to take time out for a serious relationship. Instead she seeks a man who will not demand much of her time or cause stress with his complaining. She has a full agenda, a large bank account, and little patience. When the man arrives at her condo, she expects him to submit his proposal, execute his business, and promptly leave. The older and more mature woman is also a very good Vamp. She has had enough of fantasizing about Mr. Right. Now all she wants is Mr. Right On Time, with the sex that is. After years of falling in and out of love with insensitive men who only wanted a quickie, she has adopted a new philosophy, "What the hell? I may as well get mine, too." In many cases the Vamp over forty has already been married, has children, or doesn't want any, and is settled into a comfortable routine. In her world men are strictly for entertainment purposes.

By far the most interesting Vamp of them all is the cheating married woman. Don't act so surprised, married women are out there creeping, too. Statistics show that 50-60% of them have cheated on their husbands, at least once. Some would argue the numbers are much higher. Maybe the other 40% were too busy cheating to be surveyed. No matter what the numbers, there is no doubt the married woman is Vamping. And she is often the most adamant about dating married men, only. Not just because they appear to be more stable than the single men who run the streets, but also because they can better identify with the inconvenience of her situation. After all, who can better sympathize with a married cheater than another married cheater?

The number of Vamps is multiplying every day and there is no sign of a slow down. "What is the cause of this?" you ask. One reason is the over-exaggerated male-shortage statistics. Women are scrambling like chickens with their heads cut off trying to find a good man, or any man with whom they can spend quality time. As one vamp stated, "I just want a piece of the rock; sometimes you have to chisel off another woman's boulder." Again, this is just another weak excuse women use to justify their lack of sexual and emotional control. If only they would take time out to look at the big picture, they could see the problem isn't quantity of men but quality in the man. Until they understand this fact, the cheating man will continue to play them against one another like two pit bulls in a ring and puppets on a string.

And why shouldn't he dog them out? The Vamp is constantly setting herself up as an emotional doormat and a sexual outhouse. The cheating man is simply going along with the game and treating her like the whore she is. "If it's sex she wants, then it's sex she'll get," he says. "No love, no affection, and for damn sure, no respect." Millions of men all across this country have adopted this same heartless mentality, and they have no incentive to change. Why not? you ask. Because in every nightclub, office building, and bowling alley in America there is a desperate Vamp willing to spread her legs without a cause or conscience. As a result, men have become very cocky towards women in general. For example, a 30-year-old gentleman from Chicago told his girlfriend flat out, "If you don't want to get with the program, I'll find somebody who will." And guess what? He had no problem whatsoever finding a number of desperate women who were willing to go along with that so-called program. So much for long-term commitment.

Another reason why women are Vamping these days is because of the liberal feminist attitude concerning uncommitted sex. I guess this is some form of '60s free love with a condom. The idea is to do it whenever you want, with whomever you want, as long as you use protection. But my question is, Protection against what? "Herpes, Syphilis, AIDS? That's all fine and well, but what about protection against degradation, humiliation, and heartbreak? Even the conniving and calculating Vamp has been known to get burned. Although she may appear to be secure and in control, just wait until she runs into the right man. Or should I say, the wrong man? All of a sudden her busy work schedule slows down and her casual attitude becomes more serious. When love calls, she'll pick up on the first ring.

Don't get me wrong. I've met plenty of women who are just as good at emotional detachment as men are, in some cases even better. But those women are exceptions to the rule. Most often women cannot separate love from sex. And besides, that trick only works when it's a man she's not that into in the first place. When a woman is having sex with a man she has feelings for, over time her emotions will come into play. Suddenly, Mrs. In Control wants more out of the relationship, sexually, emotionally, and in terms of spending more quality time. At that point she'll have to make a decision to move on and start over, which most women hate to do, or accept her role as the other woman, or the other other woman.

The mature Vamp usually has very specific taste in men. She prefers a mature man who has his head and finances together, not some young buck she has to make decisions for. She also gravitates to men who are well-groomed whom she can trust to be appropriately dressed for whatever the occasion. Close attention is paid to details such as clothes, shoes, brand of cologne, fingernails, etc. Just like a Sugar Daddy likes to show off his tender young thang, the mature Vamp wants her lover to be on point and represent her well in public. Just because he's somebody else's man doesn't mean she can't reap some of the benefits of the hard work another woman has put into him.

With the consideration of love aside, she wants the best physical specimen she can get. Dorothy from Atlanta said it best, "If I'm going to share a man with another woman, it's going to be someone I can look at naked without turning off the lights!" The mature Vamp also requires a man with a bit of charisma and tons of confidence. Believe it or not, many couples who are cheating attend social events together and travel. No woman wants to be seen in public with a man who's weak and insecure, and he's married, too, awe hell naw! If her girlfriends or co-workers discover that he's married or involved, at least they will be impressed with the package. On the other hand, if he's in her life strictly for sexual gratification, you'll never see him in the light of day because she will hide him like a vampire.

Which brings me to the most important attribute for the mature Vamp: her man has to bring his hard hat and lunch box to the bedroom. As one woman said, "What's the point of having an attractive, well-dressed, minute man?" Darren, who is 50 years old and married, says that Vamps approach him all the time, especially at business conferences. His last close encounter took place six months ago with Theresa and Tonya, two Vamps who thought they had everything under control. Well, we'll just have to see about that. As we began to talk about his experience, he shared with me why he thought more women have turned to Vamping. In his words, "Women have become just as low down and dirty as the men whom they criticize." Now, whatever gave him that impression?

Darren's Story

I was at a sales conference at the Eden Rock Hotel in Miami and the last speaker had just wrapped up his presentation. He was boring as hell. I headed straight for the bar to get a drink to wake myself up. As I approached the bar and took a seat on the last bar stool, I could feel the eyes following me. Although most of our VPs are men, the majority of the sales force is made up of women. Once I got my Grey Goose and cranberry, I took a long sip and exhaled. Thank God that's over! I said to myself. Through the reflection in the bar mirror I could see the show that was about to start. There's nothing more entertaining than watching corporate people let their hair down when they get away from home. It's like kids being let out for recess at grammar school. The married men and women are the most fun to watch. Once they get drunk, watch out, you see the real person come out. They are wilder than the single ones.

I casually glanced around the room to see who was watching. Every now and then I would catch the eye of an attractive older woman who was sitting at the table on the opposite side of the bar. Of course, she looked away every time our eyes met. I guess she was checking me out to see if I was expecting company before she resigned herself to coming over. I chilled out and ordered another drink to loosen up a bit.

The night was still young, and I was in no hurry. About twenty minutes after sitting down and halfway through my second drink, the bartender came over to me with a silly-looking grin on his face.

"So, would you like another of what you're having?" he asked.

"Slow down, bartender, I'm not finished with this one yet."

"Well, when you're done, the lady would like to buy you another."

"Hey, that's fine by me!"

Now, keep in mind, he never did specify which young lady it was who offered to pay for my drink. So, I assumed it was the woman whom I had been making eyes at. Wrong assumption. When the bartender came over with the drink, I lifted my glass in her direction and whispered, "Thank You." She responded by giving me a flirtatious smile and blowing me a kiss. That gesture obviously set off the woman who actually paid for my drink because a minute later I felt a set of large breasts against my back and a soft voice in my ear.

"Are you enjoying your drink?"

"As a matter of fact, I am."

"Well, aren't you going to say thank you?"

"Oh, so you're the generous woman who offered to pay for my drink? Thank you very much."

"I've been trying to make eye contact with you since you walked in," she said. "But I couldn't get you to look in my direction."

"Well, I'll have to pay more attention in the future, won't I." I said, and then extended my hand. "By the way, my name is Darren."

"I know who you are; I saw you at the New Year's Eve party in Philadelphia," she said with a sexy tone. "My name is Tonya, but my friends call me T. N. T."

One look at her body and there was no need to ask why. While this conversation was going on, the woman from across the bar was making faces at me. You know that look that says, "Why are you talking to that bitch instead of me?" I wanted to bust out laughing right then and there. I couldn't believe she had the nerve to get jealous. Not after she sat there and tried to play hard to get. "If you snooze you lose," I always say.

Tonya turned out to be rather long-winded, so I had to cut her off after twenty minutes of non-stop yapping.

"Look, I don't mean to be rude," I said while gently holding her hand. "But I'm expecting a few friends. Can we finish this conversation later?"

"Sure, I understand. Just do me a favor and stop by my table before you leave. I'd like for you to meet my girlfriends."

"No problem. Where are you sitting?"

She pointed to the tables in the back of the room, handed me her phone number, and strutted away with that vicious body knowing damn well I was watching.

"Thank goodness," I said to myself. "She was blocking like a motherfucker."

Of course, the story about expecting friends was a lie to give the other woman an opportunity to make her move. And I knew she would do just that, after the coast was clear. Oh, by the way, my wedding ring was sitting on my finger as plain as day. Tonya took one look at it then passed me her phone number. She didn't even so much as inquire about my marital status. It was going to be interesting to see how Ms. Cool would react because I had no intentions of taking it off for her benefit either.

Not long after Tonya had gone, I noticed the other woman getting up from her seat. She tried to play it off by walking casually, but I knew where she was headed. I turned my back to make her approach more comfortable. And just as I expected, she was standing behind me at the bar ordering a glass of wine. She was clearly nervous about initiating the conversation. I just sat there eating it up. Now she knows how uncomfortable it is for us men, I was thinking. After receiving her change from the bartender, she worked up the courage to tap me on the shoulder.

"Excuse me."

"Well, hello Ms. Cool Breeze," I said as I turned around.

"Ms. Cool Breeze?" she said with a stunned look on her face. "What did I do to earn that name?"

"Because I was seriously checking you out and you played the cool role on me."

"I wasn't playing cool," she said while making herself more comfortable on the stool next to me. "I was just being patient. I refuse to act all frantic like these little girls."

"Well, I prefer big girls myself. Would you happen to know one who is available?"

"That depends."

"Depends on what?"

"On how committed you are to your wife," she said while staring at my wedding band.

"Look who's talking? You're the one wearing that Elizabeth Taylor-sized rock on your finger."

"We both started laughing and slapping five at that one. It was a relief to find that she had a good sense of humor. That's an important quality in a woman, even if you're only bed partners. Which is exactly what this was leading up to.

"Wait a second, we haven't even introduced ourselves. My name is Darren and you are?"

"Theresa."

"Well, Theresa, where do we go from here?"

"To bed, I hope."

"You don't waste any time, do you?"

"Darren, I am 42 years old. I don't have time for games. Here's my job and cell phone number," she said while handing me her business card. "Give me a call on Monday if you're interested, anytime before five o'clock works for me, no strings attached."

She gave me a polite kiss on the cheek and walked straight out the door. I guess she got what she came for. And to be honest with you, so did I. After I punched her number into my cell phone, along with a description of what she looked like so I could remember who she was, I went over to Tonya's table to meet her girlfriends. I wasn't at the table for 30 seconds before Tonya sprang up and offered to walk me to my car. I guess she didn't want me and her girlfriends to get too well acquainted. Or she didn't want them in her business because she was married, too. Once we were outside in the lobby, she told me she had something to give me and asked me to follow her to her room. The minute we walked in the door, she was all over me like a cheap suit. I strapped on my condom and tried my best to impale her on my penis. I never heard a woman scream so damn loud. It was like she hadn't had sex in years, and as it turned out, it had been eight months, according to her. Just in case you didn't know, married women are some of the hottest women out there. They get less sex than single women, and when they finally decide to have sex, watch out, they will try to fuckin' kill you!

That particular incident took place about six months ago. As of today, Tonya is still in my little harem and so is Theresa. But what's interesting about both of these ladies is how much their attitudes have changed. When I started dating Tonya, for example, she told me her first priority was her career, school and eventually starting her own business. "You don't have to worry about me bugging you," she said. "I've got two or three projects going on at any given time." Again, that was six months ago. Now this so-called Vamp, who thought she had everything under control, is nagging the shit out of me. My cell phone goes off at least four times a day because she wants to know when we're going to have sex again. It seems all of her priorities got rearranged after a few orgasms. I'll let her hang around for another month or so, only because she's good in bed. But after that, she's history.

Then there was Theresa, oh brother! She turned out to be a real nut case. Our relationship got so intense that she was ready to leave her husband. You should have seen me. I was working harder at trying to keep her relationship together than her marriage counselor and pastor put together. The last thing I needed was some over-aged sex maniac chasing me all around town. And what's so funny is that she was the one boasting about turning me out. "You can't handle this," she would boast. "I don't want to put a Mo Jo on you." Mo Jo my ass, now look who's walking around like a sex zombie? She was even considering having my name tattooed on her waist. She said it was going to read, "Darren, The Cat Killer." And she's still married. That's the kind of love I don't need. When will women ever learn; nobody can be as insensitive and emotionally detached as a man. Women may try to play the game but in the end they will always come up short. Men can pick up the next day and move on to the next piece, without even so much as a second thought.

Tramps Need Love, Too!

Without a doubt, the most pitiful other woman of them all is the Tramp. Unlike the Vamp, who seeks out her victims, The Tramp is often chosen by the cheating man because of her willingness to submit to his way of thinking and his way of life. In other words, she is valuable only because she is subordinate and controllable. Women who fit these criteria don't look alike, have the same body shape, or even the same level of education. However, there is one characteristic they do have in common, low self-esteem. It can be due to physical unattractiveness, economic failure, inability to hold on to a man, or abuse from her past. The cheating man doesn't care one way or the other. He will use whatever leverage is at his disposal to alter the relationship to suit his own needs, sexual needs, to be exact. Remember, this is primarily what the game is all about. The other woman should not fool herself into believing she serves any other purpose except satisfying his sexual appetite and stroking his ego. If you don't believe me, ask yourselves these questions as a test. Do I spend more than 80% of my time with him having sex? And do we spend the other 20% planning when we're going to have sex again? If you answered yes, then you are a Tramp. It's that simple.

Seeking out the Tramp has become a ritual for 29-year-old Rodney. Every six months he sets out to find a new other woman to replace the old one. And he is very specific about what type of characteristics he is looking for. In his own words, "She must be moderately attractive, have big legs, and love giving oral sex." Oh yeah, he added one other requirement, "She has to be loyal to me; I don't have sex with women who sleep with other men."

I know what you're saying to yourself, "The nerve of this arrogant bastard to expect monogamy when he's cheating!" But guess what, most cheating men have the same attitude. And what's worse is that women fall for it! We'll get more into the monogamous and non-monogamous relationships later. Let's get back to smooth-talking Rodney. It will come as no surprise to you that he is cheating on a woman he has been dating for three years. As a matter of fact, he's engaged to be married in six months. I found this rather interesting, so I asked him, "Why would you plan to get married knowing you have no intention of being faithful?" His response was very revealing. "My fiancée is the woman I love, respect, and do nice things for. These other women are only for fun and games. They're like toys I pull down off the shelf when I'm ready to play. And once I'm done, I just put them back on the shelf until I'm ready again." Listening to this guy really makes you wonder, "What types of women would allow him to treat them with such a lack of consideration?" My guess would be, the Tramp.

Rodney's Story

These women out here are so desperate they will accept any old excuse for sleeping with you. This is why I find it so difficult to have any respect for them. They are so accommodating; you can't help taking advantage of them. Janet is the perfect example of what I'm talking about. I met her six months after I started dating my fiancée, which means this May we make it three years that we've been together. During those three years, I haven't taken her anywhere except to bed. Not to the movies. Not out to dinner. And definitely not out to meet anyone in my family. Ok, maybe we did go to a movie once or twice, but that was late at night during the week. And it was a theatre on the other side of town. She has a clear understanding of what her role is. Which is the only reason why she is still around. I can call her any time of the day or night and she will come running. As a matter of fact, she was over just last week. I called her from my job at 1:30 a.m. for a late-night booty call. The conversation was short and to the point.

"Hello, baby, this is Rodney. Are you asleep?"

"No, I was just lying here thinking about you."

"Well, I was calling because I need to have you next to me tonight. Can you come over?"

"What time is it?"

"It's about one thirty."

"Ok, give me about twenty minutes or so to get my clothes together for work tomorrow, and I'll be right over."

"Alright baby, I'll see you at around two."

The feeling you get when a woman will get up out of her warm bed to come see you at one in the morning is exhilarating. You really feel like "The Man." Think about it for a second; this woman was sacrificing precious hours of rest to come over for the sole purpose of having sex. She may have arrived at two, but she didn't get to bed until around four. After all, I didn't invite her over to go to sleep. I invited her over for sex. She occasionally complained that she was giving more to the relationship than I was. I'll never forget this one morning in particular. Janet woke up late and was trying to rush out to work. I just lay back in bed under my warm blanket without a care in the world. I didn't even bother to see her to the door. Completely frustrated and half asleep, I heard her cursing me out under her breath.

"I can't believe this bastard. Here I am running late for work and he can't even get his lazy ass out of bed long enough to make me a cup of coffee or walk me to the door."

But no matter how upset she appeared to be, when I called her two nights later, she got out of her warm bed again. It sounds cold, but a man can only get away with what a woman allows him to. And even though I am engaged, I was upfront with Janet about it. I never said I was unhappy, I never said I was leaving, and I never said I was unfulfilled. That's what some men do to make women more vulnerable; they lie about the status of their relationship. I don't do that. All lying does is create drama. It's bad enough that I'm lying to my fiancée. I'll be damned if I'm going to lie to some Jump-Off on the side.

Don't get me wrong, I care about Janet. We've been together for three years for a reason; I enjoy her company, and we're sexually compatible. But it is what it is. Every now and then she'll complain about wanting more; that's when I step back and tell her to go find it. I've told her on many occasions, "If you want to find a man who will give you what you want, then you need to pursue it!" In my experience if you can't be consistent with something, it's better not to do it. I know I can't take her out or wine and dine her on a regular basis so I don't do it at all. Again, that's where a lot of married men mess up. They start trying to treat the other woman like the wife or girlfriend. That's a big mistake. If you can't finish something, don't start it.

Last Word on the Tramp

It is obvious the cheating man has no regard for the Tramp other woman. She is worthless unless her pants are down and her mouth is shut. He could care less about her daughter's kindergarten graduation, her promotion on the job, or even how well her day went. His only concern is whether or not she wants to have sex, period. Any other discussion is a waste of valuable time and a nuisance. And don't even think about burdening him with your personal problems. He is the consummate fair weather friend. As long as the sun is shining and everything is going smoothly, he will be calling with a cordial invitation for fun and games. But let a few minor problems arise in her life, and the cheating man will disappear faster than the last cold beer at a July barbecue. He is there for the good times, not the hard times.

It's hard to sympathize with the Tramp who settles for half a man hoping it will become something more. In the end she will end up alone, heartbroken, and if she's not careful, infected. As a man with a daughter and nieces who are now young women out here in the dating world, I always remind them never to date a man for what he wants. Make sure your needs are being met. Men are selfish by nature; they want what they want, and that's ok. The only problem is that women are settling on issues that are important to them, like integrity, honesty, and yes, monogamy. The only way to survive in this climate of lies, games, and deceit is to set standards. And by standards I mean, those things that are non-negotiable. If a woman doesn't have standards, she will forever be at the mercy of the man who has already set his. Ladies, stop fitting into someone else's program and let them start fitting into yours. Men who cheat are successful because they know that they are uncompromising in what they are looking for, and because they are not looking for everything in one woman! Cheating is a team sport!

Shameless Traitor

Last but not least, there is the other woman who has absolutely no shame in her game. She is the despicable Traitor. While publicly declaring, "All men are dogs," she is behind closed doors with another woman's man. Often times that man belongs to a close friend or relative. As I mentioned earlier, women get along like ice cream and cake until that attractive man comes on the scene. When that happens, it's a free-for-all. And the Traitor doesn't care if that man belongs to her girlfriend, sister, or even her mother. She is out for herself, in it to win it and going for what she knows, his zipper. As one Traitor so wisely put it, "It's nothing personal." But what if that man just happens to be a long-time boyfriend or husband. In my opinion, that's about as personal as you can get. An example of this scandalous behavior is Michelle's story. She is a Traitor who admits to having an affair with her best friend's boyfriend. From the very beginning she had every intention of having him for herself. As she put it, "My friend did not deserve him." Boy, with a friend like her, who needs enemies?

Michelle's Story

Jo Ann and I met three years ago at the company where we both work. I was the new trainee and she was my supervisor. Being from out of town, and the youngest of the ladies in the office, I was very nervous my first few weeks. Jo Ann did everything she could to make my transition comfortable. I guess you could say she took me under her wing. Right away we hit it off. We had the same taste in clothes, food, and as fate would have it, men. She was a very attractive woman in her mid-thirties and I was a tempting twenty-five. But our age difference didn't stop us from hanging out together flirting with men. I am a Taurus and she is Sag, so you know we attracted men like bees to honey. Of course it was all talk and joking around. She made it clear that she was off the market and she blocked me from any guy whom she thought was a Dog, which was pretty much all of them.

Jo and I were getting along great in our business and personal relationship. That was until her boyfriend, Eric, returned home from his tour in Afghanistan. Now, what was strange about how this all went down was, I met Eric first. What I mean is, I met him before she actually introduced him to me as her man. We were at a bar to celebrate his homecoming. Eric was supposed to meet up with us after he picked up his buddy up from the airport. Jo Ann and I got a table and ordered drinks. We had a couple of shots of Tequila and started dancing together.

The DJ was really jammin. I guess the alcohol must have gotten to Jo because she took off for the restroom in the middle of the song. I left the dance floor and headed for our table. As I made my way through the crowd, I noticed a sexy, tall, tanned man watching me. The closer I got to him the more he smiled. I had to pass right by him to get to my seat.

"Excuse me!" I said trying not to blush. "But you're standing in front of my table."

He gestured with his hand for me to come by.

"Um, Um, Um," he said. "Now, that's what I miss most about Texas. They have some of the finest women on the planet!"

"Why, thank you. You're not too bad yourself."

Now, keep in mind, Jo Ann had only shown me one picture of Eric, but he looked totally different in person. It had been six months since he had that photo taken. He had obviously been hitting the weights because he was buffed. He was six feet tall, with light brown eyes, and a muscular build. And he had buns that made you want to thank his mamma. Yes indeed, he was fine.

I excused myself to go look for Jo Ann, but I made sure to brush up closely to him when passing him by. It wasn't too hard to do since the place was jam-packed. As our eyes came face to face, it was obvious that the connection was strong. If you've ever had a situation where you meet someone and you feel the chemistry immediately, you know what I'm talking about.

We exchanged flirtatious looks before I excused myself to find out where Jo Ann was. In my own womanly way, I left no doubt in his mind that I was interested. But as I walked away, I realized, "I didn't even get his name."

Oh well, I thought. I'll definitely run into him later.

Boy, was I ever right about that! After I found Jo Ann, we went back to the table. Before I could tell her about the guy I had just met, she was going on about some drama that was going on in the women's bathroom.

"Girl, I need a drink!" she said dragging me by the arm towards the table. "Let's have another shot before Eric gets here!"

We both ordered a glass of wine and talked for a few more minutes before she excused herself to go to the bathroom, again! Now, this is when things got really interesting. At least twenty minutes passed, and Jo Ann still had not made it back from the bathroom.

I hope she didn't get in a fight with one of those chicks in the restroom, I jokingly said to myself.

But no sooner than that thought crossed my mind, did she show up at the table with you know who on her arm.

"Hell no!" I said under my breath.

I just knew she was bringing him over to me. But this was not the case.

"Michelle, this is Eric. Eric, this is my girl Michelle."

"Hello, Michelle, haven't we met somewhere before?" he asked sarcastically.

"I don't think so. Could you excuse me for a second? I need to go to the ladies room."

"Go ahead, take your time." Jo Ann happily replied. "I've got all the company I need right here!"

As I walked towards the restroom, which I really didn't have to use, I began wondering if this was all some kind of sick joke. Ok, so he wasn't my man. And I hadn't described him to her or even told her his name. But you can understand my situation, right? Anyway I checked my attitude and enjoyed the rest of the night. By the time I went back over to the table, Jo Ann was sitting in Eric's lap looking like she had just hit the lottery.

"My man is back, safe and sound. And he's all mine!"

"Welcome back, Eric!" we all toasted.

When we lifted our glasses, I tried not to look him in the eyes, but he wasn't making it easy. Ever chance he got, he would touch me casually on the arm. And when we all went out on the floor to dance together, he turned his back to Jo Ann more than he did to me. That's a sign of flirting even Stevie Wonder couldn't miss. Jo Ann was so drunk she wasn't paying attention. Every time he turned my way, he gave me that look. I knew I wanted Eric and I knew he wanted me. But Jo had been a friend and a mentor; I was going to do my best to keep it in check.

For the next two months I made every excuse possible not to be in their company. But Jo Ann was such a chatterbox; it was easy to keep close tabs on how things were going between her and Eric. She trusted me with every intimate detail. Our late-night girl talk on the telephone was my best inside scoop. And you know how women like to talk.

"So, how are things going between you and Eric?"

"Not so good. We had another argument last night."

"What was it about this time?"

"Can you believe he wanted me to come over to his apartment in a trench coat, with nothing on underneath?"

"No, he didn't!" I replied as if to sound disturbed, too.

"Yes, he did, girl. Not only that, but last week he wanted me to give him oral sex in the car while we were on our way to dinner."

"You mean while he was driving? You've got to be kidding?"

"No, I'm not. But I told him to find him a hoochie if he wanted that type of action. I'm an old-fashioned country girl."

"Wait a minute, didn't you two have an argument just last week?"

"Aw, that was about my cooking. He complained that my red beans and rice didn't have any flavor."

She would have been better off giving this information to the CIA. Don't women know you can't trust any woman with so much insight into your relationship, and especially into your bedroom? I was licking my claws after that revealing bit of news.

The process of breaking them up was going to be a breeze. If she would have been handling her business, I would have stepped back, but what woman doesn't give head in 2012? Seriously! Now I had all the details about what she wasn't giving him,

I started hanging out with them again. I began doing all

those subtle things to let Eric know that I was still interested. You know, little things like always taking pictures with him, or playfully sitting on his lap. But my favorite move was casually putting my hand on his knee whenever we were sitting close together. Jo Ann was so blind and stupid, she didn't even notice. And if she did, she never said anything about it. I wish a woman would put her hand on my man's knee. She would be pulling back a nub.

Anyway, my plan was simple; let him know I was down to do everything Jo Ann wouldn't do, and, of course, pump up his ego. Men are suckers for that. The perfect opportunity came when they had another argument while we were at the movies. She was upset with him for checking out other women while we were standing in line. I was just as shocked as he was. I mean really, do women really expect men not to look at another woman's ass? Hell, these women today dress so provocatively I find myself looking at asses, too. And some of them look damn good! My attitude is, you go girl!

After she calmed down, we all got back in the car and drove back to his place. The minute we parked, she stormed out of his car and slammed the door. I tried to talk to her but she decided to go home instead; another stupid mistake. Now I was alone with her man, and he was fed up with her. I began my subtle attack by sounding compassionate.

"Eric, don't blame Jo Ann, she's just a little old-fashioned"

"Old-fashioned my ass, she's just boring!"

"Sometimes women need time to get comfortable with certain things. If you know what I mean!"

"Michelle, I'm a grown-ass man; I'm gonna look at women's asses. And I don't want to have to negotiate getting my dick sucked!"

I wanted to say, "I heard that!" But I stayed in the friend-zone; he had to be the one to make the move. I needed that for my conscience.

"Just give her a little time; I'm sure she'll come around. She really does love you!"

"Well, love doesn't fix everything, dammit! Every now and then you just want to be a little wild, you know what I mean?"

"I can understand that!" I said. "But every woman is different!"

"You can say that again, cause we both know you and Jo are as different as night and day!"

"Excuse me?"

"You heard what I said," he said with a sly grin. "I pay attention to everything, Michelle says."

"Everything like what?"

"Like your attitudes towards sex and relationships! Whenever a topic comes up, you are open about it, not like Jo Ann, who is either quoting Scriptures, bashing gays, or calling women who use sex toys nasty," he laughed. "I can't even get her to have sex with the lights on."

"Yeah, I know," I chuckled back. "She tells me everything!

"Everything?" he said with a stunned look on his face.

"That's right, everything. But don't tell her I told you."

"Did she tell you about the trench coat?"

"Yep, she sure did. And she told me about the request for a blow job while you were driving."

"How embarrassing."

"Don't be embarrassed. I think you're creative with your sexual ideas."

"I'm glad somebody thinks so. I can't get her to go along with anything that's out of the ordinary."

"Well, I wish I could be of some help."

"Excuse me!"

At that moment Jo Ann's car pulled up to the house. But it was too late. I had already planted a seed in the mind and in the crotch of her man. It was only a matter of time before his curiosity and his hormones got the best of him. About a week after that conversation, my prediction came true. He asked me if he could come over to my place to talk about something that was on his mind. But I knew he wanted to do more than talk, and I was right. Without even so much as a hello, we were in each other's arms as soon as the door closed behind me. We both knew what was up. After that day, I began to make myself unavailable to Jo Ann. No more shopping on weekends, no more girls' night out, and no more late-night talks on the phone. Unlike her, I know how to keep my mouth shut.

As of today, Jo Ann still isn't aware that I'm the reason that Eric left her. She still calls me every now and then to talk about how much she misses him. I just set the phone down while she pours her heart out. A couple of times when she called, Eric was in bed lying right next to me. He loves to give me head while I'm trying to keep my composure. Here I am going, "Yeah girl, um. I hear what you're saying, ah." I can't believe she hasn't caught on yet. As I said, she's so stupid.

However, I must admit, she did teach me something. And that was how to please Eric. By observing her mistakes, I have become everything to him that she wasn't. I show up at his house at least once a week without any clothes under my trench coat. Just last week he almost crashed the car while I was giving him a blow job. And as for good cooking, I put Rachael Ray to shame. Chicken and dumplings, fresh baked lasagna, and cakes made from scratch. I'll do anything to keep the man I wanted so long and worked so hard to steal.

WAKE UP!

When will The Other Woman wake up and realize the reason why she is the other woman is because she does not fit the qualifications of a wife or girlfriend? Sure, she may be attractive, but only in a sexual kind of way. She may be supportive, but the wife or girlfriend has seen him through years of hard times. And she may be good in bed, but men know that a lasting relationship cannot be built solely on good sex. The wife may not be a ten in the sack, but she is a twenty when it comes to being a good mother and a support system. Not to mention, he loves the wife, not you! There's no amount of sex, massages, or great meals that will ever change that.

No, the cheating man is not going anywhere but home, home to his wife, home to his girlfriend, and home to his children. The Other Woman should therefore pack her emotional and sexual suitcase and find a man of her own. Otherwise she will be subjected to more unnecessary pain, especially during the holidays. Every Valentine's Day will bring bitter sweets and broken hearts. Each passing birthday will see her grow older, not wiser. Thanksgiving will have no thankfulness because the chair beside her at the family dinner table will be empty. Christmas Day will be just another annual nightmare of loneliness and depression. And as for the New Year, it will only remind her of how big a fool she had been the year before.

PAY TO PLAY

On a typical Friday afternoon, the cheating man prepares himself for another getaway with his Jump Off or Mistress. First he contacts the other woman to confirm their plans. Second, he calls his wife or girlfriend to tell his usual lie about going out with the boys after work. As the clock strikes 5:00 p.m., everything is set. He rushes out of the office building and into his car. Once inside, he tunes into his favorite radio station, shifts into drive, and heads for the expressway. But he has one important stop to make before his secret rendezvous, the cash station. When he arrives at the bank, the drive-thru lines are long and moving slowly. He wants to get out of the car to use the walk-through, but he doesn't want to take a chance on being spotted by a friend or neighbor. The fewer witnesses the better. While he waits in line, he reaches for his cell phone and clicks the calculate App and begins adding up his expenses. "Let's see," he contemplates. "Motel room, cheap bottle of wine, gas money, and a few extra dollars to get me through the weekend." After waiting for what seems like an eternity, he finally makes it to the ATM. He punches in his PIN and withdraws $300. Now he's ready to get the party started.

This scenario plays itself out millions of times every weekend from New York to L.A. Men are emptying their wallets, charging up credit cards, and bouncing checks, all in the name of lust. And although the dollar amounts may vary, the cheating man will inevitably pay for his horny impulses, and pay dearly.

Whether it's for a sleazy motel room, a tank of gasoline to get across town, or twenty bucks to help pay for his lover's babysitter, the dollars quickly add up. The attitude of one man regarding this expense was typical. "You've got to pay to play!"

Well, he's right about that, but who's really paying, and how much? The cheating man may be out a few dollars, but what about the risk of bringing home a potentially fatal STD, or getting the Other Woman pregnant? And let's not forget about the fatal attractions who slash tires, smash windows and show up at the job acting a fool! Is that also a part of the price you pay to play? The economics of having an affair never matches the pleasure you get from it. For example, what price do men put on AIDS? If he knocks up his mistress, that could cost anywhere from $300 to $3,000 per month, depending on the man's income. And anyone who's been stalked knows there is nothing more stressful than worrying about when a crazy person is going to strike next.

All of these things not only impact the cheating man but his family. AIDS is not just his issue, but also his wife's or girlfriend's, since most often men who cheat don't use protection, especially if the affair is long-term, which many are. Some of these relationships can last as long as 5, 10, 15 years. You think he's strapping on every time they have sex; of course not. Making babies is also a family affair; suddenly his time, energy, and financial resources are being divided between his wife's house and some chick he was just having fun with. What's worse is that the baby becomes a daily reminder of his unfaithfulness. When it comes to crazy women, we all know they never focus only on the man who scorned them. The wife and girlfriend usually get pulled into this mess, either with rude phone calls to the house, showing up in public making a scene, or worse. There are plenty of cases where the mistress has murdered the innocent wife or girlfriend out of spite. Make no mistake about it; cheating can be a deadly game. The emotions of a woman are nothing to play around with.

However, men who cheat think they have all the angles figured out. They don't want to hear about all these what ifs, and maybes. In their minds there are no consequences if they stick to the plan! Get it, get it up, and get out! But in reality, it's never that simple unless you pay a prostitute, which some men would be better off doing in my opinion. At least there are no expectations and less drama to bring home. The problem is that too many men, while claiming it's nothing but sex, get too emotionally involved with the Other Woman or Jump Off. Instead of keeping it simple and distant, men are often the ones who get caught up and become possessive and insecure. That's right, I said it. More often than you think it is the cheating man who gets caught up and starts trippin' in the affair. And once you go down that road of expecting the Other Women to be exclusive and to make herself available, you've instantly created another responsibility and potential time bomb!

To all my male readers, listen closely to what I am about to say. Women are not made up the same as we are. No matter how much they claim to be ok with being second, third, or fourth, in your life, eventually they will expect to graduate to a higher level. If they really care about you, and if the sex is good! Because make no mistake about it, sex is at the center of most of these relationships, especially in the beginning stages. If you don't believe me, look at the jam-packed motel parking lots every weekend. Who do you think are taking up all those beds, single people? Give me a break! Single people can have sex at home. Married people are the ones racing to the nearest cheap motel every weekend to have sex with the Other Woman and Other Man. Creeping is a multi-million-dollar industry. And if you add the booze, the weed, and the porno, it all adds up to a multi-billion-dollar business. It certainly does pay to play, and the cheating man is making a lot of people rich!

Cheapskate Cheaters

The cheating man has earned the reputation as the cheapest man on earth. Though he may be blessed with good looks, an impressive wardrobe, and sexual skills, he is often one paycheck away from being on the streets. In other words, all of his assets are on his ass. Of course, you would never know this by the way he swaggers around the club as if he owned a Ferrari, and lived in a mansion. Chances are, he got a ride to the club with a friend and lives at home with his mama. But being cheap has nothing to do with income or net worth. It is more a matter of generosity. For example, if a man who earns a million dollar salary were only willing to spend $1,000 a year on his mistress, he would be considered a tight wad. On the other hand, if a bus driver earning $30,000 per year were to spend that kind of money on his lover, he would be perceived as very generous. As I said, it's not about how much a man rakes in, but how much he's willing to dish out.

Which brings us to the cold monetary reality of the cheating game. Most men who have relationships on the side don't want to spend one thin dime. Their number one priority is to get the best sexual bargain on the market. If they had to choose between a beautiful mistress who insisted on going out every weekend and a moderately attractive woman who didn't complain about staying at home, guess which one they would choose? That's right, the low-maintenance, low-budget plain Jane. But even the most unattractive lover can be a financial burden around the holidays. Therefore, the miser cheating man will intentionally shy away from any serious relationships between December 25 and February 14. And if he's already involved, then he will quickly and creatively find a way to get uninvolved.

The plan is simple; instigate a fight with the other woman just before the holidays. This argument can be over bad sex, phony jealousy, or flaky dandruff. What difference does it make? The objective is to keep as much money in his pocket as possible. And if he's really a cheapskate, he will come up with some sort of unorthodox religious restriction. "I'm a Muslim, baby," he'll say. "We don't recognize these commercialized, European holidays." Yeah right. Just last month he was taking shots of Patron, smoking cigarettes, and stuffing his face with chitterlings. As for birthdays, well, the cheapskate cheating man has a plan to avoid celebrating that one, too. Out of nowhere, he will come up with a close friend, a relative, or old army buddy whose birthday just happens to fall on the same day. What a coincidence!

This financial game of bargain basement sex will eventually catch up with him. Although he may have been successful at avoiding the direct cost of infidelity such as dinner dates and expensive gifts, he will soon discover there are indirect costs that can be even more costly. One man who can testify to that is Anthony. During the two years of his affair he has gotten away with not taking his mistress out anywhere except to fast-food restaurants and matinee movies. His wife never suspected anything because he never broke his routine and his bank account was never short.

"I've got her where I want her; the sex is good, her body is tight, and the price is right!" he boasted. "What more could a man ask for?" Of course, this was his attitude before last month's eye-opening experience. That's when he learned the lesson that so many other horny fools eventually do. Sooner or later, you've got to pay the piper.

Anthony's Story

Have you ever had one of those days that you felt like God was trying to tell you something? Well, I have. And it came on a cold day back in January. It began innocently enough with a sick call to my job. I complained to my supervisor about having stomach problems, but in reality I was just too damned lazy to get out of bed. Even though my job was ten minutes away by bus, I still didn't want to go in. After putting on my usual performance, I lay back down and tried to go back to sleep. But for some strange reason I couldn't relax. One minute you're tired as hell and five minutes after you've decided you're not going to work, you've got all the energy in the world. It must be psychological.

I decided to put my newfound energy to use with a good workout at the gym in my building. I sprang out of bed, blended a protein drink, and put on my sweats. As usual, the gym was empty. It never ceases to amaze me how people pay big bucks for all these amenities and never use them, I was thinking. After working out for about an hour, I went back upstairs and took a cold shower. By 10:30 a.m. I was bored. I felt like a kid ditching school with nothing to do. That's when I got a text from Angela, my mistress. She told me to call her when I got a break, which was odd because we usually didn't talk until afternoon.

As I dialed her number, I thought about how good it felt to call another woman from the privacy and comfort of my own home. Most cheaters have to call from work or while they're driving home. It's no wonder that traffic is always backed up during rush hour. All the married cheaters are driving slowly so they can talk to the person they're creeping with. Or they just don't want to get home to those bad kids and annoying spouses. I just wish they would get the hell out of the left lanes so I can get past! After a few rings, Angela picked up!

"Hey, baby! Thanks for getting back with me so soon."

"Wassup, Angie, something wrong?"

"No, everything is fine. I just called to let you know I used one of my vacation days to take off today. Do you want me to meet you for lunch?"

"That's funny, I took off work today, too! The weather outside is shitty!"

"I know, it's cold as heck outside and it's been snowing all morning! You wanna come over and keep me warm?" she said in a sexy tone.

"That depends!"

"On what?"

"On what I can expect when I get there?"

"We've been seeing each other for over two years; you already know what to expect."

"Why don't you remind me?" I said teasing while I was slipping on my clothes.

"The minute you come in the door I want you to put your dick in my mouth, then I want you to pick me up and take me into the bedroom and throw me on the bed and have rough sex with me! Pull my hair, call me your bitch, and choke me."

"Damn, you want me to choke you, too?"

"Um hum, but not till I pass out, just until I'm woozie!"

We both laughed.

"Ok, that's enough dirty talk. I can't get my pants on because my dick is so hard" I joked. "Let me throw on a pair of jeans and grab my garment bag and I'll be right over to punch in," I laughed. "How's noon?"

"Perfect!" she shouted. "You'll be just in time for lunch, or should I say, to be lunch. And let me warn you, I'm starving. See you at noon. Bye."

Angela was the ideal mistress. She was attractive, childless, and most importantly, affordable. Never once in two years had she asked me to take her out or buy expensive gifts. All she wanted was a little conversation and lots of sex, both of which I could easily afford. But getting over to enjoy this economical date presented a transportation problem. My wife had driven the Honda Civic to work that day and our other car, a 2009 Corvette, was stored away in our garage. We both had agreed not to drive it until spring or unless there was an emergency. But on that day, I would break my own rules. The weather outside was terrible and there was no way I was taking the bus over to the other side of town. I thought about waiting for my wife to get home with the Honda, but the idea of answering questions didn't sit too well with me. So, being the typical horny male, you know it didn't take long to make a decision. I put on my blue jeans, threw a business suit in my garment bag, and grabbed the car keys off the hook. Before leaving, I wrote a short letter lying about attending an important business engagement across town. Then I wisely called my secretary and asked her to cover for me if my wife was to call. After putting all the safeguards in place, I strolled out the door ready for a high-impact, low-budget workout with Angela.

So there I was, driving in the rain and snow; it was a slushy mess. The traffic was bumper to bumper and people were driving like lunatics. To make matters worse, there was road construction going on, three lanes were merged into one. It must have taken me twenty minutes just to get down the expressway ramp. But once I got beyond the construction area, it was smooth sailing. For the next ten miles traffic was light and moving at a constant 55 mph. That is, until I arrived at the toll way where traffic was backed up again, "Why don't you stupid people have your change ready," I shouted. After wasting another fifteen minutes of pulling my hair out, I finally got through the toll and made it to Angela's place. What a trip!

Looking at the clock in my car, it was 1:00 p.m. I was an hour late. Having wasted enough valuable time, I quickly grabbed my cellular phone and garment bag and turned on the alarm system. Don't get me wrong; it's not that Angela lives in the ghetto, but the neighborhood isn't exactly Mayberry, either. Anyway, when I made it up the front steps, Angela was waiting with the door open. As usual, she was half-naked and smelling like the perfume department at Marshall Fields. I put my things down and dragged her straight to the bedroom. It took me all of five seconds to strip out off my clothes and get between the sheets. I did slow down long enough to put on my condom.

By 3:00 p.m., we were both exhausted. My mouth was completely dried out and Angela's stomach was growling like crazy. We put on our robes and went downstairs to make something to eat. She put a couple of steaks in the oven, and I shredded a head of lettuce for a salad. By 4:00 p.m., the food was ready. While we sat across the table from one another, she made all kinds of obscene gestures with her food, licking the steak and rolling her tongue around the fork. It was clear she wanted more sex, but I was tired and my tank was empty. After cleaning our plates, she put away the dishes and guided me back upstairs to screw my brains out, again. But before she could make her move, I begged for mercy.

"Please, baby, I'm only human for God's sake."

"Aw, come on, Tony," she said while stroking my chest. "I know you have a few more rounds in you."

"Food always makes me tired, Angela, especially when it's raining outside. Just let me relax for a minute."

"Remind me not to feed your ass until after round two next time."

"Very funny. Now stop hogging the blanket and let me get some rest."

I told her to set the alarm clock for 6:00 p.m., which would have given me enough time to put on my business attire and make it home by 7:00 p.m. The day had gone perfectly, up to that point. The sex was great, the food was good, and the bed was warm. All of that pleasure and relaxation for the price of a tank of gas. What a bargain! But my celebration was premature. As I fell into a deep sleep, the price of passion was about to multiply.

It was 9:15 p.m. when I was awakened by the sound of my car alarm. I leaped out of bed and lifted up the foggy window to see two young kids going through the inside of my car.

"Get the hell away from there!" I shouted.

One of them gave me the finger while the other grabbed what he could carry, and off they ran around the corner. Angela turned on the lights and handed me my pants. I just looked at her and shook my head. She had intentionally neglected to set the alarm. This was one of her silly attempts at causing trouble. I wanted to smack the shit out of her, but there was no time for dramatics. So, without saying a single word, I ran downstairs, grabbed my cell phone and car keys and slammed the door behind me. After turning off the alarm, I inspected the inside of the car to see what damage had been done. The passenger's side window was completely busted out, and the seat was soaked with rain. Everything out of the glove compartment was gone: iPod, cologne, insurance papers, and a pair of my wife's Gucci sunglasses. Thank God they weren't professional, I thought. Otherwise I would be walking home. I cleaned the glass off the seat and headed for the expressway. I was totally disgusted. My so-called cheap date had already cost me over one thousand dollars. But the night was still young.

When I arrived at the entrance ramp to the expressway, I looked over at the digital clock inside the car; it read 9:30 p.m. My ass is definitely in for it tonight, I said to myself. How am I going to explain being out this late without calling? The frustration and anxiety of the situation only made matters worse. There I was 40 miles away from home with no window and no excuse. As I drove down the wet and slippery expressway, my foot turned into a block of cement. The speedometer read 75 mph. That was way too fast to be driving on wet pavement, but I didn't care. I had to get home and every minute counted. The chilly night air was blowing freely through the broken window, but I was so pissed, I didn't feel a thing. I was determined to make it home before ten. And just as it looked as if I was going to make it, guess what happens? That's right, I get pulled over by a State Trooper for speeding. "God, please don't let this be some cowboy who's had a bad day," I prayed. But that was asking for too much. As he approached my car, I let the window down, and reached inside my jacket to get my license out.

"Keep your hands where I can see'm, boy!" he shouted.

"Oh shit, it's John Wayne!" I said under my breath.

"Don't move until I tell ya to."

"What's the problem, officer?"

"The problem is I've got a report of a stolen red Corvette, and you are speeding like this is the damn Indianapolis 500."

"Well, if you will allow me to get my license out, I can prove the car is registered to me."

"Why don't you just do that?"

I slowly pulled out my wallet and handed him my license. I didn't want the situation to turn into Rodney King, part two.

"Stay right there, son, I'll be right back," he said with an annoying Southern accent.

He walked back to his car and punched up my license on his computer. Within five minutes he was on his way back. But this time, his attitude was less hostile and more professional.

"Look, Sir, I'm sorry about the harsh language but sometimes you never know."

"No problem, officer."

"However, I will have to give you a ticket for driving 70 mph in a 55 mph zone. And since the road is wet, I'll also have to cite you for driving too fast for conditions."

"Look, officer, can you give me a break? I've had a terrible day. I'm late getting home and my car has been broken into."

"Well, looks like your day is about to get even worse."

He handed me two tickets, and had the nerve to tell me to have a nice day. "Yeah right," I said under my breath. I put the car in drive and pulled out into traffic. At that very moment, I swear I wanted to cry. Why do all the worst things seem to happen when you're out somewhere you have no business being? I contemplated.

After that experience, I never saw Angela again. I didn't even bother going back for my suit. I simply tacked it on to the price of the lesson. As for my wife, she didn't say a single word to me that night. The look on my face was so damned pitiful she decided to have mercy. The next morning I went to the dealer for an estimate on the damage. The cost was $1,100. However, after adding on the $200 for the traffic tickets, $500 for the suit I left at Angela's, and the $3 for the tolls, it came out to an even $1,803. Let this be a lesson to cheating men everywhere; it really isn't worth it.

Knocked Up

The cheating man's inability to control his hormones will eventually catch up with him. One day he will make the mistake of not using protection and the result will be 18 to 21 years of child support. Now he will pay to play whether he likes it or not, either by choice or with a little motivation from the court system. Men who find themselves in this predicament act as if they are stunned by the choice of their mistress to go through with the pregnancy. "How could this trick do this to me?" he swears. "We didn't even have a serious relationship." It may not have been serious to him, but for her it was as serious as a heart attack. The underlying problem is the cheating man's ignorance and total disregard for the feelings of his lover. Most women are emotional creatures who equate love with sex. Her vagina is not just some outlet for his physical pleasure, but an ultra-sensitive nerve connected to her heart. So while he's on top of her moaning and groaning thinking it's all in fun, she is slowly but surely falling in love. Now she won't be so easy to get rid of. After years of climbing in and out of his bed, the mistress also feels she has made an investment, one that she has every intention of collecting on. And if that means having his baby, then so be it.

This kind of mentality is typical of women who are desper-ately lonely and have very low self-esteem. Rather than finding a man who is willing to consent to fathering their child, they prefer to set a sex trap and trick him into it. This is by far the most disgraceful and stupid thing a woman could ever do. She may have the baby and a few extra dollars, if she's lucky, but she'll rarely if ever get the man. Ultimately, she is the one who is trapped with the day-to-day responsibility of raising a child. Not to mention having to explain to her son or daughter that their father was married to someone else when they were conceived. What a jacked up way to bring children into the world. But no one is more stupid than the cheating man for allowing it to happen. He is the one who has everything to lose, his family, his peace of mind, and his money.

One year ago, Anthony and Carey, who are both in their late thirties, learned exactly how expensive cheating can be. However, it was Carey who learned his lesson the hard way. Whether by accident or design, his mistress, Stephanie, came up pregnant only two months after they started having sex. His world forever changed and his wallet forever lightened. According to the laws in this state, she was entitled to 20% of his salary, which amounts to nearly $550 to $600 a month. What a price to pay for a few nights of meaningless sex. Anthony, who is single with no kids, could only empathize with his partner and learn from his mistake. Hopefully there's a lesson in it for other cheating men out there. Strap up or pay up!

Anthony and Carey's Story

This nightmarish ordeal began in August when Carey and I met Stephanie at the mall. A mutual friend who managed one of the clothing stores introduced us. She had a nice personality, but her body was not quite up to my standards. On a scale from one to ten, she was about a six. Her breasts were too small and she didn't have much ass, either. But what she did have was a flirtatious smile and a bed that was easy to get into. As it turned out, that was all she needed to attract Carey's attention. From the very beginning, I warned him to be very careful with her. Although she appeared to be a nice person, her credentials were shaky. No college, no career, and as far as I was concerned, no future. I'm always leery of women who fit into this category because they have absolutely nothing to lose.

Like most women who are trying to trap a man, Stephanie made herself available 24-7. Carey would call her at all hours of the night and she would drop whatever she was doing to do him. On at least two occasions, he called her after 2:00 a.m. when we were leaving the club and just like clockwork she was ready to do whatever he wanted, whenever he wanted. Now, that may sound appealing to some men, but it taught me one valuable lesson.

Dealing with a woman who has too much time on her hands can be dangerous. If they are not invested in something, then you become the investment. Anyway, after about two months of dropping by for late-night quickies, he became bored with her and broke off the relationship. From that point on, her name was never mentioned again, not until three months later when she called with the shocking news of her pregnancy. Of course, he called me immediately after he hung up the phone with her.

"Tony, this is Carey. You won't believe this bullshit!"

"Wassup, man?"

"Do you remember that female we met at the mall about four months ago?"

"Which one?"

"The one I used to call and wake up at two in the morning. You know, the plain Jane."

"Yeah, I remember her vaguely. What about her?"

"Dude, she just called me a minute ago and told me she was pregnant!"

"Hell naw. You've got to be kidding me, right?"

"I wish I was. I'm getting ready to go over to her place right now and talk to her about getting an abortion."

"Wait a minute; weren't you wearing a condom?"

The phone got quiet for what seemed like an eternity. I knew then what the answer was.

"As a matter of fact, I didn't use one on a couple of occasions."

"Oh shit. You messed up big time."

"I'm not even sweating it. I'll just go over there and threaten to kill her ass if she doesn't get rid of it."

"Listen to me carefully on this one, Carey. Don't even waste your time with that approach. This woman is not going to have an abortion, trust me."

"How can you say that when you don't even know her?"

"First of all, you haven't slept with her since early October, right?"

"Right."

"Now here it is late January, and she's just now calling to tell you that she's pregnant. Come on man, what does that tell you?"

"I'm fucked!"

Later that evening he called me with the update on what happened with their visit. Just as I expected she refused to get an abortion. She lied to him and said she didn't know she was pregnant until her fourth month. Not only that, but she claimed her doctor advised her against an abortion because of medical reasons. Was that a bunch of bull or what?

As the months passed and the delivery date grew nearer, Carey became more frustrated and hostile. The thought of a stranger having his baby was eating him up inside. This was definitely not the type of woman he wanted to bear his child, and his first one at that. "Why me?" he would angrily shout. "I should go over there and throw her ass down a flight of stairs." Although this remark was meant only as a bad joke, it was clear he didn't want her to carry the baby to term. During this time, he cut off all communication with her. The way he saw it, there was nothing for them to discuss until after the baby was born. And besides, he didn't want to give her the impression he was supporting what she did. In his mind she was nothing more than a conniving bitch who took advantage of him, and that's exactly what she was. But guess what, he fell for it!

On the day the baby was born, Carey was calm, cool and collected. I guess he was just glad it was over. He even went to the hospital to see the baby; it was a boy. But I strongly advised him against signing any papers until after having a blood test. Sometimes you never know. There are women out there who will get pregnant by a bum, and say it's yours just to save face with their families. A man should always double check to make sure that a child belongs to him. I don't give a damn how long you've known a woman or how much they tell you a baby looks like you.

When he returned from the hospital, his concerns shifted from what he was going to do about the baby to how he was going to break the news to his wife.

"Tony, how am I going to look my wife in the eye and tell her I have a son by another woman?"

"Well, if I were you, I would just wait for the results of the blood test before I start running off to confession."

"You might be right."

"I know I'm right. I mean, why break the news to her when you're not absolutely positive yourself?"

"You've got a point there, I'll wait."

Two weeks after the baby was out of the hospital, he called her and demanded to have a blood test before signing the birth certificate. She had the nerve to get upset, and threaten to take him to court. When he called me back, he didn't know what to do. I simply told him to stand by his demand. "Tell that bitch you don't know her from Adam," I said. "She can't expect you to trust her when you don't even know her last name."

Apparently the idea of going through expensive lawyers and time-consuming court procedure made her more reasonable. The blood test was taken, and another wait had begun.

"I hope this test comes back inconclusive," Carey said. "I would never mess around again."

"You need to stop that damn lying."

"Ok, then let me say, I will never have sex without protection again."

"I'll let that one slide, for now."

"I'm serious, Tony. This is the most stress I've ever been under in my entire life."

"You've been stressed out? What about me? I've had to listen to your whining for the last six months. Hell, I feel like I'm the one having the baby."

A week later the results of the test came back. But unfortunately for Carey, it was 99.9% in favor of him being the father. Just as promised, he signed the birth certificate and put his son on his health insurance. After only a few nights of meaningless sex, it now seemed that Stephanie got everything she wanted, a beautiful baby, a handsome father, and $550 a month. And while he despised her for what she did, he only had himself to blame. After all, he was the one who had everything to lose, not her. He should have done a better job at protecting his own interest. Now he has to face his wife with the painful truth. And God only knows how she's going to take it, especially since she's been bugging him for years about having a child of her own. His excuse was always the same, "We can't afford it." Well, after this expensive mistake, he may be right after all.

More Drama!

Any man who has had the experience of having an unwanted child will tell you it's one of the most aggravating and powerless feelings in the entire world. The woman has all of the rights and options. She can either get an abortion, put the baby up for adoption, or leave the man out of the child's life altogether. But what rights or options does the man have? To screw or not to screw, that's what, because once he puts his penis inside of her vagina, all of his powers are instantly transferred. Now his financial fate is in the hands of his lover.

Then there are the ferocious fights over paternity and child support. "It's not mine," the man will swear. "I don't know how many other men you've slept with besides me." For the mistress who has been faithful, this is a slap in the face and an embarrassment. She knows the baby is his and demands that he support it. "If you don't want to help me out voluntarily, I'll just have to take you to court." Now the situation gets blown all out of proportion and everybody suffers. The mistress will have to secure a lawyer and take days off from work to attend court proceedings. And after all of this wasted time and money, the cheating man will end up paying retroactive child support anyway, so what's the point? It seems to me their energies and financial resources would be better spent on the innocent child, not shifty lawyers.

The cheating man's compulsive desire to have more than one woman is not only monetarily costly but also potentially dangerous. It won't be long before his web of deceit snares a woman whose venom is more poisonous than his own, and whose mind is as unstable as a rocking chair with one leg. She will be his worst nightmare come true, a real-life fatal attraction. In the beginning of the affair, she appears to be a sweet, rational, and sane individual. But when he tries to dump her, watch out! She will not react passively by crying herself to sleep listening to her Mary J. Blige CD. Instead she will become enraged and seek revenge on the one person whom she feels is responsible for causing her so much misery. And guess who that is?

Robert discovered first hand just how ferocious one of these women could be. For three months his ex-lover stalked him all over town. She followed him home, to the gym, and even to the park where he took his daughter to play. "She seemed so docile and harmless when I met her," he said. "What in the world could cause a woman to change so dramatically?" Chances are she was crazy long before he ever met her. All she needed was a little pressure to make her snap. And snap she did.

Robert's Story

L et me start out by saying, I have no one to blame but myself for what happened. I'm not one of those guys who won't take responsibility for his actions. I played the game and I got burned. But Kelly was one crazy heifer. When I say crazy, I mean Glenn Close crazy! We met at a fundraiser for underprivileged children back in June. I noticed her the minute she walked into the room because she was wearing a sharp pants suit and eyeglasses. It's something about business attire that turns me on. As fate would have it, our tables were directly across from one another. When we made eye contact, I greeted her with a hand gesture and took my seat as the speaker came to the podium. Since her back was to the stage, she had to turn her chair completely around to see him. And every now and then she would casually glance over her shoulder to see if I was looking. Of course, I was.

After the opening presentations, people began to walk around and mingle. I expected Kelly to do the same but she just sat there sipping on her glass of water. That's when I decided to go over and introduce myself. As I pulled my chair back from the table, she smiled as if to say, "Come and get it." I approached her with my hand extended.

"Hello, my name is Robert," I said as we shook hands. "How are you doing this evening?"

"I'm doing just fine, Robert. My name is Kelly. Nice to meet you."

"I guess it was pretty obvious that I was coming over, huh?"

"Well, at the risk of sounding conceited, yes it was. But I must admit, you were rather smooth about it."

"Thank you for noticing. So, what brings you out to support such a worthy cause?"

"I love helping children."

"Yeah, so do I. As a matter of fact, I have one of my own."

"Boy or girl?"

"A 3-year-old girl. Her name is Tamera."

"Aw, and I bet she's cute, too."

"Of course, I think so," I said proudly.

After going through this routine of getting comfortable with one another for about fifteen minutes, I decided not to waste any more time dilly-dallying around. It was time for the big question.

"So are you married, engaged, or in love?" I boldly asked.

"None of the above," she responded with a smile. "But what about you? I know some woman has her claws in you already. And it's probably your baby's mother."

"Well, I'm not going to lie to you. We still see one another, but it's nothing serious."

"Yeah, right. That's what they all say."

"Look, I'm not going to waste time lying to you about my situation. If I'm interested in getting to know a woman, I tell her my status upfront. That eliminates all of the unrealistic expectations and game playing."

"I don't know about you, Robert. You seem like a real bad boy. And sooner or later, bad boys have to be punished."

What in the hell did she mean by that? I thought to myself. Is she into sadomasochism? Or is she merely joking about my aggressive behavior? At the time, it really didn't matter. I was determined to get her number.

"So what are you trying to say? You don't trust me?"

"Let me share something with you, Robert. I've only been in town for two months and already I've heard that line about a thousand times."

"Oh really, where are you from?"

"Connecticut."

"Connecticut?" I said with a curious look on my face. "You

mean to tell me there are black folks in Connecticut?"

"Very funny," she laughed. "Yes, we have blacks in Connecticut. Not as many as Chicago, but we do exist."

"Let me stop cracking on your hometown and get back to the point. I want to see you again. Can't we work something out?"

"I'll tell you what," she said, "Let me have your number, and I'll think about it."

"Think about it?"

"That's right, I said think about it. I'm a delicate 28-year-old woman. I like to consider what I'm getting myself into. And so should you for that matter."

There goes another one of those odd remarks again, I thought. Is this woman trying to tell me something or what? When I think back on it, she was probably trying to warn me. But my mind was tuned into only one thing, getting her out of that business suit and under my Egyptian cotton sheets. I wrote my home number down on the back of my business card and handed it to her. At that time the people at her table were headed back from the lobby area. I charmingly kissed her hand and went back to my table. It was up to her to take it from there.

It was Saturday afternoon when I gave up on hearing from Kelly. I figured six days was plenty of time for a woman to call me if she was interested. Later that evening, I thought about calling my child's mother, Donna, to ask her out to party but I remembered she had plans to take my daughter to a birthday party. There was no way in the world she was going to be rested enough to go out after dealing with those wild kids all day. So, I called my best friend Allen instead. He is always ready to hit the clubs. I knew he would be screening his calls with his answering machine. He is so old school.

"Hello, this is Allen. Sorry I'm unavailable to answer your call. At the tone leave a brief message and I'll see if I can fit you into my busy schedule." (Beep)

"Busy my ass," I laughed. "You haven't had a date in months."

"Look who's talkin'," he said as he picked up the phone ready to signify. "If it weren't for Donna, I don't think you would ever get any."

"Is that right? Well, at least I didn't get handcuffed to a bathroom sink by two stick-up women."

I was referring to an incident that happened a year ago when two women at a motel robbed him. They promised him a threesome, a night he would never forget, and they were right. When he got to the room, a man was waiting with a gun and they took his wallet, jewelry, and even his designer eyeglasses.

After robbing him blind, they made him strip naked, pose nude while they took pictures, and then handcuffed his wrist to the bathroom sink. It wasn't until 11:30 a.m. the next morning that the cleaning lady found him buck naked, sleeping on the floor. How embarrassing. But little did I know, he would soon get the last laugh.

"Now why did you have to go there," he laughed. "How was I supposed to know they wanted to play cops and robbers instead of doctor and nurse?"

"Let me stop dogging you, partner," I apologized. "I called to ask if you wanted to go out to our favorite spot tonight?"

"You know I'm game. What time do you want to meet up?"

"How about 10:00 p.m.? That way we can get our usual table."

At that moment, someone was trying to call me on my other line.

"Is that your line or mine?" Allen asked.

"It's mine. Hold on for a second." (click)

"Hello?"

"Hello, may I speak to Robert?" a woman's voice requested.

"This is Robert. Who's this?"

"Oh, you've forgotten me already, huh?"

"Look, I don't mean to be rude, but I don't like playing guessing games."

"This is Kelly, remember me?"

"Well, hello stranger! It's about time you called. I thought you faked me out."

"No, that wasn't it at all. I just wanted to think about what I was getting myself into. Have you thought about it?"

"What's there to think about? We're two consenting adults, right?"

"I guess."

"Kelly, I'm on the other line with my friend Allen right now. We're thinking about going out tonight. Would you like to join us?"

"Sure, why not?"

"Would you like for me to pick you up?"

"No thanks, I'll just meet you there."

I gave her directions to the club and the time we would be there. I then clicked back over to Allen and told him about my unexpected date. He was anxious to see if she measured up to my physical standards. But I was more interested in whether or not she measured up to my sexual standards. She was cute, but I needed a freak.

When I arrived at the club, Allen was already there with a woman under his arm. He introduced us and ordered a round of drinks. I rested my jacket on the back of the chair and began looking around for Kelly.

"So where is your date, Romeo," Allen joked.

"She said she would try to be here by 10:30 p.m. but you know how long it takes these women to get dressed. First they have to pile on a ton of war paint. Then they'll spend an hour trying to squeeze into a dress that's two sizes too small. And don't even let me get started on how long it takes them to do their hair. It's like a major construction project!"

"Yeah, but you men love it, don't you?" his date said with her hands on her hips.

"You're damn right we do!" Allen and I both replied and bumped fist.

"So, what's Kelly wearing?" Allen asked.

"If I know her, she'll probably have on a pin-striped business suit. She seems very conservative."

By 11:00 p.m. I hadn't seen anyone who fit Kelly's description. Once again I thought she had faked me out. I walked around looking for her until a woman asked me to dance. What the hell, I thought. No sense in spoiling a perfectly good evening. We danced for about twenty minutes before I noticed this fine woman on the far end of the floor, getting busy. "If I didn't know any better, I'd say that was Kelly," I thought to myself. "But there's no way she would be wearing that short black dress." After looking harder, I could see that it was her, and she was getting jiggy with it!

"Excuse me" I said to my dance partner. "I need a break."

"Maybe I'll see you later," she said with a flirtatious grin.

"Yeah, maybe."

I quickly ushered her off the floor and headed for the area where Kelly was dancing, and there she was shaking and grinding to the music. Damn, she was looking good! I finally got her attention by waving my hands in the air. She immediately broke off her dance and came to me.

"Where have you been all night?" she said sounding exhausted. "I've been looking all over for you."

"Yeah right. I guess you expected to find me behind the woman's ass you were dancing with?"

"Well I did, didn't I?"

"I guess you've got a point there," she laughed.

"So where is your friend Allen?" she asked.

"He's at the table, you want to meet him?"

"Sure, but let me freshen up a bit first."

"You look fine, let's go."

She wrapped her arm around mine and I escorted her over to the table proud as a peacock. When we got there, Allen and his date were hugged up like two teenagers.

"Excuse me, love birds," I interrupted. "I'd like for you to meet Kelly."

"Hello, pleased to meet you," Allen's date said.

"Wait a minute!" Allen shouted. "This is Miss Connecticut? No wonder they kicked you out of the state. With an outfit on like that you're probably illegal."

Kelly reacted by laughing and slapping him five, which surprised me. She had seemed laid back and a little boring when we met. Now she was a social butterfly and dance machine, but I liked it, I liked it a lot. For the next couple of hours we talked, drank and made jokes about the people in the club. When the party was over, I invited her over to my place for a nightcap. This turned out to be a big mistake. I was about to disclose my residence to an absolute psychopath. But once again, my smaller head was doing all the thinking.

It was 3:15 a.m. when we made it upstairs to my apartment. After hanging up our jackets, I offered her something to eat, but she wasn't hungry, at least not for food.

"Do you have a towel I can wash up with?" she said.

"Sure I do," I replied while reaching into the linen closet. "Use this one."

"What about a T-shirt?"

"Ah, no problem, is there anything else I can get for you?"

"I'm not making you uncomfortable, am I, Robert?"

"Absolutely not," I lied.

I could feel the sweat pouring down my back and the bulge growing in my slacks. She casually grabbed the towel out of my hand and went into the bathroom. As the door closed behind her, I went into action. First I took my pants off and slipped on a pair of shorts. Then I selected my old school slow jam playlist on my iPod to set the mood. I love listening to The Isley Brothers, The Whispers, and Marvin Gaye when I'm having sex. Finally, I took a couple of condoms out of my drawer and put them in my pocket, just in case. Shortly after setting things up, I heard Kelly calling for me to give her a hand.

"Robert!" she shouted. "Could you come here for a minute?"

"What is it?" I asked from outside of the bathroom door.

"I need you to hand me the soap."

"No problem!"

The bathroom was foggy from the hot shower. I grabbed the bar soap out of the soap dish, and I reached my hand inside the shower curtain hoping to catch a peek.

"Here you go," I said as her hand took the soap. All of a sudden she pulled my arm and the rest of my body into the hot shower.

"Hey! What are you doing?"

"Just relax and enjoy the sights," she said.

In a very exotic fashion, she reached down and pulled down my shorts. I tried to speed up the process by giving her a hand, but she wouldn't let me.

"I'm doing this," she protested.

"Be my guest."

For the next thirty minutes we had passionate sex underneath the showerhead. Luckily for me I had my soggy condoms on hand. We did it standing up, on her knees, and against the wall. She was so flexible I could have bent her over the curtain rod. This is too good to be true, I thought to myself. When the morning came, I found out just how right I was.

When I woke up the next morning, Kelly was staring down at me with those spooky light brown eyes. I couldn't tell if she was admiring my body or regretting what had happened. Without saying a word, she sprang off the bed and into the bathroom. I assumed she was ready to go so I put on my robe and opened the blinds. It was a beautiful Sunday afternoon. Just as I was about to make breakfast, Kelly came back into the bedroom ready for more.

"Where do you think you're going, mister?" she asked.

"Well, I was about to scramble some eggs."

"I've got something for you to scramble all right!" She grabbed me by the arm and pulled me back onto the bed. After reaching inside my nightstand for another condom, we were at it again. But this time she was talking crazy while we were doing it.

"Oh, Robert, you're so fine. Give it to me, baby, come on. Deeper, deeper."

"You want it all, baby?"

"Yes, all of it, from now on. You're my man now. You're mine."

"Chill out with all that possession talk; you're killing the mood."

"I'm just talking, baby, just enjoy the ride."

I let her statement slide and went back to getting busy. She was a complete wild woman, growling and screaming, "Fuck me, fuck me!" After an hour of this unappealing session, I got up and went to the bathroom. That's when the telephone rang and the answering machine picked up. It was my girlfriend, Donna.

"Hi honey, it's me. I just called to remind you to meet us at the park at 2. Tamera has been asking about you all morning, so don't be late. Oh yeah, how did it go last night at the club? I know Allen was acting a fool as usual. Sorry I couldn't make it. Anyway, I'll see you later, bye."

From inside the bathroom, I could hear Kelly mumbling under her breath. When I walked into the living room, she was rushing to put on her clothes.

"Hey, what's the rush?" I asked.

"I can't believe you, Robert."

"What are you talking about?"

"I guess I was the back-up date for last night, huh?"

"Look, all I did was ask you out. What's wrong with that?"

"Nothing except you lied to me about the status of your relationship with your baby's mother. You two have something serious going on. I may be young, but I'm not stupid."

"How in the hell can you gather all that by listening to a phone call? All she did was remind me to come see my daughter. I do that every Sunday afternoon."

"I don't want to talk about it right now, I'm a little upset," she said as she grabbed her purse and headed for the door.

"Wait a second," I shouted. "I don't even have your number."

She stopped momentarily to write down her cell number. I convinced her to give me a minute to put on my shorts so I could walk her downstairs. After I escorted her to the lobby, I dashed back to my apartment and threw on a pair of old blue jeans to meet Donna and Tamera at the park. As it turned out, that would be the last time I enjoyed myself at the park without looking over my shoulder.

For the next three days, I was out of town on business. I called home every night to check my messages but Kelly hadn't called. I didn't want to give her my cell number. I had that number for years and I don't give it out until women pass the thirty days crazy test.

Just so happens Kelly hadn't passed her probation period. I

was thankful that she hadn't called. She was a little too dramatic for me.

When I got back in town on Wednesday afternoon, I stopped by the apartment, dropped off my bags, and went to the office for a short conference. By 4:00 p.m., all of the meetings were wrapped up and I had received time off for a job well done. All I had to do was meet a client downtown at 7:00 p.m. and have him sign some papers. After that, the next five days were mine. When I called to check my messages at home, there were three messages from Kelly. I dialed in my code to retrieve my messages.

"Hello, Robert, this is Kelly. Why haven't you called me? I really need to talk to you. Call me back right away." (Beep)

"In case you didn't get my first message, this is Kelly again. I need you to call me back immediately, this is urgent!" (Beep)

"Look, Robert, I don't know what kind of game you're playing but you're fucking with the wrong woman. Either call me back this instant, or I'll come see you. And you won't like it!" (Beep)

What is this woman's problem? I asked myself. I blocked my cell number and dialed the number she left me on the pager twice, but no answer. When I called my answering machine at home, there were three identical messages on it. She was seriously trippin'. But I didn't have time to deal with her at that moment. I had an important meeting downtown and I needed a quick shower and a nap. I collected all of the contracts, threw them into my briefcase, and headed for home.

When I drove up to my apartment building, Kelly was parked out front in a red BMW. I parked my Audi in the underground lot and went to see what she wanted. As I approached her car, she jumped out with her hands on her hips. She looked pissed and ready to pop. I insisted that we go upstairs to my apartment so we didn't make a scene for my neighbors. She locked her doors, grabbed her purse, and followed me to the elevator. I lived on the 25th floor, so the conversation began immediately after the last person got off on the 5th floor.

"What is your problem leaving me those kinds of message?" I shouted. "Are you out of your mind?'

"What else was I supposed to do? she replied. "You didn't call me for three days, or return my messages."

"That doesn't give you the right to call me up talkin' crazy. And it damn sure doesn't give you the right to stake out my apartment like a detective."

As the elevator doors opened onto my floor, we held our tongues until we got past the nosy neighbors who were in the hallway. Once inside my apartment, I sat her down on the sofa, and played back her messages on the machine. Can you believe she had the nerve to start crying?

"I'm sorry, Robert. I didn't mean to say those nasty things. I just wanted to talk to you, that's all."

"Get up, and come with me!" I shouted.

I walked her into my bedroom and pointed to the unpacked suitcase lying on the bed.

"I've been out of town on business for the last three days. I can't just drop everything I'm doing to call you, understand?"

"I said I was sorry," she sighed. "What else do you want me to say?"

"Right now I'd like for you to leave."

"But I don't want to go," she said as she put her arms around my waist. "Let me make it up to you."

"I don't think that's possible, Kelly."

"I'll do anything you say, Robert," she said as she began to unsnap my pants. "Just don't ask me to leave."

All of a sudden my complaining stopped. She pulled down my slacks, dropped to her knees, and began giving me oral sex.

And while I was standing there moaning and groaning trying to keep from biting my lip off, she somehow managed to undress herself and maneuver me onto the bed. I couldn't believe it. There I was having unprotected sex with this deranged lunatic after she had threatened me over the phone and come over to my house unannounced. What am I doing? I asked myself. So, I snapped out of it long enough to pull a condom out of my nightstand and slip it on. I should have ended it right then and there; that flesh took over my common sense.

I must have dozed off because when I looked up at the clock on the headboard it read 6:30 p.m. I had to hurry to make my seven o'clock appointment.

"Kelly, get up!" I shouted

"What's wrong?"

"I have somewhere to go."

"I'll just wait here for you to get back."

"That's not a good idea. I need you to leave with me."

"Come on, Robert, I'm comfortable. How long are you going to be anyway?"

"Look here, I'm not going to go through interrogation when I'm ready to leave my own house. Now get up and put your clothes on."

That did it. From that point on I would see the real Kelly. She quickly slipped on her sundress and strapped on her sandals. While I ironed my shirt, she started mumbling under her breath and giving me the evil eye. I had a feeling she was about to snap!

"I bet you let Donna's ass stay here when you're gone."

"What did you say?"

"You heard what I said you no good bastard. I bet Donna doesn't get kicked out after she's been fucked."

"That's it!" I shouted. "Get your crazy ass out of here before I throw you out."

"Don't worry, I'm leaving. But remember what I told you in the beginning, you should've thought about what you were getting yourself into. You're not going to treat me like some street whore and get away with it."

"Just get the hell out of here before I call security and have you thrown out!"

She gave me the finger and slammed the door so hard one of my paintings fell off the wall. Now I've done it, I thought. After all these years of playing games, I've finally run into a real-life fatal attraction. I had seen that movie three times and knew Kelly definitely had Glenn Close potential. I didn't want to admit it, but I was scared. From that day forward, the hunter became the hunted.

For the next three months, Kelly made my life a living hell. She would call at all hours of the night, leaving crazy messages about getting even and teaching me a lesson. She even threatened to cut off my dick off like Lorena Bobbitt did to her husband. Ouch! After a month of these disturbing calls, I had my number changed. But somehow she managed to get the new one. I figured she had to know someone at the phone company. Luckily my cell phone service was with Verizon. After the phone calls stopped, the stalking began.

Every weekend she would park outside of my apartment and sit there as if she was at a drive-in movie. I was tempted to send her crazy ass a bucket of popcorn and some Milk Duds but I didn't want to provoke her. The last thing I wanted to do was let her know she was getting to me. I just ignored her and went about my business as usual. That was easier said than done. When I pulled out of the underground parking, she began to tail me all over town. She followed me to the grocery store, to the gym, and to church. But she finally crossed the line when she showed up at the park one Sunday afternoon while I was visiting my daughter.

Donna had to be told about what was going on. There was no way of knowing how far Kelly would go. But somehow, I had to come up with a convincing story to explain why this crazy woman was stalking me. Telling her the complete truth was not an option. I decided to drop the news late one Sunday evening after visiting with Tamera. As her phone rang, I took a deep breath and prepared to go into my act.

"Hey sweetheart, how are you doing tonight?" I politely asked trying to soften her up.

"Fine baby? What's up? Did you forget something when you dropped off Tamera?"

"No, I just wanted to talk to you about something that's been on my mind. Is Tamera still awake?"

"No, she's asleep. What's with all the mystery?"

"Ok, remember last year when that guy from your job kept calling you and sending you flowers?"

"Yeah, what about him?"

"Well, I have a woman who's fixated on me."

"So that's why you've changed your phone number twice in two weeks. I knew something was going on. How serious is it?"

"Very serious, I think. She followed me to the park today while I was with Tamera."

The phone all of a sudden got silent. I could hear what sounded like footsteps and then a door squeaking shut. I'm sure she went to make sure Tamera was asleep and then to her bedroom before she went off.

"If that bitch comes near my baby, I'll kill her! I mean it."

"Calm down, Donna."

"Calm down, my ass. What's going on, Robert? Are you telling me everything?"

"Look, this woman was just a client who wanted to mix business with pleasure. When I turned her down, she became obsessive. That's it."

"I'm going to trust you on this one, Robert. But don't let me find out you're lying or it's over between us, I'm serious! Now tell me what this crazy woman looks like so I can watch out for her."

I told her everything I knew about Kelly. How she looked, how she talked, and what type of car she drove. All I could do was hope this whole thing would end before the stakes got too high. I had already lost my peace of mind; I wasn't about to lose my family. But Kelly was a very sick young woman who was bent on revenge. She felt rejected and disrespected. How does the old saying go, "Hell hath no fury like a woman scorned?" I was living it!

Three weeks had passed since the incident in the park and it seemed that Kelly had finally moved on. I was hoping she was stalking some other poor soul. I decided to take Allen and Donna out to our favorite spot for drinks. I told Donna we were celebrating a successful business deal, but in actuality I was just happy to drive out of my building without seeing that damn red BMW parked across the street. Allen and I met inside the club at 10:00 p.m. We grabbed our usual table and ordered Coronas while we waited for Donna to arrive.

"So where's Donna?" Allen asked.

"She had problems finding a babysitter, but she's definitely coming."

"How is she handling all of this drama?"

"So far everything has been going pretty well, especially since Kelly stopped trippin'."

At that moment the waitress came over with our beers. I thought it would be the ideal time to propose a toast. I lifted my bottle and stood up from my stool.

"To Kelly, may she find another man to terrorize, or move her crazy ass back to Connecticut."

"Amen," Allen toasted.

For the next half hour we sat there sipping on drinks and checking out the beautiful women coming in. Of course, all I did was look, but Allen was foaming at the mouth. I had to remind him that Donna was very tight with one of his girlfriends. He checked himself and ordered another round. Shortly after we finished our second beer, the waitress came over with another drink on her tray.

"Excuse me," she said politely as she set the drink down in front of me. "This drink is from a secret admirer."

"What is it?" I asked.

"It's a Bloody Mary."

"Where is the woman who paid for this drink?" I urgently asked.

"Right over there," she replied while pointing in the direction of the bar.

When I looked over, I couldn't see anyone who resembled Kelly. But I knew for a fact she was the one who pulled this sick joke.

"What did she look like?" I demanded.

"She was kinda short, with a petite build. And she had light brown eyes. Can I get you anything else, sir? I have to get back to work."

"No, thank you," I said.

As the waitress walked away, I could see Donna making her way over to the table. She was looking good, too. Her hair was freshly cut, and the dress she had on was hugging every curve. For a 32-year-old woman with a child, she has a great figure. I tried to remain calm but I had a feeling something was about to go down. I wasn't going to hang around long enough to find out if I was right. So when Donna walked up to the table, Allen and I immediately started making excuses to leave.

"You're looking good tonight, baby," I complimented. "Let's go get something to eat instead of sitting around here."

"Good idea," Allen agreed. "I'm starving."

"That's fine by me," Donna said. "But let me have one drink before we go."

I quickly flagged down the waitress hoping to order the drink and get the hell out of there as fast as possible. While Donna sipped slowly on her strawberry daiquiri, Allen and I practically stood guard until she finished. And just as we were about to leave, guess who shows up? Kelly. She stood directly in front of the table with a bottle in her right hand and her left arm tucked behind her back. She was clearly drunk and looking spooky as ever.

"Hello, Robert," she said. "Aren't you going to introduce us?"

"I don't think so," I said as I positioned myself in front of Donna.

"Well, the least you could do is thank me for the drink I sent you."

"Look, Kelly, I don't have time for your bullshit."

"Kelly?" Donna shouted. "Are you the sick bitch that's been following my child into the park?"

"No, I'm the sick bitch who's been following your man into the park. I have no interest in your nappy-head child."

"So what the hell do you want?" Donna shouted.

"I want to teach your cheating ass man a lesson about toying with a woman's emotions. He's not going to treat me like some trick and kick me out after he fucks me."

"Woman, you are out of your mind," Allen said.

"You shut up, four eyes, and mind your own business!" Kelly screamed.

That's when she lifted the bottle over her shoulder, swung

it once at Allen, and then hurled it in my direction. Everybody ducked. After the bottle smashed against the wall, I looked up to see Allen's bloodied face. She had hit him directly in the eye. His eyeglasses cut through his skin and he was bleeding profusely. The yelling began immediately.

"You crazy bitch!" I shouted. "Look what you did."

"You should be more concerned about what I'm going to do to you."

In one motion she swung her arm from around her back and began violently throwing what felt like large steel darts. I quickly pulled Donna down onto the floor and shielded her with my body. I felt two sharp objects pierce my backside; one hit me in the upper back and the other in my buttocks. Once she was out of ammunition, Donna jumped up and ran towards her like a mad woman. Kelly tried to run but Donna grabbed her by the hair and slung her to the floor. By this time, the music had stopped and all eyes were focused on the catfight. Even the bouncers stood by and watched.

"I'll kill you, bitch, I'll kill you," Donna threatened as she ripped Kelly's blouse off and smashed her face against the floor.

"Let me up," Kelly begged.

"Not until I knock some sense in your young ass."

I ran over to where the fight was taking place with the two darts still inside me. I started to break it up, but Donna was giving it to her good. So, I stood by like everybody else and watched. After a few more scratches on the back and punches in the face, Donna let her up and the security guards moved in. We were all escorted to the back office where the owner was waiting. Allen and I knew him personally so the police were not called. Kelly admitted to starting the whole thing and offered to pay for the damages. I chose not to press charges since Donna kicked her ass pretty good and nobody was seriously injured. Allen, on the other hand, was holding a cold towel over his right eye. He tried to grab her by the throat as she was escorted out of the club. But this wasn't the end of it. When I got to my car, three of my four tires had been sliced and the windshield was smashed out. On the hood there was a message carved in the paint that read, "Now we're even, motherfucker."

Burned

The most fatal attraction of all is not the woman with a weapon in her hand, but a disease within her body. While the cheating man swears up and down his Mistress of Jump Off is clean and healthy, she could be burning with herpes, syphilis, or even HIV and AIDS. And just as he neglected to wear a condom to prevent pregnancy, he will likely neglect to protect himself from contracting an STD. It is well known that many men who cheat become comfortable with the Other Women and foolishly stop using protection, sometimes weeks into the relationship. That's a hell of a decision considering whose life is at stake. His own and the life of the innocent wife or girlfriend who is dumb enough to continue to trust him. This is why the cheating man must slow down, take a step back and ask himself, "Is it worth it?" This is an important question for any real man to face up to because it's only a matter of time before the high cost of infidelity hits his wallet, his conscience, and his home. When that happens, he will lose his most valuable asset of all, the woman who loves him. And she won't be as easily replaced as money. Nor will her loss of respect be remedied with a shot of penicillin. Sometimes women don't give us a second chance, and judging by how reckless and irresponsible we can be at times, she may be wise not to.

Wake Up!

Why do so many women get involved with men whom they suspect are cheaters? And more importantly, why do they remain in those relationships even after their suspicions have been confirmed? The answer to that question would depend on which woman you ask. Some claim it's because of love, or the kids, while others openly admit, it's all about the money. But these so-called reasons are nothing more than lame excuses for the timid wife or girlfriend to hide behind. In my opinion there can be only one common denominator for tolerating this kind of disrespect, and this is fear; more precisely, the woman's fear of being alone.

This paralyzing dread of waking up to an empty bed and growing old alone is all the leverage the cheating man will need to take full advantage of his relationship. He has predetermined there will be no consequences for his actions so he continues to take risks with his life and hers. The men I interviewed for this book are the perfect examples. They bragged about their methods of cheating with no regard for who might read it. And although names have been changed to protect the guilty, there was an air of arrogance that the games would continue in spite of what was said. As one gentleman boldly put it, "It doesn't matter what I tell you about how I cheat. Once a woman falls in love with me, she's not going to listen to anyone telling her anything. She won't even listen to herself." He is clearly depicting women as too stifled by emotion to act on any proof of infidelity, and he's not alone. Several men promised to purchase a copy of this book to give to their wives and girlfriends as gifts. What audacity! I'm not sure whether it's the ratio of men to women that have men so cocky or how much mess the women in their lives have put up with, but the cheating men of today are on a rampage. They are going through women like a hot knife through butter. Even the truth about how the game is played is not a threat to them. Chris Rock said it best in his stand-up, "Let a playa play!"

Open Relationships

Earlier in the book I mentioned open relationships, which is defined as couples where both or one of the partners have intimate relationships with other partners. In fact, I have done several topics about it on my radio show. Each time, women shut down and became defensive believing it was just another male trick to justify sleeping around. It's understandable that women would look at it that way since they only see relationships from one of two perspectives. One, all men do not cheat; therefore, they will hold out for that man who also possesses other qualities that make them compatible. Or two, most men will cheat at some point, and if they choose to be with that man they will weather those storms, usually with the hope that he will get tired, grow up, or whatever, which normally never happens. For some strange reason, women have this idea that our desire to have sex with other women is like the chicken pox, that it will go away after puberty. Ladies, please listen loud and clear. It's not a disease; it's in our genes. Just accept it and let's move on for God's sake!

I personally don't believe every man cheats, but I do believe the majority will at some point in their relationship, and so will most women. If we can agree with that assessment, then we can move forward and stop approaching relationships the same way over and over again expecting a different result. We all know the definition of insanity, right? Let's face it, most relationships are open anyway. People either don't know it, or they are in denial. And if women are going to tolerate their man being involved with other women, then they should reserve the same option to see other men, if they choose to. Every statistic about infidelity shows that over 70% of men have cheated once and over 50% of women have stepped out. Why are we afraid to tackle an issue that's staring us right in the face?

Besides, not having the open relationship talk is to the man's advantage and the woman's disadvantage. Why? Because men know that if a woman is into him sexually and emotionally, she most likely won't desire sex with other men, but women who are honest with themselves know that most men will exercise that option whether the woman agrees to it or not. It's not until men are faced with the possibility that their woman will be sexing other men that the reality of what they are asking the woman to put up with becomes real. As a married woman in New York put it, "It's called, put the shoe on the other foot! Or what's good for the goose is good for the gander!"

I think part of the problem is women give in to the ideal of monogamy too easily, without any agreement or understanding that the man will do the same. Ladies, please stop making it so damn easy for us, geesh! It should be clear from day one to every man who wants to play the field that you will exercise your option to do the same damn thing. And I promise you that your relationships will improve immediately. But you must start out with the conversation on day one! Try it and let me know how he responds. You can reach me on BaisdenLive.com, BaisdenLive on Facebook, and BaisdenLive on Twitter.

A Man Is Going to Be a Man

Teaching a woman not to tolerate infidelity in their relationships is not a simple task, especially if she was raised in an environment where it was normal behavior. Karen, who is 28 years old, can relate well to this type of programming. At a young age she was brainwashed by her mother, aunts, and other female family members into believing, "A man is gonna be a man!" For years she accepted this philosophy as gospel and quietly went along with the program. But after years of being neglected and disrespected, she finally woke up and smelled the coffee.

Karen's Story

My mis-education about men began at age fifteen. That's when I first started to notice my father was staying out late and going away for long weekends, supposedly with his fishing buddies. My mother never once complained. She just went about raising my brother and me as if nothing was wrong. But sometimes I could see the frustration come out. She did a great job of disguising it by fussing at him about leaving his empty beer bottles on the living room table or playing the music too loud in the basement. This was her only way of getting back at him, at least as far as she was concerned. My mother was an attractive and intelligent woman. She had a Bachelor's degree in English and a body that would have given a 25-year-old a run for the money. That's why I never understood why she put up with my father's cheating for all those years. It was obvious that his affairs were annoying her, but she never threatened to leave him. I'll never forget what she used to tell me when we were alone. "Marriage is forever, baby, no matter what." By the time I was seventeen, she began to preach about a few other things as well. Things that had a dramatic impact on the way I would view my own relationships.

What family would be complete without a gossiping aunt or a know-it-all friend of the family. I had both. My Aunt Dorothy, and my mother's girlfriend Carolyn were one helluva duo. Every Sunday afternoon they would come by the house while my mother cooked dinner. Of course, this was the signal for my father and my older brother to escape to the basement, and my cue to get lost. However, on one particular visit no one asked me to leave. It was obvious by the way they were all grinning that this was my indoctrination into the Woman's Club, but my young mind was ill-prepared for their bold conversation. As usual, my loud-mouth Aunt Dorothy started in on me about my boyfriend, Jason. Everybody all of a sudden got quiet.

"So I hear you've got a man, Karen," she said while picking the ends off the green peas.

"Dag, why are you all in my business Aunty? Momma, I told you not to tell her."

"Girl, your momma can't keep a secret," Carolyn laughed. "If you want something broadcast to Europe, just tell your mother and watch the ten o'clock news the next day."

"Carolyn, you'd better be glad my daughter is in here," my mother responded. "Otherwise, I would tell you to kiss my ass."

"Let's not get off the subject," Aunt Dorothy said. "Tell us about him."

I wanted to run out of the kitchen, but being allowed to hang out with the girls was too much to give up. And besides, you know how young girls like to boast about their boyfriends. So I leaned back against the counter, poked out what little chest I had and started bragging.

"Well, since you insist, "I said. "Let me give you the scoop. He's a senior, his family owns their own business, and he's as fine as Boris Kodjoe."

"Oh my goodness, you'd better put a chastity belt on her Joanne!" Carolyn shouted. "Her panties are on fire."

"Yeah, Sis, I think you need a drink," Dorothy said while

comically pouring my mother a glass of water. "Puberty has finally kicked in."

My mother just looked at me and smiled. She knew I wasn't a loose young woman. And she and my father trusted Jason not to pressure me. But shortly after the jokes stopped, the education started.

"So what are you going to do when he starts fooling around on you?" Carolyn asked.

"Get rid of his butt," I declared.

"Is that right? And then what?"

"And then I'll find a man who's not going to cheat on me."

They all busted out laughing. My mother spilled her water and Carolyn damn near fell out of her chair. Aunt Dorothy walked over to me, and sympathetically put her hands around my shoulders. "Baby, ain't no such thing as a man who don't cheat!"

"Amen to that," my mother added.

At that moment the phone rang; it was Jason. After excusing myself from all the playful teasing, I went into my room to talk. We had plans to get together later that evening, but he said he couldn't make it.

As usual, I didn't complain. But I must admit that the idea of him cheating on me did enter my mind. A seed had been planted in my head about trusting men, or should I say, *not* trusting them. And it still affects me to this day.

Growing up watching my older brother David cheat on his girlfriends also had an impact on me. He and his friend Chris would talk about women as if they were toys to be used and thrown away. And since I saw them as fairly decent men, I figured whatever they had to say was representative of most men, including Jason. One day, not long after Aunt Dorothy's lecture, I dipped in on a conversation they were having on the porch. Needless to say, I was more attentive than ever.

"So what's up with that young lady you met at that club a couple of weeks ago?" Chris asked.

"You mean Debbie?"

"Yeah, whatever happened to her?"

"She's still around, but I don't think she's gonna make the cut."

"Why is that?"

"Well, for one thing, she asks too many questions. And secondly, she's not giving it up!"

That really made me mad. They had some nerve dissing that poor girl just because she wouldn't have sex. And if she had screwed him on the first date, they would have called her a slut. Why are men like that? I angrily contemplated. What really bothered me was the thought that Jason might possibly start feeling the same way about my holding out. How long do I have before he dumps me for some whorish college student? He was graduating next year and I would still be a skinny high school girl. For the moment I put those thoughts aside and continued to take notes.

"What about that little chick you met at the skating rink?" my brother asked.

"Oh, you're talking about Rhonda," Chris said, sounding cocky. "She's on her J-O-B."

"You mean she's in your B-E-D," my brother laughed as they slapped five.

"Yeah, she could definitely be a keeper, if only she would stop coming over while she's on her period."

"Man, don't you just hate that?"

"That's alright though, I've figured out when her time of the month is. I'll just put off our dates until I know it's over. Which reminds me, I need to run to the store to pick up that new iPad. Let's roll down to Best Buy!"

Those words cut through me like a hot knife through butter. Was Jason avoiding me for the same reasons? I wondered. There was only one way to be sure. I tiptoed away from the back door and ran upstairs to check my calendar. Like most young women, I kept track of every event from our first kiss to our last argument. If there was any relationship between canceled dates and my menstrual cycle, I would find it. And sure enough, there it was in black and white.

He called me the day before my period to cancel our dates for the last three months. My heart dropped, and my eyes watered. "I can't believe Jason played me like this," I cried. This was the turning point in my attitude towards men. I had completely bought into the "All men are dogs" theory. The way I saw it there was only one thing left for me to do, secure mine.

Within three months, I was popping birth control pills like Tic Tacs and having sex. I was determined to hold on to Jason at all costs, which I did long enough to get married to him. I was 21 years old in my third year of college, and he was 23 and about to graduate. What a fairy-tale relationship, right? Wrong! Five years of marriage and two beautiful children later and Jason was still up to his same old tricks of putting me off to see other women. He was real smooth with it, too. Not once in seven years did I ever find any physical evidence of his cheating, but there were plenty of other signs that he was out creepin'. On Saturday afternoons, for example, he always refused to take the kids with him when he claimed to only be going shopping. Then there were the Masonic meetings that lasted for five hours on Friday night. When I went over to my mother's house to express how I felt, she went into her usual speech about keeping the family together at all cost.

"Mom, I don't know if I can handle much more of Jason's game playing."

"What exactly do you mean, sweetheart?"

"Come on, Mom, you know what I mean, his affairs. And I mean affairs with a capital A."

"Look baby, I know Jason isn't perfect, but he is a good man. Doesn't he provide well for his son and daughter?"

"Yes."

"Doesn't he come in at a decent hour?"

"Yes, momma, but—"

"But nothing child," she said as she stopped cooking and came to sit down at the table. "You've got to learn that a man is going to be a man. And as long as he's giving you your respect, you've got to leave him alone and concentrate on keeping the family together."

"Giving me my respect!" I shouted. "Every time he leaves the house to see one of his whores he's disrespecting me. Why should it make any difference because I don't have fingerprints or videotape? I know damn well when my husband is cheating,"

"Keep your voice down, Karen," she said while gesturing with her hands. "Your father is right downstairs."

"Good, maybe he'll get the hint and stop messing around on you."

Smack! In one motion she leaned across the table and slapped me dead in the mouth.

"You watch your mouth when you talk to me, young lady. I'm still your mother!" she shouted. "Don't you worry about how with your father. We've managed to stay together for twenty-six years and put two kids through college. When you can say the same, then you can stand in judgment of me."

I sat there in total shock with tears pouring down my face. That was the first time she had ever laid a hand on me since I was twelve. Without saying a single word, I stood up from the table, grabbed my coat, and headed for the door. By this time she was crying, too. I'm sure she was as stunned as I was by what had happened. As I walked out the door, she tried to apologize. "I'm sorry, Karen, I just want you to be happy."

I looked back at her barely able to speak and mumbled, "That's exactly what I've been trying to tell you for years."

During the twenty-minute ride home, I reflected on what my mother said. But no matter how hard I tried to make sense of it, I couldn't. There was no way in hell I was going to spend the rest of my life sharing my husband, and seven years of marriage and two kids didn't mean a damn thing to me. I wanted love and trust out of my relationship, and I wasn't getting either. "This must all end," I declared. "I'm sick and tired of waiting, worrying, and crying over this man." It was time to stop playing the fool. After wiping my face and blowing my nose, I decided the next time he slipped up would be his last. All I needed was one tiny reason to explode. That opportunity came two weeks later during the Fourth of July barbecue at my mom's house.

I hadn't' spoken to my mother since the incident took place. When Jason and I arrived with the kids, she quickly ushered me aside and apologized for everything that happened. Like most women, we got all sentimental and started crying. I'm sure everyone was wondering what all the drama was about, but this was strictly between mother and daughter. Once the entire family was there, we sat down to eat. As usual, the food was outstanding. My mother really knows how to put her foot in some collard greens and potato salad.

After everyone was full, the family split into three groups. The kids went outside, the women gathered in the living room, and the men flocked to the basement. It wasn't long before Carolyn and Aunt Dorothy went into their act about no-good men. Needless to say, I wasn't in the mood, so I went into the kitchen to refill my drink. Right away I noticed the door to the basement was wide open. As I went to close it, I could hear my drunk brother and husband boasting loudly about their sexual escapades. I just stood there and took it all in.

"Man, it's impossible for any man to be right with so many temptations out there," my brother said.

"Who are you tellin'?" Jason agreed. "Just last week a woman came into the office wearing a skirt so short half her ass was showing."

"Did you inform her that her attire was inappropriate for corporate America?"

"Hell no, I complimented her on the outfit and asked for her phone number."

The room exploded with laughter. I could hear the customary high fives and foot stomping. But they weren't through putting their feet in their mouths.

"What about the sex drives some of these young women have?" my horny 45-year-old Uncle Frank joked. "This 23-year-old filly I just met damn near threw my back out at the motel last night."

"Well at least she's working hard to please her man," Jason said. "That's one thing I can honestly say about these women on the side; they serve you better than your own wife."

That was the straw that broke the camel's back. I slammed my glass on the counter and rushed downstairs with smoke coming out my ears.

"You all have a lot of damn nerve bragging about your whores right under the same roof as your wives. I have never seen such disrespect. Daddy, you should be ashamed. And as for you, Jason, let me educate you about real life before I divorce your no-good ass. Sex at home has responsibility. I have two kids to raise, a house to clean, and a lazy man to clean up after. Not to mention school and work."

"Hold on, baby, let me explain."

"Shut the hell up, I'm not finished yet!" I shouted. "And if you would have just once offered to cook breakfast, wash a dish, or take care of the kids for just one morning, I would've given you the fuck of your life, but no. You preferred to rush out of the house to do your business elsewhere, fine! From now on let your part-time slut take on some full time responsibility and let's see how desirable she is in six months."

I stormed upstairs, told my mother I was leaving and got my kids together. Jason tried to stop me, but one look into my eyes and he could see I was on the verge of seriously going off. He wisely took his ass back into the house while my mother helped me to the car. Once the kids were strapped in and I was preparing to pull off, she suddenly reached inside the car and gave me a firm hug. "You were right, baby," she confessed. "You do deserve better. Call me if you need help getting settled." I kissed her goodbye and drove away with my two kids to start a new life. As I headed for home, confident that I had made the right decision, I looked in the rear view mirror at my kids playing in the back seat. I swore right then and there to teach them to take marriage commitment more seriously than their father did. I promised to raise my son to cherish and respect women. And as for my daughter, I vowed not to create another victim, so help me God.

You Can't Change a Man

For too many women in our society, leaving their cheating husbands and boyfriends is not an option. Again, they are too afraid of being alone to seriously confront him and issue an ultimatum—"Either stop fooling around or it's over!" This is the warning that should be coming out of the mouths of fed-up women, but doesn't. Instead they remain quiet, hoping and praying their man will grow up or slow down long enough to realize he has a good thing at home. However, most men are convinced the grass is greener on the other side of town, at least green enough to go grazing in once or twice a week. They have become bored conversationally and sexually with their mates and feel compelled to seek satisfaction elsewhere. "I need a change," they declare. But the person who really needs a change is the faithful wife or girlfriend, a change of men to be exact.

And it is this issue of change that is at the heart of many failed relationships. The woman is looking forward to it, while the man is fighting against it. "I'll be your husband or boyfriend," the man thinks, "but my lifestyle isn't going to change." Meanwhile, the infatuated woman is presuming, "Once we get together, everything will change." For whatever reason, women are under the impression that just because a man says, "I do," that all of his desires to be with other women will magically disappear. How ridiculous! The man who cheats before getting married will cheat afterwards. It's that simple. And all of the good conversation, good cooking, and good pussy in the world isn't going to stop them.

But don't try to tell that to the hardheaded woman who's blinded by love, or whipped. She is determined to solve every riddle, heal every wound, and right every wrong. She refuses to accept the fact that her man cannot or will not commit. Why is that? you ask. I believe it has a great deal to do with the woman's instinctual need to nurture and pamper. Some women perceive infidelity as an emotional disease that can be remedied with a little patience and her overwhelming love. "He just hasn't found the right woman," she declares. However, the reality is that he has found the perfect woman, one who will stand idly by and keep her mouth shut while he does his business.

STARTING OVER!

L ike a moth to the flame burned by the fire, 35-year-old Denise also fell in love with a cheating man who would inevitably violate her trust and break her heart. When she first met her boyfriend, Kevin, the challenge of changing him seemed exciting. But as the years rolled by and his cheating persisted, the magnetic lights grew dim and the attraction faded. "My pampering and rehabilitation days are over," she declares. "I need a real man who has made up his own mind to be faithful, not some immature jerk who needs to be watched over like a damned baby." Clearly, she has had enough of fixing broken men. With the support of her girlfriends, who were also fed up with the infidelity in their relationships, she finally woke up and put her foot down. Well, it's about time!

Denise's Story

S ometimes I look in the mirror and ask myself, "Denise, how could you have been so stupid?" For years I was in love with a man who seemed more like a spoiled child than a grown man. Instead of holding him responsible for his actions, I made excuses for everything he did wrong. When he came over with lipstick on his collar, I ignored it, telling myself, "It's nothing; don't make a scene." The time he accidentally called me by another woman's name, I had a logical explanation, "That's probably the name of one of his co-workers." And when he couldn't get it up in bed, I was right there with his defense. "He's just tired from working overtime." Boy was I right about that one.

My relationship with Kevin lasted three long and painful years. During which time he must have dumped me on at least six different occasions. He would conveniently start a fight over something stupid just to get away to spend the holiday or weekend with his whore. And just like a fool, I would be right there waiting when he was ready to patch things up. The last time this happened was about a year ago. I can't even remember what it was about. When the argument was over, he was storming out of the door, swearing it was over between us for good. I didn't know at the time, but he was right. However, this time it was going to be over on my terms.

There I was, on yet another Saturday afternoon, alone. As usual I was crying and totally pissed with Kevin for the one-millionth time. I decided to call my girlfriends April and Monica. If nothing else, I can curse his ass out and get an Amen, I thought. And God knows those were two women who would co-sign on anything negative to say about a no-good, two-timing dirty dog. April's husband, Tony, worked for the post office, and Monica's boyfriend, Raymond, was a police officer; both were fooling around on the side. And my boyfriend, Kevin, worked for the Transit Authority; talk about three whorish occupations. As I dialed April's number, I tried to gain my composure, but the minute I heard her voice, the tears started pouring again.

"Hello?" April's voice inquired.

"Hello, April, it's me," I sobbed.

"Denise, is that you? What's wrong girl? Don't tell me, it's Kevin again, isn't it?"

"You know it. We just had another argument and he broke things off, again."

"Well, good riddance. You should be celebrating and not crying," she said with an attitude, "Those damn Transit men are the biggest whores in town."

"You're right, but look who's talking," I said trying to lighten things up. "You were crying on my shoulder like a baby last week when you found a condom in Tony's wallet. I guess he's been delivering more than the mail lately."

"Aw, so now you want to crack on me, huh?" she said as we both laughed. "Hold on while I call Monica and put her on the three way."

It never took long for me to snap out of my misery when I talked to my girls. We took turns cheering each other up when things got rough, sort of like a battered women's group. Lately, it seemed the support was needed more than ever. As I wiped my face with a towel, April clicked back over with Monica on the line.

"Hey baby girl, you all right?" Monica asked in a motherly tone.

"Yeah, I'll be fine. I just need time to chill out."

"Well good, now let me tell you about what Raymond tried to pull on me yesterday," she said out of nowhere.

"Dag Monica, we haven't even dealt with Denise's problem yet," April said.

"No, April, let her go on. Maybe listening to someone else's drama will do me some good," I said jokingly.

"Ok, check this out. You know Raymond was supposed to have a patrol assignment at The United Center for the Bulls game, right?"

"Right," April and I said in unison.

"Well, I went by his house to drop off his birthday card because I couldn't find the one I wanted soon enough to mail it on time. When I drove up, I saw him and another woman coming out the door. They were both in civilian clothes all hugged up."

"You've got to be kidding, girl," April said sounding totally shocked.

"Wait, that's not the good part. Can you believe he had the nerve to tell me she was his assigned partner, and they were working undercover?"

"They were working undercover all right," I said. "Under the covers."

"Then what happened?" April asked. "Did you maintain your lady-like composure?"

"Well, of course I did. I politely threw the card in his face, called her a bitch and drove off."

"It must be something in the water." I laughed. "First April finds a condom in Tony's wallet. Then Kevin dumps me for no reason. Now you bust Raymond in the act. What a week."

"Wait a minute, April," Monica interjected. "You went through Kevin's wallet?"

"You're damn right I did. It was lying right out in the open."

"Out in the open?" Monica asked. "Exactly what do you consider out in the open?"

"At the bottom of his dresser drawer, under some drawers."

"Well baby, let me tell you. Once you start going through a man's belongings, you're already out of control and on your way to divorce court."

"Whatever, Monica. All I know is he better get his act together, or my daughter and I will be flying the friendly skies without him."

April is a 28-year-old flight attendant, and very attractive. I really couldn't understand why Tony was cheating on her. Any man would kill to be in his shoes, and in his bed. Now, Monica was the mother hen of the group. She's 37 years old, well educated with hips and a walk that could stop traffic. Again, I couldn't understand why Raymond was trippin'. Monica was a class act who could pick and choose any man she wanted. But she loved Raymond's dirty drawers and he probably knew it. As for me,

I've been told I have it going on, too. Although I may be slightly overweight, some men insist on having a woman with a little meat on her bones. Kevin just didn't know how good he had it.

So why were we putting up with these three knuckleheads, you ask? The answer to that question was the topic of conversation at dinner that evening. We decided to treat ourselves to a nice meal and then go out to the club to release some of our frustration, and burn off a few calories. April had to rush to find a babysitter; Monica was determined to get her hair done; and I wanted to go to Bally's to work off some of my frustration.

It was 5:00 p.m. when we finally got off the phone. The plan was to meet at the restaurant downtown at 8:00 p.m., and I had every intention of being on time and dressed to kill.

The moment I returned from the gym, I pulled my sharpest outfit and four-inch pumps out of the closet. I was determined to squeeze my wide ass into that tight dress, with Crisco if necessary. Fortunately for me, twenty minutes on the Stairmaster and thirty minutes in the sauna did the trick. After taking my shower and oiling down my body, I slid into that dress with no problem at all. Next I put on my makeup and painted my nails. As I looked in the mirror at the finished product, I saw a confident, voluptuous, full-figured woman who had been deprived of a good man and good lovin' for way too long. Not once in three years had Kevin ever taken me out to a nice restaurant and then dancing. It's like he was ashamed of being seen in public with me. "But that's all right though," I proudly said to myself. "Never ask a boy to do a man-sized job."

It was 7:30 p.m. before I stopped admiring myself and decided to leave. Once in my car, I turned the rear view mirror towards myself and confessed, "April and Monica may only be going out to unwind, but I'm on the hunt tonight." And what a night it turned out to be.

To my surprise April and Monica were waiting at the bar when I arrived at the restaurant. They were sitting with their backs towards me surrounded by men, so I couldn't see what they were wearing. "Please God, don't let them be dressed too conservatively," I thought. What a waste of a prayer that was. When they stood up from their stools and turned around to greet me, I damn near fell out. April's fast behind had on lace stockings and a strapless mini-dress that barely covered her ass. Tony would have killed her if he saw her in that outfit. Monica was sharp as usual. Her 5'10" frame made her look like a fashion model. She was wearing a hot pink halter dress with a push-up bra underneath that made her 32 Bs look like 36 Ds.

Needless to say, we didn't pay for any drinks that evening. As a matter of fact, we didn't pay for dinner either. When the waitress came over to take our order, she told us it was on the house. The manager, who was fresh on Monica, flipped the bill. All he wanted in return was a minute of her time before dinner and her phone number. I was ready to give it to him myself. Since he was a little cute and we were a lot broke, she went along with his request. But the second the food arrived, she cut him off with quickness and came over to eat.

"Well, that's that," she nonchalantly said. "Dig in girls, it's on me."

"You are cold-blooded, Monica," April said. "You have no intention of calling him, do you?"

"Of course not. Hey, I didn't ask him to spend his money. I can't help it if men like to show off with their wallets. And besides, they throw out tons of food every night anyway. He's just trying to impress me, but I'm not easily impressed."

Monica always had deep words of wisdom, except when it came to explaining why she was putting up with Raymond. I had always been curious as to why women as beautiful as they were put up with men who treat them so badly. No doubt, they were probably wondering the same about me. It didn't take long before all the free drinks began to loosen our inhibitions and our tongues, especially mine.

"Monica, you mind if I ask you a personal question?"

"No, go right ahead."

"Why do you put up with Raymond's B.S. when you could have any man you want?"

"To be honest with you, Denise, sometimes I don't know myself. I guess I don't have the patience to train another man. Raymond may be a dog, but he's my dog, and he's predictable."

"That's so unfair!" April asserted. "Men can sleep around with all the women they want, but let a man look sideways at their wife or girlfriend and all hell will break loose."

"That's because men know they have women right where they want them, especially black men," I said. "I recently read a study which stated seventy percent of black males are unavailable."

"Unavailable, meaning what?" April asked.

"Unavailable to the heterosexual black female for a relationship, that's what."

"To hell with that survey, I think it's more like ninety percent. These men out here are a total disaster!" Monica laughed. "Either they're locked up, doped up, unemployed, under-employed, married, homosexual, or just too damned ugly to look at."

April laughed so hard she nearly spit her drink out. Her face got all red, and tears started streaming down the side of her face. For a minute I thought she was choking to death, but she was all right.

"Girl, are you trying to kill me?" April said after composing herself. "Don't ever say anything that damned funny while I'm trying to swallow."

"But it's the truth, and you both know it. Look at our men,

for example. All of them are good looking, have good paying jobs, and are surrounded by hundreds of skeezers everyday. And you know they're the biggest skeezer pleaser in town."

"You may be right, but I know how to put Tony's ass in check," April said.

"And how's that, may I ask?"

"I'll just go on strike. No cooking, no laundry, and definitely no pussy."

"Well, I've got my own methods for getting Raymond to behave. My Louisiana friend at work taught me a little voodoo. She told me to get one of his pictures, cut the head off, and place it face up in the crotch of my panties."

"And what's that supposed to do?" I asked.

"I don't exactly know, but the first two weeks I tried it, Raymond was wearing my thighs like ear muffs every morning."

"Stop fooling around, Monica, this is serious," I said.

"Ok then. Why have you put up with old bucktooth, big nose, two-timing Kevin for the last three years? He must have a gold-plated dick to keep you coming back after all the hell he's put you through."

"With me, I think it's a matter of how I feel about myself. Kevin has been telling me for so long that nobody else would ever want me that I actually started believing him. When we first met, he would compliment me on my figure and my outfits. Now, all of a sudden I'm showing too much cleavage, or, I'm getting too fat. I think he's just trying to lower my self-esteem so he can control me."

"Ok, that's enough of this depressing conversation," Monica said as she reached inside her purse. "I've got something for you to read and then we're out of here."

"What is it?" April asked.

"It's an office joke being faxed around town."

She pulled out two pieces of paper with large typing on it and handed it to us. It read:

MENopause

MENstrual cramps

MENtal illness

MENtal breakdown

Ever notice how all our problems begin with men?

After getting a good laugh and a spirit boost, we freshened up and were on our way. It was 10:00 p.m. and way past all our bedtimes, but the conversation and the alcohol had us hyped. As we drove the few blocks to the club side by side, I rolled down my window and rowdily shouted, "Look out men, here we come!"

It had been several months since any of us had been out on the club scene. The music sounded louder and the men were more attractive than I remembered. We tried our best not to look uncomfortable or unfamiliar with the surroundings, but men can sniff out new meat like bloodhounds. As we strutted past all the jealous looks and turned up noses, it was obvious things hadn't changed much.

Women still spend most of their time checking out each other. After finding a table and getting ourselves situated, we began scoping the place out for good prospects. Right away I saw a gentleman who was just my type: tall, dark, and, most importantly, alone. When I tried to make a seductive gesture to get his attention, the guy next to him thought I was flirting with him.

"I saw that," Monica said. "You got the wrong one, didn't you?"

"Damn, and here he comes," I said under my breath. Like a snake crawling out from under a rock, this Jerry baldheaded midget slithered through the crowd towards our table. I turned my back to discourage his approach, but it was too late.

"Excuse me, Ms. Lady," he said while tapping me on the shoulder. "My name is Lenny."

"Hi, Lenny," I said trying not to choke from the smell of his cheap cologne.

"Can I buy you a drink?" he asked.

"No thank you, I'm waiting for my boyfriend."

"Well, baby, if you change your mind, remember I'm Lenny and I've got plenty."

As he walked away he looked back and smiled at me with that annoying gold tooth protruding halfway out of his mouth. April busted him out the minute he was out of hearing distance.

"Hell naw, no he didn't say he was Lenny with plenty. He needs to quit with his countrified, fake Isaac Hayes lookin' ass."

Monica was bent over in her chair crackin' up. She had to put both hands over her mouth to keep from laughing in his face. And who could blame her? Some of the lines you hear are so weak you've got to laugh to keep from crying.

"Lord, I need a drink," Monica said as she wiped her face with a Kleenex.

No sooner did she say that than the waitress arrived at the table with anonymous drink offers. We all accepted and ordered our usual, double shots of cognac. After receiving the drinks, we sat up straight on our stools and waited for the man or men who paid the tab to make the next move. Please Lord, don't be another clown like that last one, I was thinking.

"Whoever paid for this Martel better get over here in a hurry," April said.

"Why is that?" I asked.

"Because this drink is like an hourglass. Once it's empty, his time is up."

Right on cue, two fine-looking men walked up to the table. One of them was light skinned, with a stocky build. And the other, who just happened to be the man I was trying to flirt with earlier, was slim with hazel eyes and tight buns. Mmm, Mmm, good.

"Hello, ladies," the slim one said, "my name is Lawrence; this is my partner Dexter. Mind if we join you?"

"Hell no! I mean, be my guest," I said enthusiastically. "My name is Denise; this is April, and the tall, beautiful one over there is Monica."

"I hope you're enjoying your drink," Dexter said as he purposely looked in April's direction.

"Yes, I am. Thank you very much."

"What about you, Denise?" Lawrence flirtatiously inquired.

"You're fine, I mean it's fine, thank you."

It didn't take long to tell that April and I had been chosen. Monica was the odd man out this time, which didn't happen all that often. Not surprisingly, she took the opportunity to make light of the situation.

"So what am I, some kind of charity case?" Monica joked.

"Oh no, sweetheart, that's not it at all. I just figured a woman with your height would prefer a taller man," Lawrence apologetically explained.

"You're right about that, sweetheart. So do you have any friends who are 6'5" and over?"

"As a matter of fact I do, but unfortunately, they're not here tonight."

"Oh well, be sure to tell them what they missed."

Monica was ready to party, but nobody would ask her to dance. The men were obviously intimidated by her beauty and height. For some reason it seemed as if all the men in the club were less than six feet that night. April joked with her saying. "Didn't you know this was six foot and under get in free night?" Finally, after several good songs played, a cute guy who was about 5'2" asked her to dance. At that point, all she needed was an escort out onto the floor; after that he could drop-dead. The minute she hit the floor, she started showing off. Her nieces had just taught her how to do a new dance and she was giving lessons. Oh yes, Monica could dance her ass off.

April and I were waiting for the DJ to play a Steppers song. We were completely out of practice on the latest dances, but Steppin' was smooth and simple. It's like riding a bike; once you learn, you never forget. For those of you who don't know what Steppin' is, ask someone from Chicago or the Midwest. In some cities it's called Bopping, Ballroom, The Hustle, Swinging Out, or Hand Dancing. But nobody does it better than we do in Chitown, nobody. As I was saying, we were too far behind the latest dances to go out there and embarrass ourselves, but that didn't stop Monica. She was having a ball and showing her age. While the entire crowd was swaying back and forth to the rhythm shouting, "Hey Ho, Hey Ho," Monica's old ass was yelling, "The roof, the roof, the roof is on fire." It was apparent that she was a little tipsy and out of party practice.

Finally, after what seemed like forever, the DJ played a couple of Steppin' records, "Forevermore" by Anthony David and Algebra, and a classic steppers cut, "Imagine This" by Mike James. We quickly assigned Monica to purse-watching duty and slid onto the floor. April and I were shocked to discover that both Dexter and Lawrence could really throw down. They were shuffling and turning so precisely you would have sworn the practiced all their moves together. I was impressed, and so was April. When the songs ended, we returned to the table laughing and joking like old friends, I was really having a great time. For the next two hours we were pampered and flattered more than we had been in years. Kevin, Tony, and Raymond were distant memories, or so I thought.

I didn't notice right away, but Monica was running back and forth to the bathroom every ten to fifteen minutes. I just figured she either had a weak bladder or was checking somebody out. Then it dawned on me she was making a booty call to Raymond. I was sure of it. Why else is she peeking inside her purse to see if anyone is calling her cell at 1:00 a.m.? I thought to myself. My suspicions were confirmed when she pulled me aside and told me she had to leave.

"Denise, I hate to be a party pooper, but I've got to go."

"I don't believe you, Monica," I said with disappointment. "You just caught Raymond fucking somebody yesterday and you're running back to him today, and at 1:00 a.m. in the morning."

"You don't understand, girlfriend. Raymond just needs his space every now and then. And just like I told you, I've invested too much time into training him."

"You're the one who's trained, Monica, or should I say, dick whipped?"

"Look, I don't have time for this right now. Tell April I'll talk to her later, bye."

She kissed me on the cheek and shot out the door like her house was on fire, or should I say, her pussy? All I could do was shake my head while walking back to the table. For the very first time, I realized just how pitiful I must have sounded trying to defend Kevin all those years. This was too deep. My mind was reeling; how do women allow themselves to become so caught up? I was thinking. Needless to say, my night was ruined. I asked Lawrence for his number, gave him a hug, and went home with plenty to think about. April was enjoying herself and decided to stay a while longer. She was flying out of town the next afternoon and wanted to make the most of it. I didn't blame her one bit. Dexter was cute, fun to be around, and a perfect gentlemen.

First thing Monday morning, I called my job and requested a week's vacation. During the next few days, I didn't talk to anyone. I switched off my cell phone and didn't open my e-mails. I needed time for myself. Every morning at 7:00 a.m., I got up and went to the gym for a heavy workout and swim. I even treated myself to a nice dinner a few nights just to celebrate being me. But what I enjoyed most was taking steamy hot bubble baths by candlelight. Yes, I was really beginning to feel good about myself; for the first time in a long time I made myself top priority.

By Friday afternoon, I was ready to return my calls, which had piled up considerably over the last five days. I quickly fast-forwarded past the telemarketers and annoying family members. The remaining messages were truly shocking.

(Beep) "Denise, this is Monica," she said sounding depressed. "I just got back from seeing my doctor. He told me I have Herpes. I'm too old for this shit! Raymond has got to go! Please call me as soon as possible, bye"

(Beep) "Denise, if you're there pick up; this is April. Oh well, I guess you've heard the bad news by now. Poor Monica, when will she ever learn? Anyway, I have some great news myself. I'm flying to Nassau for the weekend. No, not with Tony; I'm going with Dexter Saint Jock," she laughed. "I had a couple of tickets lying around that my neglectful husband was too busy to use. Now, I know what you're thinking; two wrongs don't make a right but it damn sure makes it even. Call you when I get back, bye girl!"

Before she hung up, I could hear the Bob Marley song playing in my head, "I Shot the Sheriff." April was on cloud nine and I couldn't have been happier for her. She deserved all the love and attention she could get. Too bad Monica didn't wake up before she got burned. Anyway, there was still one final message to retrieve, one that would test my self-respect and my resolve.

(Beep) "Denise, this is Kevin. I just called to tell you I'm sorry. I know I haven't been right lately, but I miss you, baby. Give me a call so we can work things out. I'll be waiting; I love you."

Boy I hated it when he did that. Every time we broke up, he tried to sweet talk me into forgiving him. And like a fool, I fell for it each and every time. I told myself over and over again: "Not this time, Denise. Don't let your heart sell out your brain." I didn't know what to do. Should I call? I contemplated. Or should I just let things fade? I decided to think it over for another day. Besides, Monica had provided me with enough drama for one day. When I called her later that evening, she had already confronted Raymond about the STD and accepted his apology for slipping up, as he put it. There was no point in wasting my time dogging him. Her nose was wide open and he could do no wrong. After giving her two cents' worth of advice, I turned my attention to how I was going to respond to Kevin's apology.

When I woke up Saturday morning, I decided not to bother calling Kevin. I figured I'd leave him hanging the way he had done me on so many occasions. With that settled, I went about my routine of working out and relaxing. I felt like a new woman. My mind was at peace and my confidence level was high. All I needed was someone to talk to, not Monica or April either. I needed to hear a man's voice. Yes, Lawrence was definitely on my mind, but I wasn't ready to get deep in another relationship so soon. He made it perfectly clear he wanted more than a friendship. As he put it, "I'm not interested in being some woman's girlfriend with a penis. Either you're sexually attracted to me or you aren't." At the time I was offended, and a bit disappointed, by his attitude. I assumed he only wanted to sleep around with every woman he met, but I was wrong. What he was trying to get across was, "My time is valuable and I prefer to spend it with a woman who is interested in having an intimate relationship with me." At the very least, I should have respected his honesty, which I do now.

By nightfall, I was curled up on my leather sofa listening to V-103 on the radio. The dusties were sounding great and a cool breeze was blowing through the patio window. I was feeling so good that I decided to break out my six-month-old bottle of wine and get drunk while rereading Terry McMillan's, "Waiting to Exhale." And just when I was getting to the good part where Bernardino sets her husband's BMW on fire, the phone rang. Without thinking, I instinctively picked it up. What a mistake that turned out to be; it was Kevin.

"What's up, baby, why didn't you return my call?" he said trying to sound hard.

"I've been busy," I replied with an attitude.

"Well, can we talk?"

"I don't have anything to say. You're the one who dumped me, remember?"

"Yeah, I know, and I'm sorry."

"You're sorry, alright, sorry and tired. I'm sick of being on this emotional rollercoaster!"

"Don't be like that, baby; you know how much I care about you."

"If this is how you treat someone you care about, I can do without it. And stop calling me baby; I'm a grown woman, and it's about time you found that out."

At that moment an old song by the Jones Girls came on the radio, "You Gonna Make Me Love Somebody Else." I stopped listening to Kevin's begging, sat the phone on my lap, and tuned into the song. The opening lyrics said it all.

You gonna make me love somebody else, if you keep on treating me the way you do.

I ain't did nothin' to you. I just love you with my heart,

heart and soul.

Every time I need some lovin', why do you turn cold, turn cold?

Now, I ain't dumb and I ain't stupid, I know you need love like I do.

Cause if you ain't lovin' me, I wanna know who in the world you lovin'? Tell me if you don't want me around.

Amen to that! I shouted, "These sisters must have made that song especially for me." When I picked up the phone, Kevin was still begging and going on about how much he loved me.

"Denise, you know I love you, baby. Nobody will ever love you the way I do," he boasted. "Don't you still love me?"

I paused, took a deep breath, and thought about all of the hell he put me through over the years. And in a calm and convincing tone, I responded.

"You must have the wrong number; love don't live here anymore," and hung up.

AFTERWORD

In the game of cheating there are no happy endings, only rude awakenings and hard lessons, lessons that I hope men and women will apply to their own relationships to help build them up and not break them down. It took me over forty years of making mistakes and taking women throughout hell before I finally understood how much damage lying and cheating can do. The baggage our women carry in their suitcases is often put there by us. We criticize them for being dramatic and defensive without realizing that we are writing the script. It's funny when I think about it. Not once in my entire life have I ever heard a single man say to me, "Michael, always be honest with women; it will make your life so much easier." Like most young men growing up, honesty was never an option for me. Lying has become second nature to most men. We never consider that a woman will be okay with dating us even if we're involved with other women. We take away their choice when we start out the relationship with a lie. And even if she turns you down, at least you have her respect. What's bigger than that?

Honesty also has its price. If men are going to exercise their option to see other women then they have to be prepared to accept that women may want to exercise that same option to date and have sex with other men. This is where things get complicated for most men. While they point fingers at women for being possessive and insecure, they are the ones who really have the problem. You see, men are more possessive and more insecure than women, at least when it comes to sex and sharing. Until men are mature and secure enough to take in what they dish out, we will repeat this vicious cycle over and over again. Freedom for one must mean freedom for all. If you can't stand the heat, then get out of the kitchen, fellas. It's time for us to man up and be honest about who we are and give women the choice to share or not to share.

But in all fairness, women must also be open for the truth. I was recently at a film festival in Miami. I asked all the single ladies to stand up. There were approximately three hundred in the theatre. I instructed them to sit down if my qualifications for a partner were not compatible with theirs. My first requirement was that they not want more children or to be married. About two hundred of them immediately sat down. Then I said they must be sexually adventurous. Another fifty took their seat. Then I told them I needed a woman who accepts that I could not promise to be monogamous. As you might expect, there were only four women left standing. Three of them were over forty and the other young lady appeared to be in her mid thirties. So, out of three hundred women, it only took four different criteria to eliminate ninety-eight percent of the single women in the room. No kids, no marriage, sexually adventurous, and no monogamy. But the real lesson was yet to be taught. Moments later a gentleman stood up and shouted, "I want to be married and I'm monogamous!" The theatre erupted in cheers. After the applause died down, I asked the women, "Why didn't you cheer when I was being honest about what I wanted?" A woman sternly said, "Because women want honesty until you tell them something they don't want to hear!"

I've been echoing this point throughout the book because it is crucial in moving our relationships forward. Until women are cheering just as loudly for the single man who admits he doesn't want kids, marriage, or monogamy, the cheating man will continue to tell the love-starved woman the things that make her cheer, trust, and eventually open themselves up to be hurt. Honesty can be a difficult thing for a man who doesn't have a lot of options. But it can be made more difficult by women who say they want it and then only celebrate it when he's singing their song. Honesty is honesty, and women have to be prepared to embrace it even when it's not what they want to hear.

Lastly, to all the young men out there who've been listening to all this nonsense about being a player, pimp, or ladies' man, it's all a bunch of garbage. Real men are honest with women. From day one they tell them, "This is who I am. This is what I want. And this is who I am seeing." At that point, the woman can chose to get involved or just remain friends! Either way, there's no loss of respect and nobody gets hurt. If the relationship doesn't work out, your conscience is clear! That's how a real man operates! Don't let anybody tell you different! Practice being honest for the next fifteen or twenty years, and I promise it will get you much further with a lot less drama! Because the truth is the best game in the world!

ABOUT
MICHAEL BAISDEN

Michael Baisden is undeniably one of the most influential and engaging personalities in radio history. His meteoric rise to #1 is redefining radio with the numbers to back it up. The show is syndicated by Cumulus Media and is heard in over 78 markets nationwide with over 8 million loyal listeners daily. His career began when he took a leap of faith to leave his job driving trains in Chicago to self-publish his book, and began touring the country selling books out of the trunk of his car. Through the power of his sheer determination, Michael carved a unique niche as a speaker, radio personality, and social activist. He is always in the lead when it comes to helping those who don't have a voice. "I'm not one for just talking; either do something or get out of the way!"

Baisden, who now has four best selling books to his credit, has hosted two national television shows, and has recently produced three feature films.

Nationally Syndicated Radio Personality

Baisden Communications: His radio career began in 2003 when 98.7 KISS FM in New York City offered him a position as the afternoon drive-time host. Because of budget constraints the station was unable to offer him a salary. Michael's response was, "Just give me the mic!" And sure enough, within six months, their afternoon drive ratings went from number 9 to number 1.

After eight months of consistently high ratings, Michael suggested taking his show national, but management was apprehensive, suggesting that New York wasn't ready. A few months later, Michael threatened to quit if management did not pursue a syndication deal. "There was no doubt in my mind that I could have one of the hottest shows on radio! I knew the impact it would have on people all across the country and I wasn't taking no, for an answer," Michael rebutted.

Since his radio show debuted nationally in 2005, Michael has captured the hearts and minds of millions of Americans with his provocative mix of relationship talk, hot topics, politics and the best of old school with today's R&B. When it comes to entertaining, enlightening and educating, no one in talk radio compares. His high energy and love for interacting with his listeners are just two reasons for the popularity and success of "The Michael Baisden Show." Michael ignites heated discussions with explosive episodic themes like: Infidelity In The Church, Deadbeat Parents, Talking To Your Children About Sex, and Do Women Know What They Want?

Best Selling Author

Baisden Publishing: According to Simon & Schuster, Michael Baisden is "probably the most successful self-published African-American male author out there today." With nearly 2 million books in print, both hardcover and softcover, his books blend the perfect combination of entertainment, humor, provocation and sexuality. Michael's vibrant personality on and off the air has made him a people magnet.

He began attracting attention with primarily female followers as author and publisher of the highly successful best selling books: *Never Satisfied: How and Why Men Cheat, Men Cry in the Dark, The Maintenance Man, God's Gift to Women* and, most recently, a hot new book, *Never Satisfied: Do Men Know What They Want?* Two of his titles ultimately were adapted into stage plays playing to sold-out crowds across the U.S.

Television Show Host

The author and relation-ship expert previously hosted a nationally syndicated talk show, "Talk or Walk," which was a compelling and fast-paced reality series that com-

bined the emotion of talk, the conflict of court shows and the fascination of a relationship series.

Another dream was to host a Late Night Talk show. He got that chance in the fall of 2007, when he partnered with TV One to host and co-executive produce *Baisden After Dark*, featuring comedian George Willborn and band leader Morris Day. The show was a smash hit, breaking records for viewers on the network. The show currently airs weekdays.

Producer / Filmmaker

Baisden Film Works: Michael has two successful national stage plays (based on his novels), which toured the U.S. playing to sold-out crowds; an award-winning feature-length film presentation documentary titled *Love, Lust & Lies* that deals with relationships and sexuality based on the perspective of people of color; and two seminar tapes, *Relationship Seminar* and *Men Have Issues Too.*

His television career kicked off in 2001 with "Talk or Walk" distributed by Tribune Broadcasting, which was a nationally syndicated Daytime TV Talk show he hosted that dealt with relationships. In 2006 he created, hosted and executive-produced a Late Night TV Talk show with co-host comedian, George Willborn, and band leader, Morris Day, which aired on TV One titled "Baisden After Dark". In 2011 Michael produced a TV Special titled "Do Women Know What They Want?" that is currently airing on Centric of the BET Network and is based on his upcoming film. In 2011 Michael struck up a distribution deal for 3 feature films with TimeLife: *Do Women Know What They Want?*, *Love, Lust & Lies*, his two relationship films, and a comedy show titled *Turn Around* featuring his radio show co-host George Willborn.

Motivational Speaker

Baisden Entertainment: The Love, Lust & Lies Relationship Seminar Series attracts thousands of standing-room only, sold-out crowds nationwide as he tours the country. As a motivational speaker he has been an inspiration to hundreds of thousands attending his seminars and events. As well as numerous national Baisden Live Tours, he has also produced international Island Jam events in Jamaica and has an exclusive upcoming trip to South Africa.

Philanthropist

The Michael Baisden Foundation: A non-profit organization was formed with a goal to eliminate illiteracy as well as promote technology and is dedicated to education, support and advancement in our communities. Michael's own passionate testimony as to how books changed his life gives hope to those who have been enslaved by the shackles of illiteracy.

In December 2009 Michael called for a National Mentor Training Day and announced his plans for a 2010 nationwide campaign. He pledged up to $350,000 of his own money to be donated in over 72 markets he would visit on a bus tour. The outreach was named "One Million Mentors National Campaign To Save Our Kids." Michael challenged his listeners to match or beat his donations and get involved.

In October 2010 President Barack Obama publicly congratulated Michael on his efforts. He founded the Michael Baisden Foundation focusing on education, literacy and mentoring.

Michael believes "books change lives" and he is living proof!

Social Activist & Community Leader

Baisden's proudest moment came on September 20, 2007, when he passionately and skillfully spearheaded the famous Jena 6 March in Jena, Louisiana. This historic and momentous occasion garnered tens of thousands of citizens of all races to peacefully march in support of six young men who have been unfairly treated by the justice system. In addition, he urged millions of listeners to wear black on September 20 in protest of unequal justice. The news traveled throughout the country. Everyone from college students of all races to corporate executives wore black in support of the Jena 6.

Another historic year was 2008.

In late January Michael endorsed Sen. Barack Obama in the Democratic Primary. He celebrated President Obama's victory with over 4,000 fans at a watch party in Miami on election night. The Obama  camp along with millions of listeners credited Michael with being one of the major forces behind this historic victory to elect the first African-American to the Presidency of the United States.

In 2009 he once again stepped up and answered the call of the National Association of Free Clinics. With Michael's help they were able to get more volunteers than they needed and get the word out to the countless thousands that needed the free health services.

Michael continues to entertain, enlighten and educate as he pursues one of his first dreams, to have his novels adapted to major motion pictures.

In 2011, Michael continued to expand his media reach when he produced, wrote, and directed a groundbreaking relationship film titled, *Do Women Know What They Want?* The reviews have been amazing! "It was time for something new and exciting, and no one else was doing it, not like this!" Michael said. Get ready! It looks like the baddest man on radio and late night TV will be in theaters near you soon!

Stay tuned—it's just the beginning of the Baisden legacy.

Follow Michael on Facebook, Twitter or YouTube @ BaisdenLive.

www.MichaelBaisden.com
www.BaisdenLive.com
www.MingleCity.com

Congratulations
Michael Baisden
The *MOST* Influential Man In Radio

THE MICHAEL BAISDEN SHOW
Informative, Engaging...Funny!

The show is syndicated in nearly 80 markets nationwide making it easy for you to get connected and  stay connected with Michael no matter where you are! Keep up with all of the latest and get first notification of exclusive online events, contests, activities and tours. The show airs weekdays from 3-7 p.m. EST. Listen live online or via app, download podcasts and check out the daily show features.

For more information, go to the office show website at: **www.BaisdenLive.com**

SOCIAL NETWORKING:

www.MingleCity.com is the online community for drama-free adults. It is a place for singles, couples, groups and friends to interact with other  like-minded members in their area, across the country and the world. Create your own personal webpage, invite your friends, start or join groups, find events, chat, blog, post your favorite photos and videos.

SOCIAL MEDIA @ BAISDENLIVE:

Follow Michael @ Twitter:
BAISDENLIVE

Be A Facebook Fan @
BAISDENLIVE

Tune In on YouTube @
BAISDENLIVE

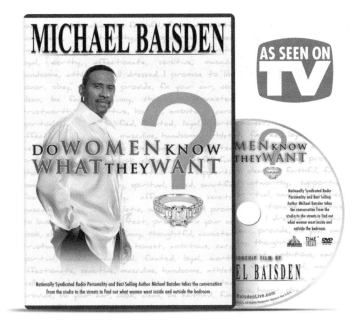

DO WOMEN KNOW WHAT THEY WANT?

What started out as a cordial conversation with one simple question "Do Women Know What They Want?" exploded into a battle of the sexes that will have you laughing hysterically one minute and shouting at the screen the next!

No longer anonymous voices on the radio, can men be honest about their multiple relationships, interracial dating, and why they choose to date but not marry some women? And can women admit to having afairs with married men, take responsibility for their bad choices, and explain why they fake it?

Suggested Retail Price: $16.95
Available in Cut and a *Too Hot for TV,* UN-CUT version!

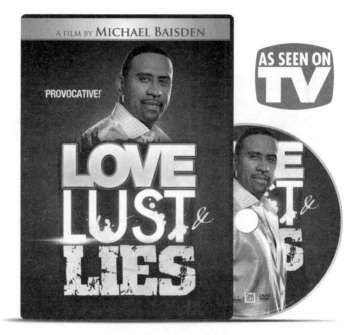

LOVE, LUST & LIES

We've all seen documentaries that deal with relationships and sexuality, such as "Real Sex" on HBO. But if you're like me, you've thought about how exciting it would be to experience a program that deals with these issues from the perspective of people of color. Well the wait is over.

"It's amazing to me how many people are afraid to be open about what they want inside and outside the bedroom," Michael says. "Hopefully, after watching these interviews they'll be more willing to explore their sexuality and to discuss issues such as infidelity, adult toys, and the swinging lifestyle."

Suggested Retail Price: $16.95
Available in Cut and a *Too Hot for TV,* UN-CUT version!